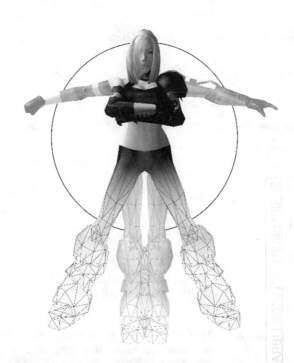

Modeling a Character in 3ds max®
Second Edition

Paul Steed

Wordware Publishing, Inc.

Library of Congress Cataloging-in-Publication Data

Steed, Paul.
   Modeling a character in 3ds max -- second edition / by Paul Steed.
   p. cm.
   Includes index.
   ISBN 1-55622-088-X (pbk., companion cd-rom)
   1. Computer animation.   2. Computer graphics.   3. 3ds max (Computer file)
   I. Title.
   TR897.7.S74 2004
   006.6'96--dc22

2004027074
CIP

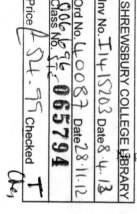

ISBN 1-55622-088-X
10 9 8 7 6 5 4 3 2 1
0411

All inquiries for volume purchases of this book should be addressed to Wordware Publishing, Inc., at the above address. Telephone inquiries may be made by calling:

(972) 423-0090

For Marion, Trent, and Brianna,
who put up with me and like me anyway.

Contents

Part III: Texturing

Acknowledgments

Writing a book is a labor of love, so an updated second edition should have been a piece of cake. Yeah right! The hardest thing for me to do was just like what I wrote five years ago. Why did I ever think I could write? I feel like a second-grader struggling with tense and just making sense. Do all writers go through this? Am I really even a writer?

Everyone's a writer when you think about it today. We all write novels one email at a time. We add chapters to the book of our lives by having a meaningful conversation or even a tedious lecture (given and received).

I wrote this book the first time because I couldn't find anything like it and owe the privilege of having it published to the fine folks at Wordware Publishing. Tim, Wes, and Beth all have put up with my crap for quite a while now, and I'm honored they feel the book has been successful enough to warrant a second edition.

I've been in the industry now for nearly 14 years and wouldn't be here without a few heroes: Chris Roberts, Dennis Loubet, Den Beauvais, Cyrus Lum, Kevin Cloud, Jim Lee, and James Cameron. Also a few friends: Craig Halverson, Dean McCall, Erin Roberts, Jason White, Tim Miller, Mynx, and my id Momma 4ever — Mrs. Donna Jackson.

Many more people have helped me keep my drive, enthusiasm, and dedication to trying to improve each year (even if only a little). However, the best friend I can make is the one who feels my books or my tutorials have helped him or her get over that hump of learning and growing as a character modeler.

Never stop learning.

Introduction

Writing a book is a very rewarding experience...over time! It is a commitment to many hours of head-banging frustration and the pouring of one's thoughts into a medium discernible by others. Normally, the point of revising a book is to update it to be useful with the current state of the technology to which it refers. In this case, the techniques I discuss and the instructions I give are just as relevant with max 7 as they were with max 3. What I've tried to do is augment what I've already laid down by dropping into the mix tips and tricks that are possible with the latest versions. While not ground-shaking in its introduction of new material, this second edition of *Modeling a Character in 3ds max* will hopefully reinforce what the first book teaches with the little bits of value-add that recent versions of max bring to the field. It also adds some insight I've gleaned as an artist that only could have happened over time.

Like most of my peers in the computer game industry, I'm self-taught in what I do. Manuals, tutorials, and simply putting hours into working in the gaming industry have been my teachers. I've written this book because I couldn't find one like it to teach me what I wanted to know. By buying it you also have decided to subscribe to a self-teaching attitude and have what it takes to surpass me or anyone else in the field if you put your mind to it. While it does take a certain level of talent to become successful at creating great and effective game characters, perseverance and willingness to learn new things are just as important to your chosen career.

I've approached this book as if we're both sitting down learning together. I want you to *watch* me do my thing. I'll share what I've stuffed into my head and fingers over the past thirteen years, six companies, and fourteen games because I'm confident you'll learn a few things in the process. Be forewarned, though, I'm not just adding another didactic, strictly educational, dry technical manual to your collection. I wanted this book to reflect a little more personality. I've included occasional anecdotal "authorized digressions," small tales of life "in the trenches" as a developer. I've also included

FYIs, For Your Information factoids or observations that pertain to the material being covered. File them away for reference or skip past them — it's up to you.

The computer books on my shelf that I like the most and recommend to others are the ones that focus on completing a specific task or project. That's why I've written this book the way that I have. I wanted to make a useful guide for creating a low-polygon, *real-time* character in max for use in a game like *Unreal* or *Quake III: Arena*. Don't look for this book to cover lighting and rendering techniques. Although I do get pretty basic at times, *Modeling a Character in 3ds max Second Edition* is not a replacement for your max manuals and tutorials...it's a *companion* to them.

I've tried to satisfy both the novice and experienced modeler, but I have taken for granted you've bought this book because you're new to creating low-poly characters. If you want to completely recreate the character I've built by following along *exactly*, great! By all means do that. If, however, you're somewhat experienced and/or learn like I do by riding tangent to the beaten path instead of in its ruts, you'll use what I've laid out as a *workbook* to build your own character. This last approach is going to benefit you the most, but depends on your learning ability and experience level. In other words, if you're experienced, you may just want to use it as a reference guide, skipping to whatever sections you need.

Since I'm an artist I've probably included more illustrations than a typical book on max. This is because I have a pet peeve with some books not having *enough* illustrations, but it's also because I wanted to make it *readable*. That is, you can learn from it even if you don't have max running in front of you. It's instructional and conversational. If you're tired of huddling in your office poring over the words and images printed here, sit on a park bench out of the office somewhere and read over the material at your leisure. You'll not only feed your brain, but remember what sunlight feels like on your skin and what birds sound like when they chirp. As far as building a buxom female character instead of a male or creature character...it was just a personal decision. Any and all of the methods I introduce will work on whatever gender or species you prefer.

It's my fervent hope that you'll find this book useful in your self-education and not just another addition to that row of books on your shelf that looks good but never gets read. Good luck and good modeling!

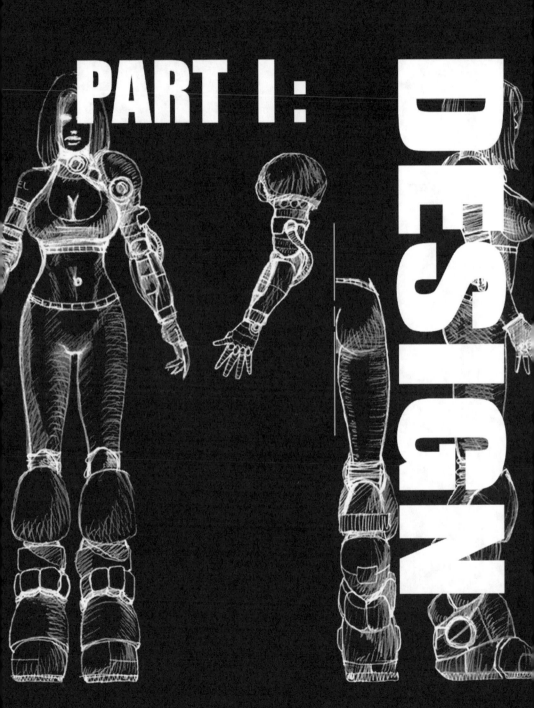

PART I : DESIGN

Part I: Design

CHAPTER 1
Design Fundamentals

Defined, *design* is "the arrangement of elements or details in a product or work of art." Of course, given a large number of elements, they can be arranged in an almost endless way with a plethora of results. Many things can impact the design of your real-time character, but the most impacting and unavoidable one is *limitations*.

Limitations

By limitations I don't mean limitations on your imagination. I mean hard limitations like making a convincing human or creature out of a thousand triangles or less. However, with the growth of the hardware and computing power of the PC and the next generation of consoles like Xbox 2 and PlayStation 3, polygon limitations are becoming less severe. Still, characters for real-time games can rarely afford to have flowing gowns or octopoid tentacles. Organic shapes that undulate and look "squishy" are hard to pull off, as is cloth or long, flowing strands of hair when you have to represent them with triangles. Designing real-time characters requires much more thought than a character destined *only* to be rendered, as in a movie. With lower-polygon meshes it's usually best to keep the designs compact and simple using transparency mapped onto two-sided, segmented planes to create the illusion of hair or scraps of cloth.

Even as polygon limitations ease and characters that are 10,000 triangles or more are possible, other limitations like number of bones in a skeleton, number of possible morph targets, and amount of texture resolution will always exist. For example, this real-time character done for a recent XNA demo for the Xbox is over 80,000 triangles:

However, even though it seems like her triangles are "limitless," she was still confined by a hard limit of 75 bones per unique object in her geometry.

In most cases "low-poly" refers to less than a thousand triangles, but today with the proliferation of 3D accelerator cards and faster CPUs low-poly is becoming an almost antiquated term. Still, technically if there has to be any thought put into the number of polygons it takes to create a character and make it look like it does in the reference drawings, it's low-poly. For example, if the character being designed is going to be in a game like *Quake III: Arena* or *Unreal Tournament*, it *can* be up to 2,000 triangles and still work. But, unless you have the latest machine with the latest pimped-out 3D accelerator card, you'll experience a serious performance hit if the character is much bigger than the normal 800-polygon range.

Even when there's no polygon limit per se, real-time characters are subject to additional limitations like the bone count and morph targets mentioned above. Another limitation imposed by the nature of rendering things "real time" includes transparency. For example, the "Eva" character was designed to wear a sheer dress that had bits of reflective "triangles" attached to it to provide contrast like they did in movies back in the black and white *film noir* era of the 1930s and 1940s.

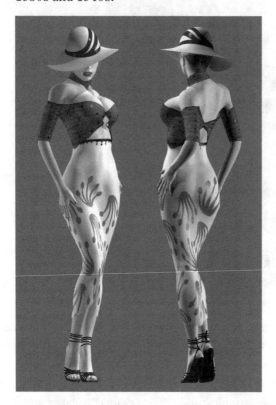

But when it came time to implement her, Eva had to undergo a costume adjustment because the cost of figuring out shadows *through* a transparent object was just too high. So her dress was made opaque and the geometry hidden by it deleted.

Genre and/or perspective (the view at which the characters will be seen) also affects your design. By genre I mean a first-person action game versus a third-person action game or a top-down isometric strategy game. Obviously if the characters are in your face and can be scrutinized or appreciated, more attention and polygons have to be placed on smaller details like blinking eyes and moving mouths. *Half-Life 2* features very realistic characters that are definitely higher resolution than the average real-time character. Just the heads of some of these characters will be close to a thousand triangles! In games like *Warcraft III*, the characters remain a relatively fixed distance from the camera and they're never more than an inch or two high on the screen. They can be lower-poly because you'll definitely never get close enough to discern facial features!

The animation system the character will be dropped into limits the design of your character as well. While I don't cover animation in this book, you still need to think about it since it affects the functionality and geometry of the character. For example, when I designed a character for id Software's *Quake III: Arena* it had to fit a three-part formula dictated by the animation system. Dividing the character into three distinct parts — head, torso, and legs — made it impossible to create something that appeared to be made out of one fluid piece. Of course this didn't stop cool characters from being created, but it did become a major design consideration.

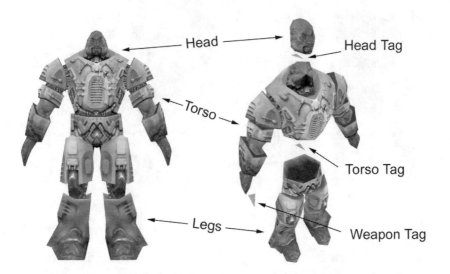

'Keel' Copyright id Software, Inc.

This illustrates how each character in *Q3A* had to be broken down before being animated and implemented in the game engine. There had to be a head object that was connected to the torso by a small invisible triangle or "tag" that represented connection and point of rotation. The torso was in turn attached to the legs via another tag that also described connection and rotation. It had to be built this way because the animation system allowed the head and torso to move independently of the legs in response to the mouse movements provided by the player. In other words, when you look around in the game by moving your mouse around, the head of the character looks around too (i.e., "free look"). To accommodate this sort of arrangement, the head and torso had to be built with a rounded bottom and the neck and legs rounded at the top. This definitely limited the design of the characters in *Quake III: Arena*. However, with some creative thinking there were ways around the system that allowed me to come up with some pretty weird results.

This little guy in particular took advantage of the animation system by having his parts swapped around:

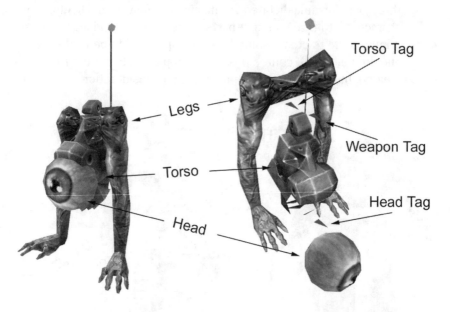

'Orbb' Copyright id Software, Inc.

While Orbb is freaky looking and does illustrate a creative use of the animation system limitations, the real reason I made him that way was purely because I wanted to do some cool hand and finger animations. The limitation of only 800 faces made it impossible for me to add fingers to the more conventional characters like Keel. Another reason is that the bulk of the animations for the characters occurred in the legs since they were at the top of the hierarchy or "parents" to the rest of the body. Since I couldn't animate the hands in the small number of animations in the upper body, I satisfied the urge to see fingers moving by designing Orbb.

AUTHORIZED DIGRESSION: *ORBB VS. CARMACK*

When we were making *Quake III: Arena*, John Carmack —
co-founder, co-owner, and chief coder at id Software — found
Orbb very disturbing. The character just didn't *seem* like it
should be running around in the Quake world firing rockets at
you. John Cash (a former programmer at id) relayed to me
one day that Orbb freaked Carmack out so much that he lost
games because of it. For a period of several days we all tested
this theory by chasing poor Carmack around on the tournament levels with the very disquieting and (apparently) creepy
Orbb.

FYI: *FUNCTIONALITY OVER FORM*   I'm always experimenting with different ways to do things in order to see if I can
squeeze a little more performance out of the creation process.
When I did the XNA Film Noir demo that featured Eva I wasn't
happy with how her hands animated. When I had her rigged
(e.g., mesh attached to a skeleton for animation) her fingers
just didn't line up right. Thus when I started my next character
I designed and built her hands a little differently. I worked out
the *function* before I did the form and let the design of the
palm be influenced by the movement of the fingers.

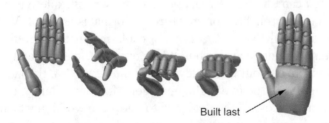

Built last

This type of design approach is unique to modelers who animate, but if you are a modeler who has never animated how
can you be sure your character will animate properly? How
can the design look good and *move* well? While I encourage
artists to master each area of the creation process individually,
you still need to know enough about the respective modeling
and animation parts to create an effective design. Allowing
your design to be influenced by function results in the most
effective character you can create.

Finally, the last limitation on your character design is...the game design itself. If the character design is someone else's sketch or based on someone else's description, then you have to satisfy their vision of what that character's supposed to look like. Sometimes this is easy and sometimes this is hard. It's easiest when you have a great rapport with the person communicating the description of the character. It's hardest when you can't get good reference or the person with the vision keeps changing his or her mind. It's worst of all, however, when you ask someone what they want a character to look like and they simply say "Just make it *cool*."

Make It Cool

While it's true you'll have some limitations to deal with like face count, game engine, and description, the main thing you need to think about when designing a character is whether or not it's *cool* — because in the end, that's what's going to make the design stick in peoples' minds.

Now everyone has their version of cool...their own definition for hip. It may even change over the years and be influenced by whatever new trend is, well, *trendy*. For me, it's simple. A design is cool if it stands out, if at first glance I say, "Wow. *That* is damn cool." It's because I can't help it. A reaction or some sort of expletive is yanked uncontrollably from my throat. Normal is not cool. Mundane is not cool. BORING is *definitely* not cool. Imaginative, interesting, different, well-done art is cool. Whether you studied art at a prestigious school or from your television or movie screen, the fact is "coolness" is in the eye of the beholder. More importantly, the real key to the success of the design is to know the world in which you plan on plunging your character and whether or not it will fit in that environment. That is how you know your version of cool will work.

Here are some sketches of characters I've designed and built over the years:

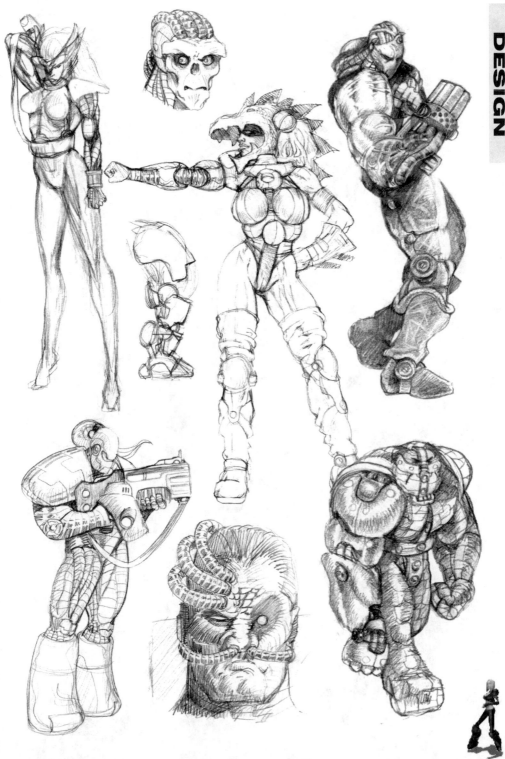

Drawing Skills

Speaking of sketches, character creation in the computer starts with being able to render and understand basic drawing principles like dealing with lines, volume, form, and perspective, especially when it comes to the human form. Good drawing skills are a must and can't be overlooked if you want to design and make better than average characters. You need to practice as much as you can...and then practice some more. In order to do this you need a sketchbook, a drawing tool, and the desire to do something with it. Granted (like in my case), after you spend so much time with your nose glued to your monitor or in your manuals, your sketching skills tend to atrophy (as you can tell from my sketches in this book). Don't let that happen! Make time for drawing as much as you can. Do it at least an hour or so a week (or more!).

There are several different ways to practice your drawing skills. Copying illustrations from books or magazines and/or performing exercises in a traditional art class are examples of good ways to become a better "draw-er." However, the best practice for improving your figure drawing and overall drawing ability, whether it's for character creation or not, has to be life drawing.

Life drawing allows you to understand shape, form, volume, light, and shadows better than any other sort of practice. It compels you to try to reproduce one of the hardest things you could possibly draw: the human figure *right there in front of you.* You don't even have to be an art major to attend life drawing classes. Sometimes you can even have the life drawing class come to you by chipping in with several fellow artists and hiring a model to pose for you. Just make sure you hire your models on their ability to hold a creative range of poses for extended periods of time and understand what you're asking of them.

Have a warm, well-lit environment as well so they're not shivering while striking that pose for 30 minutes.

 AUTHORIZED DIGRESSION: *NAKED COFFEE* When I worked at Origin in Austin, Texas, we got several artists and programmers together who wanted to hone their art skills. We started having weekly, after-hour life drawing classes in one of the meeting rooms on the third floor. Well, the Quality Assurance (QA) department was also on the third floor. After about a month of Wednesday night life drawing classes, experienced QA people would initiate some of the newer QA people by sending them into the meeting room for coffee (meeting rooms always have coffee machines) during our sessions. Needless to say when some 19-year-olds walk into a very quiet room to find an attractive, *naked* woman standing on display...well, you can imagine the look on their faces, especially when we'd all just ignore them and keep drawing!

Another good way to practice your figure drawing is to open up any magazine and just start drawing the people in the ads or articles. If anything, it gives your memory something to "draw" on for future reference, giving you more range and helping your sense of lighting.

These drawings were done from reference I found in *Shape* magazine or something...

I had to design a character for a driving game called *Propaganda* and basically used these sketches to represent her as an illustration in the design doc. Later I built and textured a model based on the design using even different reference. The drawings helped impart some life into the character and even resulted in putting shades on her when the original description didn't call for them.

When it comes to drawing, just remember there's no hard-and-fast rule for making that idea in your head tangible. I recommend a pencil and a sketchbook to start with, but an ink pen on a restaurant napkin can work just as effectively to capture that thought for a character. I know of people who sketch exclusively on their WACOM tablet (a digitizing palette that transfers pencil movements on a special "board" into a program like Photoshop). More and more I find I'll use max as a sort of sketchbook to quickly pose or light characters and either sketch them from there or build them out a little more and just render them as a drawing.

Proportions

Of course you can't make cool characters if you don't understand the principles of proportions and anatomy. Think of proportions as landmarks to gauge lengths and widths and features against. I get artwork from people all the time to critique, and the first thing I see is that it just doesn't *look* right. The forearm is too long, the feet are too big, the head is too big, etc. The character just doesn't look proportional. One of the best ways to improve your sense of proportions is to use your eyes. Once you draw or build a character, look at it and ask yourself if it looks right. Be completely honest. Ask the opinion of someone else just to make sure. If it doesn't look right, keep hammering on it until it does. Sometimes even the slightest changes can make really big differences.

Of course in the game development industry, and the entertainment industry in general, there's this pervasive adherence to, uh, "larger than life" proportions. While it's unlikely an athletic woman would be running around, shooting, diving, and rolling if her breasts were larger than her head, or with her pouty lips and hip cocked suggestively, the demographic nature of the people who see the characters sometimes dictates otherwise. Same goes for the square-jawed hero with biceps larger than his head.

Here is a normally proportioned male figure:

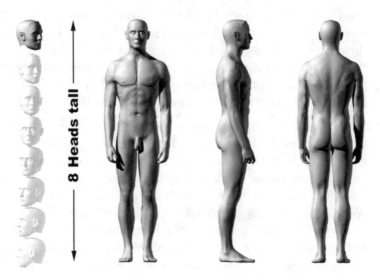

Like I said, *normal.* He's about eight heads tall and at least seems like a regular guy.

Now check out a more heroic figure:

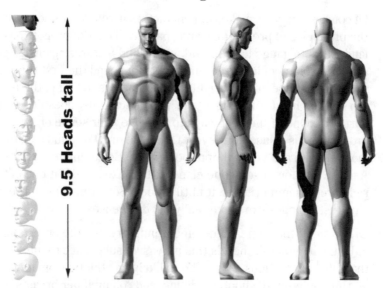

Proportionally, his biggest difference is the relationship between his head and the rest of his body. For guys and monsters, *head size* is crucial to adding that "comic book" heroism to your buff character.

Just scaling Normal Man up doesn't change the head-to-body ratio. Our hero is nine and a half heads tall; normally the male figure is much shorter.

Notice also how the hero has larger hands and feet. Resizing these extremities helps make this type of character seem tougher and ready to fight. Keep in mind, the "heroic style" is just one of many. The key is to know the real proportions so that mechanically at least the character will approximate something recognizable and animate properly. Manipulate the proportions as you will but keep in mind what's *real*.

When it comes to the female figure, the areas of exaggeration are obviously a little different than those seen in the male. A normal woman's proportions:

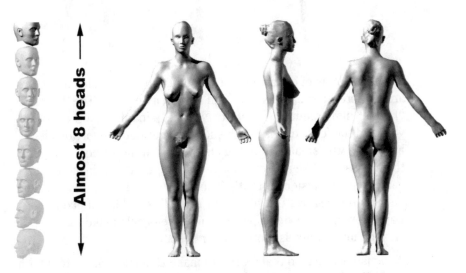

Notice just how *asymmetrical* the model is. The right breast is larger than the left and even her arms are slightly different in length. This is a common theme in reality that doesn't show up in computer graphics enough. Too often we use symmetry as a crutch due to the powerful Mirror function (just build half and flip!).

Here's a more heroically proportioned example:

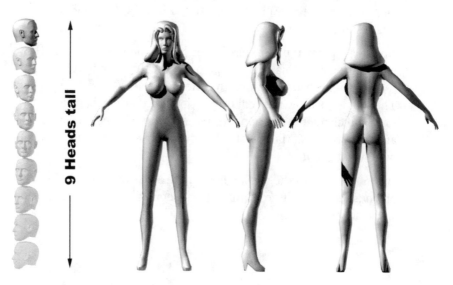

The main areas of enhancement you make to the female character are to increase the breast size and lengthen her legs. This fits that "heroic" style mentioned before. Now keep in mind another reason we build the female mesh with such exaggerated proportions is because of the small size of the characters on the screen. Okay... that may seem like a stretch for rationalizing the typical computer game female physique, but it's true! Viewed from far away it would be nice to recognize the sex of our little 25 x 25 blob of pixels. Larger breasts, curvier hips, and longer legs help make that arrangement of pixels more gender specific.

To be fair, there's no real reason to make all female characters with triple F cup sizes. Normal breasts are fine and very attractive in the flesh. 3D artists (like comic artists) each have their own preference. I try to experiment and mix it up a little. Having a *variety* of models both male and female in various physiological configurations (i.e., ectomorph, endomorph, and mesomorph) in your character stable is never a bad thing. If your intent is to make a sexy female character, then whatever experience or preference you have will influence your design and ultimately your model.

Reference Material

I've mentioned life drawing and magazines as sources from which to draw inspiration when drawing, but overall *reference* material is very important to have. Not only does it help you improve your design skills, but it also gives you ideas and a sense of what's been done as well as what *can* be done.

I rely on any source for inspiration — books, movies, or life in general. For reference I turn to books (movies are great sources of reference, too). Books rock. Aside from educating me, they're definitely a great source when I design characters. It's rare that I'll just pull something out of my head and not use any reference. Most of the time, I go to my collection of favorite books for a little spark to fire up the imagination or cultivate an idea.

What types of books do I have? As a general rule I make it a point to pick up any book on the making of movies that I dig. I also grab any art books specifically done by prominent sci-fi and fantasy artists. Books on paper gaming can be great for ideas and/or cool illustrations too. I especially like the War Hammer stuff, GURPS, and the FASA Shadowrun material. I also have books on basic drawing and the use of other media like oils, pastels, and ink. These books, various magazines, and the Internet provide me with enough reference or inspiration to design any sort of character I want.

Comic books, however, are the *real* root and source for any proficiency I have when it comes to creating interesting and believable characters. I've always been into comics. In fact, I was *so* into comics when I was younger my collection reached nearly *ten thousand!* I even went so far as to apply to and be accepted at the mecca for comic book artists: The Joe Kubert School of Cartoon and Graphic Art. The love for creating these characters of the imagination and the desire to make them come alive beyond splash pages and sequential panels are why I'm a computer graphics artist today.

As far as specific books go, the following are invaluable to me. They provide serious help and motivation when it comes to conceptualizing, creating, and animating 3D characters:

- *How to Draw Comics the Marvel Way* by Stan Lee and John Buscema
- *Atlas of Human Anatomy for the Artist* by Stephen Rogers Peck
- *Modelling and Sculpting the Human Figure* by Edouard Lanteri

I consider these books a must simply because they've had the most impact on me. The first time I went through the exercises in *How to Draw Comics the Marvel Way,* I thought they were stupid. Stick figures? Cylinders, cubes, and spheres? Dynamic storytelling and action framing? I thought I already knew everything about drawing characters; then again I was fifteen years old.

As far as anatomy goes, almost any book will do, but *Atlas* is very effective and has been around for quite a while. Edouard Lanteri's book on sculpting is superb with helping understand mass and volume in the human figure, not just with clay but when building it in the computer as well.

I'm sure you have a bunch of art books on your shelf as well (you might even have some of the ones I've mentioned). Since I've been building my collection for nearly twenty years it's pretty big. If you're just starting out and/or have a limited budget you're not going to amass a wall of books overnight. These additional books aren't as crucial as the three I mentioned before, but I find them very useful nonetheless:

- *Pencil Drawing* by Gene Franks
- *Color and How to Use It* by William F. Powell
- *Drawing the Head and Figure* by Jack Hamm
- *Techniques for Drawing Female Manga Characters* by Hikaru Hayashi
- *Superheroes: Joe Kubert's Wonderful World of Comics* by Joe Kubert
- *How to Draw in Pen and Ink* by Susan E. Meyer and Martin Avillez
- *The Figure in Motion* by Thomas Easley
- *The Art of Comic Book Inking* by Gary Martin and Steve Rude
- Any of the annual "Spectrum" sci-fi and fantasy anthology books

I'm a firm believer in "there's no such thing as having too much reference," so there's no way I can list *all* the books I'd recommend even if you were interested in hearing about them! All I can say is that there are so many great artists and teachers who can help you go to the next level, it behooves you to seek them out.

Influences

Whether you attend art school or have taught yourself how to draw, paint, or sculpt, one thing is common to all artists: They have influences. Before Dali and Picasso got bored with traditional artwork they were influenced and inspired by the masters before them. My influences are definitely more contemporary. Fantasy painters like Frazetta, Boris, Michael Whelan, Don Maitz, Chris Achilleos, Virgil Finley, and Jim Burnes influenced my budding interest in art with their amazing novel covers or illustrations. Recently I've latched onto other amazing artists like Luis Royo, Brom, Oscar Chichoni, and Juan Jimenez. These and others never cease to inspire awe and wonder when I browse through their work.

 AUTHORIZED DIGRESSION: *OSCAR CHICHONI* While still at Origin in 1995 I worked with/for my friend Chris Roberts (of *Wing Commander* fame). He was trying to pitch a sequel to *Privateer* for which I was slated to be art director. One of the enticements of joining the project was when he told me I could seek out any artist I wanted to help with the production design. I chose Oscar Chichoni. His *Heavy Metal* covers just astounded me with their texture and vivid *coolness*. After almost two weeks of trying to get in contact with him, I finally found his agent in New York and arranged a meeting.

Oscar is Argentinean and doesn't speak English so his manager did most of the talking when they flew in to Austin. We went to lunch and communicated as best we could, mainly commenting on how summer in Austin was very pleasant (especially all the summer *dresses* in Austin). We went back to Origin and he rolled out his work for us to look at. I was simply stunned. Some of the work was from the illustrations he had done for the movie *Restoration* starring Meg Ryan and Robert Downey Jr. that won an Academy Award for Art Direction the following year (and after seeing his drawings and paintings done for the film it was easy to see why). He even signed a *Heavy Metal* poster I had bought with a very cool "Con afecto — Oscar."

While painters like the aforementioned modern fantasy art masters impress me greatly, the artists who have had the greatest influence over me since I was a kid are comic book artists. These people are the ones who made me spend many hours drawing characters that

could compete with Conan, Spider-Man, and Daredevil. They're the ones I owe my love of character creation and enthusiasm to learn how to become a better artist. Barry Windsor Smith, Gil Kane, Neal Adams, Bernie Wrightson, Michael Kaluta, John Byrne, Michael Golden, Frank Miller, and Richard Corben each have had huge impacts on my development as an artist. They were my heroes and still are to this day. Along with the masters from the "Silver Age" of comics, the works of artists like Jim Lee, Simon Bisley, Adam Hughes, Jason Pearson, Joe Madureira, Joe Quesada, Kevin Nowlan, Mike Mignola, Alex Ross, and Kev Walker just blow me away and fill me with inspiration.

FYI: *HIRE A PRODUCTION DESIGNER* Often, game artists do all phases of creation when it comes to their characters. Personally I love building other people's designs. When I came up with the idea for Film Noir and the Eva character I hired painter and production artist Richard Hescox (www.richardhescox.com) to flesh out my ideas. He came up with reams of ideas for her costume, and by mixing and matching we arrived at the final design. This illustration is what I used for reference when I built her:

Finally, I have to mention how much I dig animé and manga. The very stylized Japanese-style animation and comics that many Americans are starting to enjoy is so *different*. Masamune Shirow's work blows me away, but there are many others equally as good. I would love nothing more than to create an entire game filled with animé and manga characters. A consistent, stylized (yet realistic) universe that has 3D characters built and animated in this style would make people's jaws drop. The challenge of making characters that would consistently fit that sort of style would also test the mettle of any 3D artist.

The bottom line when it comes to influences is that all artists have them whether they admit it or not. Other artists influence not only our designs, but our texturing style and animations as well. Any artist whose painting compels me to try to capture the essence of that work with vertices and polygons makes me want to dig as deep as I can into their work and see why I find it so appealing. Don't get me wrong — I think I have great ideas for characters and (when I take my time) can execute a pretty cool design on paper, but after pounding the stuff out for a long time I sometimes feel like my ideas are stale and my designs flat. Seeing fresh new stuff from all kinds of artists is very exciting and leads me to do even better *original* designs.

Work Environment

While it might be a stretch to include a blurb about work environment in a design section of a book on making 3D characters, I have to stress what an important role I feel it plays on the creative process.

If you've ever had to study for an exam, I'm sure a teacher or counselor handed you a list of recommended study techniques. Of these things that are supposed to help you digest and properly assimilate that impending deluge of information you'll never use (or forget once the test is done) I only kept one pearl of wisdom — the one about your study environment. It basically suggested that in order to make your time and effort more effective you needed to pick the same quiet, comfortable place to study each time.

I guess it makes sense if you think about it. How can your brain focus on the extreme mental gymnastics of learning *anything* if the rest of your body isn't comfortable in your surroundings? But that's what it's really saying: The comfort of your surroundings allows for optimal learning. The more at ease you are as you sit at your desk, master of your domain, the quicker your brain slips into kick-butt mode. No task is insurmountable, no project is out of your reach. As you stare off into space trying to come up with that spark of an idea or the elusive answer to a tricky problem, your eyes fix on that familiar drawing, statuettes, action figures, or configuration of stucco on the ceiling that looks like an imp's face, and the answer just *appears*.

My office is my oasis, my sanctum. It may be a guy thing, but my office is my fortress against the rest of the world. Even as a kid I was always making tree houses or forts to get away from the world and call my own. My office is so important to me that once I basically came to the decision I didn't feel comfortable sitting at my desk, couldn't be *creative* enough because I hated everything about my office. So I got rid of all the furniture, ordered new desks, built new shelves from scratch, bought and framed a bunch of new prints, and painted all the walls a deep burgundy color. It was great! I felt much more comfortable and definitely more creative. I shocked my environment and shocked myself into being more creative. Having my little slice of creative comfort is crucial to me to say the least. I must...have...my...space.

CHAPTER 2

Callisto Designed

I've talked about design in a general sense. Now let's talk about design as it applies to the character you're going to build in this book. When designing something from scratch I usually think about the purpose of the character first. This gives me a starting point to assign some sort of personality and motivation to it. Knowing or inventing a history and background as well as nailing down the personality and characteristics of a character from the beginning helps make it a better character. Once I start animating it I can keep true to whatever form I've assigned to it beforehand and make sure it stays *in character.*

Background

In Greek mythology Callisto was a close friend of Artemis, goddess of the hunt. She was supposed to be a very fierce warrior and a hunter without peer. I thought it was a cool name for a character, so that's how she got the name. She didn't, however, come into existence to star in and help me write this book. Callisto was actually conceived about a year before this book as an entry in an online modeling contest. I didn't even do a concept sketch for her because it didn't seem necessary.

FYI: *MODELING WITHOUT A NET*   As I mentioned in the previous chapter, I've been experimenting with designing characters and their parts by working out their function first. This leads to a lot of modeling experiments without any design reference...sort of modeling without the "safety net" of a reference sketch. Callisto started out this way...as an attempt to satisfy the rules of a contest by being generic and appealing to women by not being so stereotypical. Although Callisto wasn't based on any real person and didn't even get a design treatment until I wrote this book, I've had people come up to me at GDC and swear I based the character on them!

The point of this particular modeling contest was to try to come up with a model that appealed to the growing number of female "Quakers" out there, yet was generic enough to be broadly customized in texture only. Women gamers could have a fully animated model of their own to frag with online and not be offended by the typical male-centric attributes found in most female character models (think Lara Croft).

This was my original design/model for her:

Again, I tried to make her generic and non-distinct while retaining some attitude and uniqueness. Any female gamer wishing to personalize the character could easily make her unique just by customizing her texture. Unfortunately I didn't win the contest, but it did plant the seed for the character that Callisto turned into for this book. Why did the initial design lose? Who knows. Sure she got second place and people dug her. She seemed to fit the bill the contest rules asked for — something that could easily be modified into a number of iterations, be distinct yet obviously still be the same model with the same animations.

Makeover

In retrospect she didn't win because she was a little *too* non-distinct... too bland (the winning entry was a girl in a *trench coat* with a sword on her back). Therefore I got together with Callisto and did a little makeover (she wasn't too happy about losing, either). We had a couple cold ones at Hooters and she quickly went from being a confident butt-kicker in the name of female gamers everywhere to being very *angry*... with *everyone*. She grew some major Pamela Anderson Lee/*Barb Wire* attitude.

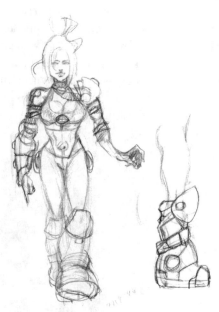

Since I get tired of always making and seeing symmetrical designs, I wanted to make her have different arms. Not to go *too* crazy on the poly-count (I decided 1,500 was a nice round number) I did keep her legs symmetrical since I had given her such big... boots. She was right-handed so I decided to armor up her left arm for defensive reasons. With the *contest* version of Callisto, I made it a, uh, point to keep her breast size relatively normal. I didn't want to turn off the female gamers for whom the design was intended. The new Callisto didn't care about stepping on toes — male or female — and definitely got some of that Pammie Lee sexy she was asking for (like I said, I was at Hooters when I redesigned her).

I gave her cleavage because any-one can model a nude female character and then paint clothes on her à la comic book super-heroines. Besides, it's more distracting to a potential opponent and sexier, too.

Of course these sketches are pretty loose and not very refined, so I had to go back and eventually clean her up to use her as reference to build into a 3D model. Usually I just scribble out ideas like I did in the previous sketches on whatever's handy (preferably my sketchbook if I can find it) and then build it. The rationale behind not doing a "prettier" sketch is that the time it takes me to sketch something out nice and neat is time I could have spent building it.

Basically I was being lazy.

Taking the time to do character studies of the character you're going to build is most definitely time well spent and helps you build the mesh even faster and understand the biomechanics of it even better. Eventually you need to have the character laid out so that it provides the optimal reference for building it in 3ds max. Another compelling reason to do a clean, useful sketch is when someone else will be building the model instead of you.

A Pose to Build By

For Callisto's reference I didn't go for a da Vinci pose because for the most part I've found that during their animations, characters keep their hands and arms down or slightly out. You could argue, however, that the da Vinci pose helps make sure your character model has the right amount of range in the shoulder and hip area.

FYI: *THE DA VINCI POSE*   Often you'll load up a model or see an illustration from a model (or for a model design) and it'll be in a jumping jack kind of pose referred to as a da Vinci pose. Back in 1511, an architectural book covering the ideas of the famous architect Vitruvius was published. A sketch done by Leonardo da Vinci to show the correct proportions of the human body was used to try to verify Vitruvius' various mathematical formulas concerning the use of mass and geometry in architecture.

The reason you'll see many people model their characters in this da Vinci pose — arms and legs wide just like Leonardo's sketch — isn't because first-time animators have to make their characters do calisthenics or back up architectural geometric theory. It's for the attachment of the mesh to an underlying bone structure, or "skeleton." Arms and legs outstretched allow the vertices of the limbs to be automatically (almost) assigned to the right bone. Rarely does an artist animate a mesh without a skeletal joint system like Bones or Biped in the max plug-in character studio. Even if it were possible to animate like this it wouldn't be practical. While I do ascribe to the usefulness of the da Vinci pose when dealing with a high-polygon mesh, lower-poly models under 1,500 faces can be built however you want. For me, having the arms and legs spread makes it too difficult to see the character. Besides, how many times in real life do you see people in that position? Most of the time, I model characters with their legs in a solid shoulder-width stance with their arms halfway at their side. I also always weight the vertices of lower-poly characters in max manually, so the utility of the da Vinci pose for fast and proper weighting is lost on me.

After refining and thinking about the sketches I made at Hooters, here's what I came up with for the model building reference for Callisto:

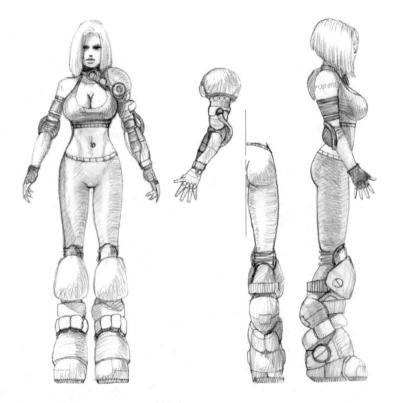

Note the breakdown of the figure. I changed the redesign somewhat from the rough sketches, but see how this sketch is explicitly for *building* a model in 3ds max? I know I've been harping on your drawing skills and not being lazy with your sketching, but functionality outweighs prettiness when you set up your reference to build. This drawing, or "template," is going to be used as a background to lay down splines that trace the lines of the design. Note that I only sketched the right side and then the back of one leg. I did this because the legs are symmetrical and I'll work out the detail in the back when I texture Callisto. Detaching and rendering just the left arm instead of the whole side is an example of the practical functionality I was talking about earlier.

Since the head is important for identity and expression, I did another drawing separately for it (lips are kinda big but what the hell)…

I changed her hairstyle from a wild bun thing to a shorter bob for the reasons of limiting design factors I spoke of earlier. I knew I couldn't pull off the free-flowing design very easily with a limited number of triangles.

To make her look more like a Gen-X scrapper, I made her bangs hanging down on the right side of her face. I started drawing them in and erased them because they obscured the eye too much in the reference drawing. Note the guidelines of the head shape beneath the hair. This isn't absolutely necessary, but it's better to have too much in the reference than too little. The front and one side view are good enough to build it. Normally I don't design reference for the back of the head unless there's something weird going on at the top or at the back.

Getting Her into the Computer

Once the basic guide sketches are done and they have the utility of providing you with what you need to build, it's time to bring them into the computer. The best way to do this is to use a flatbed scanner. I'm pretty partial to HP scanners so I use the ScanJet 6300C to do my scanning. However, any scanner will do and if you don't have access to one, you can get them fairly cheap right now. Some copy places have a scanner you can use like a copy machine as well.

Step 1: Scan the Sketch

When I bring a sketch in I generally just scan it in at 100% and downsize later as necessary. Start with the head sketch:

For potential use in other applications like a design doc (or a book) I always bring sketches in at a higher than normal resolution. It can always be knocked down to whatever resolution you want later on.

Step 2: Save It

At this point you'd save your scanned image to the proper directory using a rational naming convention. Since I've taken the liberty of providing you with the images you'll need on the companion CD, you don't have to do this. I just thought I'd go through the motions with you to show you how I do it.

FYI: *NAMING CONVENTIONS* I have to admit I can be pretty anal when it comes to naming conventions and directory structures. Nothing is more frustrating than trying to find a texture map on someone else's machine and having to sift through all their directories for crap15.tga before the scene can be rendered. Logical and consistent naming conventions are your *friends*. Use them.

Since the files are already saved for you, now's the perfect time for you to create the same sort of project directory I've done for this project on the CD. Go to your root directory (probably C:) and create a new folder called Callisto. Go into that folder and create two more folders: Images and Meshes. If you had just scanned your Callisto images you'd have saved them where? Riiight...under Callisto\Images...very good.

Step 3: Resize the Images in Photoshop

If you have a copy of Adobe Photoshop, fire it up. If you don't, then at least read over the next section before moving on to Part II: Modeling and get yourself a copy of Photoshop as soon as you can. It is the tool of preference when it comes to texturing characters for games.

Go to the CD that came with the book and under Callisto\Images\...
load cal_headbuild.tif.

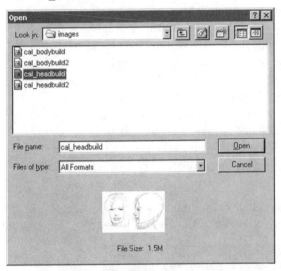

Go to Image | Image Size in the pull-down menu (or hit Alt+I, I) and
bring up the Image Size window:

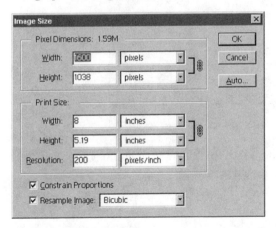

Enter 512 in the highlighted Width box and hit OK (the largest
image you can bring into max and see accurately is 512), making
sure the Constrain Proportions box is checked. With the width set
at 512, the height is now 332. This makes the file size smaller, but if
you brought it into max right now it wouldn't look very clear.

The main reason you downsized the image to 512 is because the dimensions of any image used in a program like max or as a texture for an in-game, real-time 3D object needs to be a "power of two" to be viewed properly under 3D acceleration. The width is 512 and a power of two, but the height has to also be a power of two. You *could* increase the canvas size so the height is 512, making the total size 512 x 512. This would work, but would waste a lot of texture space. A better solution is to make the image 512 x 256. This knocks your resolution down a bit, but it shouldn't affect the line quality too much and it saves memory as well as texture space. What you're doing is playing to the best "aspect ratio" for the image (in this case it's a rectangle instead of a square). The image needs to be resized again.

Hit Alt+I, I to bring up the Image Size window again. Hit the Tab key twice to scroll down to the Height box, enter 256, and hit OK.

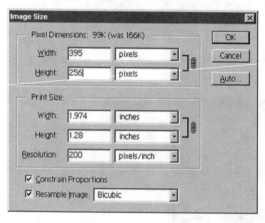

This changes the width to 395, so now you have to change the canvas size to add the extra space in the width to make the image a power of two.

Go to Image | Canvas Size (or press Alt+I, S) and bring up the Canvas Size window. Enter 512 in the Width box and hit OK. Now the image is 512 x 256. It still wastes pixels, but not as much as it would have at 512 x 512.

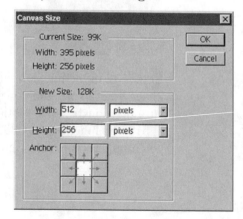

FYI: "POWERS OF TWO" Hardware-accelerated video cards are quickly becoming the norm in helping make games look amazing. Combined with the right code, they allow real-time rendering feats such as beautiful explosions, awesome reflectivity, and disturbingly real lighting and shadows. As artists, our contribution and limitation when it comes to making this visual magic happen is to make sure our textures adhere to the rule of "powers of two." In other words, the image you'll be using to texture the face will obviously be square, but what about the actual dimensions? They have to be powers of two: 2 x 2, 4 x 4, 8 x 8, 16 x 16, 32 x 32, 64 x 64, 128 x 128, 256 x 256, 512 x 512, etc. "Powers of two" simply comes from the number 2 multiplied by itself into infinity. Just be aware of the limitations graphics cards place on us.

Any game that has characters that use an off size (say 320 x 200 like we did in *Quake II* unfortunately!) as a texture page will look blurry or "muddy" when run under hardware acceleration. The reason for this coyote ugliness is because the hardware will take that 320 x 200 image and resize it to 256 x 256 to process it, stretching and compressing the carefully placed pixels of color... not good.

Step 4: Darken It

You're almost ready to save the file, but there's one more thing you need to do: darken the image. White backgrounds are bad for reference images in 3ds max since the default color for a selected line is white. White on white doesn't do much for visibility. Select Image|Adjust|Brightness-Contrast (or hit Alt+I, A, C). Enter a value of –50 in Brightness...

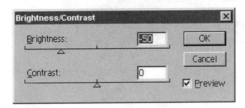

...and hit OK.

Step 5: Save It Again

Now you can save and use the file to make a material in max. Go to
File|Save As and save the image as cal_headbuild2.tif under the
Callisto\Images directory you made earlier.

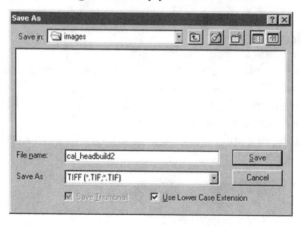

If you have Photoshop, repeat steps 3 through 5 for cal_bodybuild.tif from the CD. (Hint: This image is more square than the other one.) If you don't have Photoshop or you don't need the exercise, don't worry about it. Both cal_headbuild2.tif and cal_bodybuild2.tif are on the companion CD.

So that wraps up the 2D part of the book.

Hopefully I've got you thinking about honing your drawing skills, learning more anatomy, and finding all sorts of inspiration for your next real-time character. Seriously try to make it a point to draw at least once a week. It doesn't matter what you draw because learning the basics of design like perspective, lighting, and creating the illusion of mass on a piece of paper will make you a better 3D artist.

Keep in mind everything that will be done with your character as you design it, and as you make it envision it being animated and true to its nature. Now let's do something with our reference!

PART II: MODELING

Thoughts on Modeling

The relative differences between modeling packages today get smaller and smaller. Maya, max, LightWave, and XSI are mostly differentiated by their user base and target markets. As the similarities and modeling methodologies become closer, the greatest thing that distinguishes one package from another is simply *user preference*.

With the evolution of scanning and digitizing technology, even actual modeling methods are becoming less important as more and more developers can afford to start with a cyberscan of a model or real human being for their character models. This leads to the next part of why people use one technique over another or even one package over another: *user interface*.

Thus, what you the artist bring to the table and the results you get are becoming more important than the tools you use and how you use them. Since writing the first edition of this book I have learned more about modeling and thought less about the tool. At some point in your career as a 3D modeler your interface becomes less noticeable and you're able to translate your thoughts into electrons via your fingers, eyes, keyboard, and modeling package. When that happens, you know you are getting the results you want...every time you try. When that happens, the art package becomes irrelevant and the mechanism that is allowing you to create great art is purely your talent.

My goal with this book is to give you specific help with a specific modeling package — 3D Studio MAX 6 (3, 4, and 5 too) — *combined* with my personal approach to learning and teaching. I've discovered over the years that successful learning depends upon a series of successes that increase as your instruction continues. In other words, 5 + 5 = 10. Yet (22 – 2)/ 2 = 10 too... See my point? There are always several ways to do things. I will show you one that works and sometimes hint at or suggest others that will as well. But I didn't make the package or help develop it. I confess I'm not as proficient in it as I want to be. In fact I feel like I'm sometimes using my PC like a crude hammer to pound in nails by hitting them with the bulk of it instead of digging around for the right hammer. In other words, I tend to learn just enough to get the job done and then do the job. This is primarily a time and schedule issue and isn't wrong or incorrect, but it is depriving me of some more useful tools in max so I try to make time to learn new things as I find the potential need for them.

Strive to learn at least one new thing a day in max or any tool; you'll thank yourself for it later. In this revised edition of my first book I've tried to toss in things I know you'll find useful and maybe even *insightful* as you make your models. There's plenty of useless crap in all tools because the creators always want to cover a multitude of bases. Therefore you do have to strike a balance between being an intrepid explorer finding new paths and a common grunt hacking your way through the weeds of redundancy and less-than-useful ideas.

Never be afraid to explore, though. Dig in and hit the button you've never hit before just to see what it does. It can't hurt and it may give you one more weapon to add to the arsenal. Regardless of which tools you use or which techniques you employ, always think about and apply one simple rule to your modeling: Make Every Vertex Count. If it doesn't contribute…get rid of it.

Now let's get crackin'…

CHAPTER 3
The Guide Objects

Now that you have your respective reference material into the computer in some way, it's time to put it to use. In other words, how do you get it into max? Once you get it into max, how do you use it from there? You begin by loading the image into a viewport and then using the Line tool  in max to trace the image. These line objects or 3D drawings are going to be your actual guides for building the mesh.

Step 1: Bring the Image into max

Start up max, go to the Front viewport by clicking in it (or hitting F), and hit W to maximize the view (I prefer to almost always work in one window). Go up to the pull-down menu Views|Viewport Background and click on it (or just hit Alt+B).

Once the Viewport Background window pops up, select Match Bitmap under Aspect Ratio. To the right, check both Display Background and Lock Zoom/Pan so that when you zoom or pan in view, the image will zoom and pan with you.

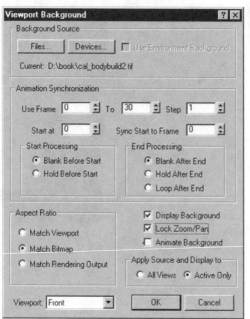

Note: If you are in a *Perspective* viewport, the lock zoom/ pan part doesn't work. It does work in a *User* viewport, though.

Next, click on Files and load cal_bodybuild2.tif either from the directory you made earlier or from the companion CD (Callisto\ Images).

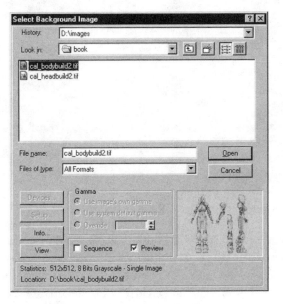

Note: If for some reason you don't see the image files, click on the small triangle to the far right in the Files of type menu and click either All Formats or TIF Image File [*.tif].

Hit Open and then OK. The image is now mapped onto the background. If the file shows up but nothing happens onscreen, hold down the Alt+Shift+Ctrl buttons and hit B to update the background image.

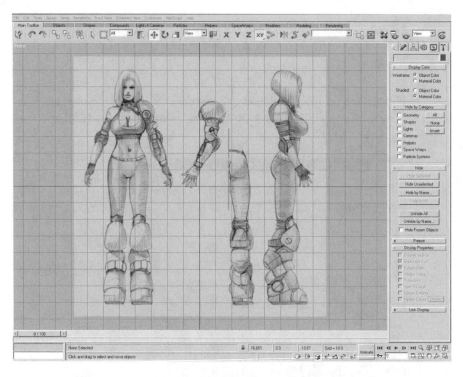

Hit G to toggle the construction grid off for clarity, then zoom in by hitting the zoom icon to make it active . Move your mouse up and down to zoom in and zoom out respectively. (Normally I just hit Z to activate the Zoom mode, and right-click to deactivate Zoom mode.) Zoom out slightly so the image is centered in view.

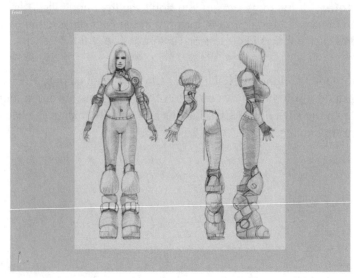

Mapping the background in max is easier and much more useful than in previous versions but hasn't changed from max 3 to max 6. To overcome the inability to see the image in a Perspective viewport and get the most out of your reference you need to turn it into a 3D drawing or reference guide *lines*.

FYI: *CHANGED HOTKEYS IN max 6* For some wacky reason the folks at Discreet decided to change some of the default hotkey assignments in max 6. If you're upgrading from an earlier version of 3ds max, take a sec and check to see if your frequently used hotkeys still work. The Scale Transform and Rotate View mode will be different for sure, but there may be others.

Step 2: Create the Guideline Objects

In a 3D package like max it's sometimes easy to forget that you can create a line drawing just like you can create a 3D object. I use this function in max all the time to create simple line art for use in everything from an ad idea to a design doc illustration to a tattoo idea! It's more functional than using a mapped plane to build because it allows you to always see through the drawing to the encompassing mesh as you build it...whether you're in wireframe or faceted viewing mode.

Zoom in to the upper torso of the drawing.

MODELING

FYI: *MAPPED IMAGE CLARITY* The lines of the image in my view look smooth because I've configured my GL driver to make them that way. Experiment to get a handle on what the combinations of Texel and MipMap Lookup do to your in-view image. Selecting Linear under Texel Lookup makes the image look the best but may make your machine run a little slower. Under MipMap Lookup, None is the best choice for making characters for real-time gaming. If you're doing hi-res cinematic work with high-poly meshes, select the Linear box to get the best image. If for some reason you don't have a 3D accelerator card, you need to get one *now*. You just cannot expect to build characters for today's games without a nice card like one of the nVIDIA Quadro FX family of cards or the ATI Radeon 9700 or 9800 cards. nVIDIA always optimizes its drivers for the current art packages so it's generally your best bet.

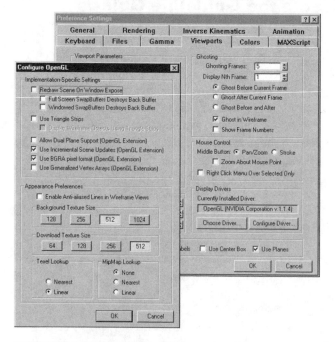

If it isn't already active, click on the Create panel tab and click the Shapes menu active . Go down to the Line button so it turns green and active . Starting with the top of Callisto's head, trace over just the lines of her hair and face and then stop. Right-click to end a line and left-click to start another. Be as gratuitous as you want with the vertices in the lines since they're only going to be used for reference.

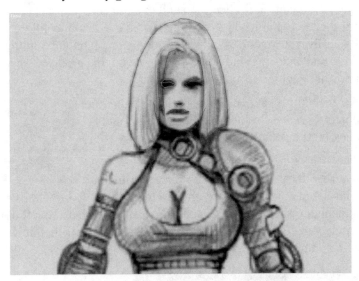

It's hard to see in a black and white illustration, but max automatically assigns different colors to each new line object (or mesh) that you create.

FYI: *UNDO & REDO VIEW* In max the Undo (Ctrl+Z) and Redo (Ctrl+A) functions are well known and well used. Most people forget there are also viewport versions of these commands. If you zoom in too far or arc rotate at the wrong moment, simply hit Shift+Z and the view will go back to the previous viewport position. Hit Shift+A to redo it again.

MODELING

Step 3: Attach the Lines

Each time you right-clicked to end one line and left-clicked to start another, max thought you wanted to make a new line/object. Basically, you've ended up with a collection of unique, multicolored lines instead of just one. You want to make this group of separate lines or "segments" one line or object.

For visibility's sake, pick the darkest of the line objects, go over to the Modify panel , and click on the Attach Multiple button .

This brings up an Attach Multiple window where you can highlight more than one line in a hit list of objects that are eligible to be attached to the object selected. Click All at the bottom left of the window to select all eligible shapes that can be attached to your selected line.

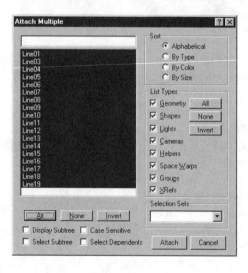

Hit Attach and left-click anywhere onscreen to deselect the line. It's now all one color.

 FYI: *START NEW SHAPE BUTTON* Instead of attaching the other lines to the one you have now, you could have avoided all that by simply unchecking the Start New Shape box on the

Create Spline panel before you began making the line. With this box unchecked, any line made while in the Create panel is part of one spline.

Select the line again, open the General sub-menu on the Modify panel  and under Interpolation, enter 0 for Steps to turn the shape into a series of lines instead of curves.

Even though I find it easier this way, you might actually prefer to use curves to align the shape to the reference, so this step is optional.

Note: Another way to turn your shape into curved lines or make it all linear *regardless* of the shape Steps setting is to select all the vertices of a shape, right-click over one of the vertices, and click on the vertex type you desire: Bezier Corner, Bezier, Corner, or Smooth from the pop-up menu.

Step 4: Create the Rest of the Guidelines

Now that you understand the ins and outs of creating lines, finish the rest of the guide. With the object selected, scroll the Modify panel up by holding the left mouse button down and dragging upward (you'll see the little hand icon). Click on Create Line Create Line under Geometry so it's green and active.

With the Create Line button active you can finish drawing in the rest of the guidelines and they'll automatically be a part of the existing line. Don't forget that you can pan the view around by holding the middle mouse button down and dragging the direction you want. Hitting the Z key allows you to interactively zoom in and out; just right-click to release the zoom mode.

FYI: *SCREEN PANNING WITH "I"*   As you find yourself approaching the edge of the view while drawing a line, hit the letter I and max will pan the screen automatically, centering your view on the position of the cursor. This is a very useful feature, just not too "I"ntuitive.

Completely trace all the lines of the image, making sure they're all attached into a single line, and name it Body Guide by going to the Modify panel and clicking once in the name field of the object (the current name should be Line something). The currently assigned name of the object is highlighted in blue...

...allowing you to type in the new name of the object: Body Guide.

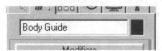

Right-click on Front in the upper-left corner of the viewport. Turn off the background image by sliding the cursor down to the currently checked Show Background and click on it. Now the background is image-less and your Body Guide object should look like so:

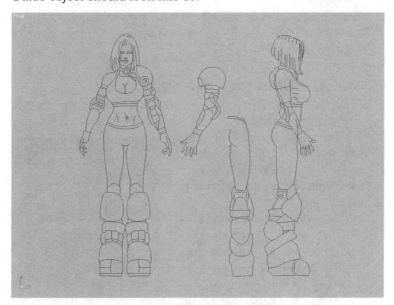

Now you've turned a 2D drawing into a 3D line.

Save your work or, if you want to save time, load up Callisto01.max from Callisto\Meshes on the companion CD.

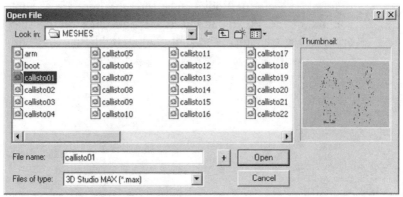

Step 5: Scale the Guideline

With the Body Guide built you now have an overall picture of the scale of the character and her body parts. Now make sure that the scale is correct. It's true that at any given point you can scale a character to whatever is appropriate; however, I've found that it's always a better idea and a good habit to establish the right scale as soon as possible. I work in feet and inches, so I have my Home Grid set to reflect that.

FYI: *CHANGING THE HOME GRID* To change the Home Grid spacing units to inches and feet, go down to the Snap icon and right-click to bring up the Grid and Snap Settings window. Click on the Home Grid tab. In the Grid Spacing field, enter 1. For Major Lines every Nth, enter 12. Leave everything else as is.

This means that you have now set the size of each little "box," or unit, to 1 and set the "heavy," or major, grid lines to be every 12 of those boxes/ units. The grid system in max is very useful and has several options like AutoGrid, so explore them!

Before you scale the Body Guide, though, there are a couple things you need to do. Zoom out a little and right-click on the object to bring up the transform shortcut menu. Highlight Move with the cursor...

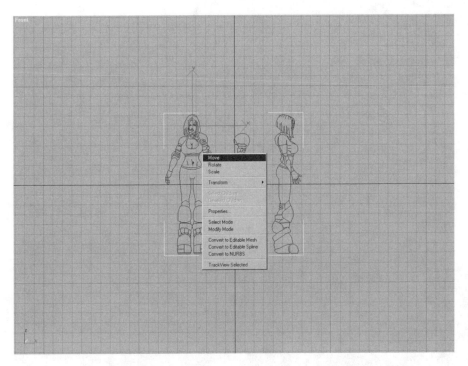

...and left-click. This changes the cursor to the four-arrowed move icon ⊕ and is the quickest way to change to another transform icon or access an object's Properties menu. Hit F8 until the active axes are both X and Y ⊠. Or you can right-click on the axis icon until the axis flyout appears:

Then simply click on the XY axes, YZ axes, or ZX axes — whichever you need. It's always easier to just keep hitting F8 until the right axes show up.

Move the object up and over so it's sitting on the dark construction line:

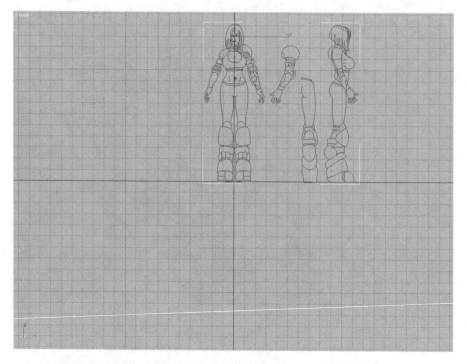

The feet should rest on the horizontal line (think of it as the ground plane) and the vertical line should bisect the front-facing render of Callisto (right down the middle).

FYI: *USING THE TRANSFORM GIZMO*   You may be wondering why I don't use the nifty transform gizmo that is available in max 3 and above by simply hitting the X key.

The reason is I just don't like it. Call me hard-headed, but I just prefer the F5, F6, F7, and F8 hotkey approach. Sometimes an old dog doesn't *want* to learn new tricks!

Next you need to adjust the pivot placement for the object so that when you scale it, it scales properly in reference to the grid and to the object itself. Go up to the Hierarchy tab 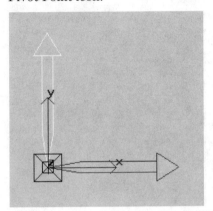, click on it, click on Pivot [Pivot] , and click on Affect Pivot Only [Affect Pivot Only] so it turns purple and active.

The normal axis icon is now replaced with the large and colorful Pivot Point icon.

This lets you know that any transform done (move, rotate, or scale) will now affect just the pivot point. The pivot point has a lot of functions, but for now think of it as the center of rotation and scaling when you select the Pivot Point Transform icon [▣]. Hit your Spacebar to lock the selected pivot [▪] so the cursor doesn't have to be right over the pivot to move it.

Right-click on the Snap icon [▪], making sure the Grid Points box is checked.

MODELING

Left-click to turn Snap on (or just hit S) and move the pivot point down to the origin point (0,0,0) between Callisto's feet.

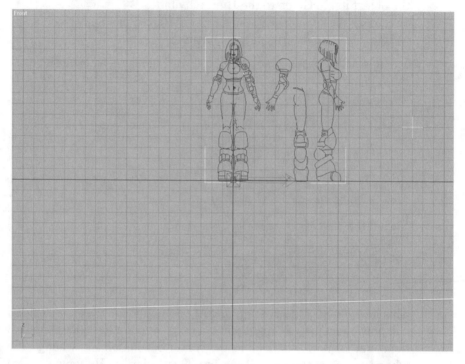

Click on the Zoom Extents icon and hold it down:

Scroll up and let go at Zoom Extents Selected . Hit it and Body Guide now fills the screen, centered in view.

FYI: ZOOM EXTENTS VS. ZOOM EXTENTS SELECTED
I've always used Zoom Extents Selected since if nothing is selected it acts the same as Zoom Extents, but it has the added benefit of zooming into view whatever object or sub-object has been selected. It only becomes a pain if you have a single vertex selected, but you'll figure that out for yourself eventually.

Right-click on the object and select Scale from the pop-up menu.

Left-click to activate the Uniform Scale ⬛ (or just U Scale) transform icon and scale Body Guide down by about 46% or until it's six major lines (six feet) tall. Hit Zoom Extents Selected again and you should have something like this:

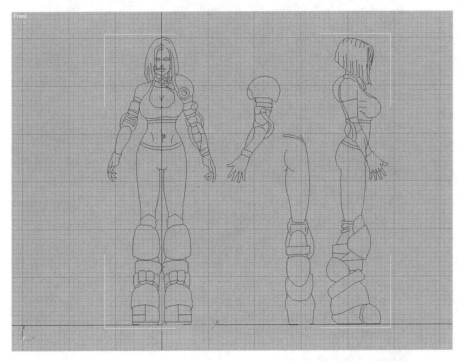

As I said earlier, the reason for doing an overall body reference is for relative scale and to build the mesh. For important parts such as the head, it's necessary to create an additional reference object for it since it normally has more relative detail and you need to zoom in to work on it. This holds true for any part of your character you feel is an important part of its identity. Heck, you could do a close-up shot for *all* the limbs and it wouldn't hurt.

Step 6: Make and Adjust the Head Reference Object

Normally you'd hide the Body Guide and repeat steps 1 through 5 for the Head Guide object, aligning it as best you can to the Body Guide. Instead, just load Callisto02.max from the Callisto\Meshes directory on the companion CD to save yourself some grunt work.

I've scaled Head Guide to match the now-hidden Body Guide. Again, starting your characters by laying out their general proportions and then a more detailed head allows you to establish a relative scale for the character.

Select Head Guide. Go to the Modify panel if you're not already there and click on the Spline sub-object icon ∧ so it turns yellow and active.

Select all of the splines of the profile part of Head Guide and make sure the pivot is set for Use Selection Center ▣. Do this by holding the left mouse button down over the Use Pivot Point Center axis icon ▣:

Scroll down the Use Center flyout and let go at the Use Selection Center icon ▣. Now the axis icon goes to the center of the selected splines.

FYI: *WHY I DON'T LIKE "USE PIVOT POINT CENTER"*
max defaults to the Use Pivot Point Center axis icon  90
percent of the time. I find this pretty annoying since I find
myself changing it to Use Selection Center  95 percent of
the time.

Right-click over the selected splines and choose Rotate from the
pop-up menu.

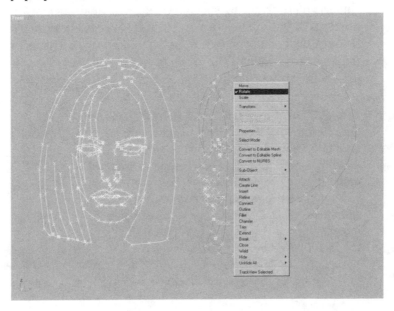

Hit F6 to restrict the axis of rotation to the Y-axis , hit A to turn
Angle Snap on , and rotate  the selected splines 90 degrees.

FYI: *TYPING IN TRANSFORMS* If you're rotating an
object or sub-object by a
known and exact number, you
can alternately enter a value
in the Rotate Transform Type-
In window by right-clicking on
the Select and Rotate icon
at the top of the viewport.

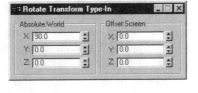

 Simply enter a value to indicate how many degrees you
want to rotate the selected object or sub-object.

MODELING

After you rotate the splines you'll be asked if you want to weld coincident endpoints.

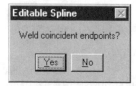

A good rule of thumb when this message pops up is to click No. Unless you're targeting specific vertices to weld, clicking Yes sometimes cause the splines to warp if their vertices are Bezier or Bezier Corner and you *haven't* set your steps to 0. This is a bad thing since it will alter the shape of some of the segments and defeat the purpose of the guide object.

FYI: *GETTING RID OF THAT ANNOYING MESSAGE* An easy fix to avoid getting that "Weld coincident endpoints?" question is to set your Weld threshold to 0. This just means that no matter how close coincident vertices get, you won't be prompted to automatically weld them. This is a useful trick when dealing with higher-res meshes using a set of modifiers called Surface Tools. In the Modify panel, go over to the Vertex sub-object 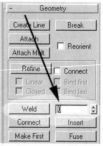 of the shape and type 0 for the value beside Weld.

FYI: *RESIZING YOUR VIEWPORT* If you have a large enough monitor or good enough eyes or just like to get as much onscreen as possible you can work at a screen resolution of 1600 x 1200 pixels or greater. If you like to work at a lower resolution like 1280 x 1024 you often find yourself scrolling up and down through the menus to the side. If that annoys you as much as it does me simply resize the viewport by holding down the left mouse button over the far right-hand side of the viewport frame and drag left to expand the menu to two columns (or more) instead of one...

▼

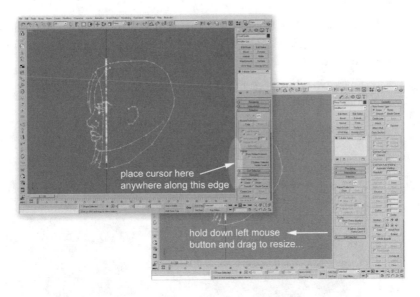

place cursor here
anywhere along this edge

hold down left mouse
button and drag to resize...

Restore the single column in the same way by holding the left
mouse button down while over the edge and sliding it back to
the right.

Right-click on the line again and choose Move from the transform
options. max has graciously defaulted back to the Use Pivot Point
Center axis icon ▦ but for a move like this it doesn't matter.

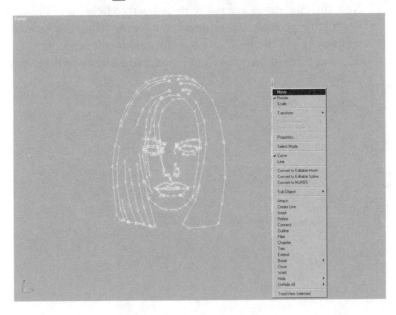

MODELING

Hit the F5 key to restrict the movement to the X-axis [x] and slide the selected splines to the left so they're approximately in the center of the face.

Click No when it prompts you to weld stuff. Head Guide should now look something like this:

Now the guidelines are ready to be used to help build the character. Recreating your sketch or detailed drawing using the Line tool like you've done is the best way to utilize your reference. It makes the drawing three-dimensional and useful in a User or Perspective viewport.

Next up — building a head.

CHAPTER 4

The Head & Face

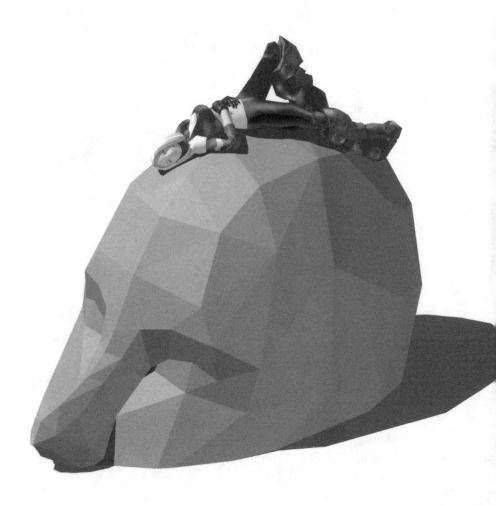

You're ready to begin building the head, but just where do you start? You have your guide objects done, built from the reference you've created, but what's next? Well, when it comes to modeling low-poly objects, one of the best ways to build anything is to start with a "primitive." Primitives are basic shapes in max that serve as a starting point to quickly build more complex objects. They have adjustable parameters that can be tweaked on the fly and are power-ful modeling allies. For me, primitives supply the raw material necessary to quickly visualize and create mass.

In max 6 there are 23 primitives to start with. Ten of them are known as the Standard set of primitives. They consist of a box (1), a sphere (2), a cylinder (3), a torus (4), a teapot (5), a cone (6), a geosphere (7), a tube (8), a pyramid (9), and a plane (10).

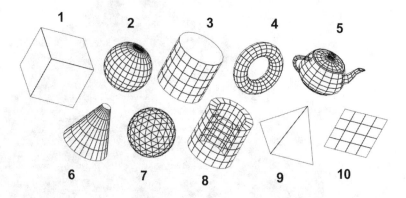

The others are accessed by clicking on the small black arrow beside Standard Primi-tives and bringing down the additional menus under the Create panel.

The Extended primitives are: a hedra (11), a chamfer box (12), an oil tank (13), a spin-dle (14), a gengon (15), a ring wave (16), a torus knot (17), a chamfer cylinder (18), a capsule (19), an L-extent (20), a C-extent (21), and a prism (22).

Note: In max 6 there's an additional Extended primitive called "hose," which presumably (?) is designed to help you quickly build a fire station.

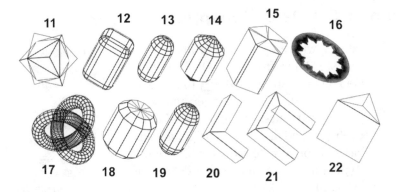

11 12 13 14 15 16

17 18 19 20 21 22

It depends on what result you're after when choosing which primitive to use. In the case of the head of this character, you're going to use a Standard Primitive called a geosphere.

FYI: *GEODESIC SPHERES*   When you want to make a sphere primitive in max you can make the default latitude/longitude sphere or you can make a geosphere. The "geo" in geosphere stands for "geodesic." Geodesic is mainly an architectural term applied to domed structures that are formed by interlocking polygons. Another way to think of geodesic is that it pertains to the geometry of a curved surface. Basically, in the Pollyanna land of low-poly, curves are the enemy. They eat up polygons quicker than a dragon munching on the local villagers when they run out of sacrificial virgins. Geospheres are the shining knight of curves in max. They slay the face-count dragon quite handily and I recommend you take them to task whenever you can. Here's why. Compare the spheres at right made in max.

Their silhouettes describe the same number of segments: 16, *but* the geosphere on the left has128 faces while the lat-long sphere to the right has 224 faces — nearly double the face count. So while the sphere is useful, it's not very efficient for low-poly modeling when you think about it.

MODELING

Step 1: Create a Geosphere

Pick up where you left off or load Callisto03.max from the CD. Click the GeoSphere button GeoSphere to make it active GeoSphere . Create a geosphere by putting your cursor right between Callisto's eyebrows and dragging your mouse until it has an approximate radius of 3.86 units (type it in the Radius box if it doesn't quite hit 3.86).

Make sure it's centered on Head Guide, moving it if necessary.

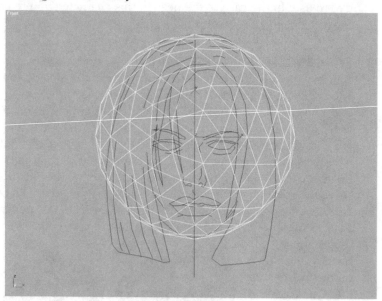

Whenever you create a geosphere primitive, the default setting is four segments, Icosa geodesic. ("Icosa" is short for a 20-sided icosahedron.) This results in too many faces so you need to change it from Icosa to Octa.

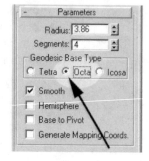

The geosphere changes accordingly, reducing the number of faces and giving you a nice vertical line running down the middle of the mesh.

Now you have an eight-sided octahedron with substantially less faces. Octa is the setting I prefer because it results in a nice bisecting line down the middle of the mesh, which makes it easy to delete half of the mesh later on.

FYI: *INITIAL PRIMITIVE DIMENSIONS* All the primitives in max are referred to as being "parametric." This just means when you first build them in max, you can type in values to change their settings and dimensions at the time you first create them. If you deselect them or create something else, then the only way to change the values is by going into the Modify panel [icon].

Step 2: Scale the Geosphere to Fit the Guide

Now Non-Uniform (NU) Scale  the sphere along the X-axis by 65%.

By shaping the geosphere, you're establishing a rough approximation of a human head using a primitive shape. Like I mentioned earlier, I use primitives as the starting point for building low-poly characters all the time. It definitely saves time and since the engineers at Discreet went to all that trouble to put them into the program, why not use them?

Step 3: Delete Half the Geosphere

Go to the Modify panel and apply an Edit Mesh modifier Edit Mesh to your geosphere. Hit the Vertex sub-object icon .

Select all the vertices on the left side of the geosphere, and delete them by hitting the Delete key on your keyboard.

 FYI: *CONFIGURING YOUR MODIFIER BUTTON SETS*

Take the time to put the modifiers you need in plain view. In max 3 and above, to change the modifier buttons that are displayed in the Modify panel, click on the Configure Button Sets icon  Set the number of buttons you want to display:

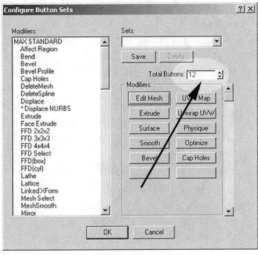

MODELING

Slide a desired modi-
fier or two from the list
on the left to the but-
ton set on the right.

Hit OK; your
button set will now
grow to the new num-
ber of modifiers on
display.

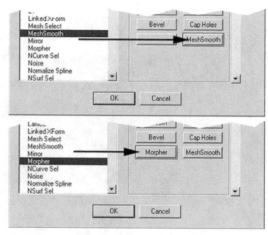

Now go to the Right viewport by hitting R and move the geosphere,
centering it so that its volume rests nicely between the forehead
and back of the head.

Rename the geosphere Head.

Since you're going to be adjusting the shape of Head from now on, you can freeze Head Guide to avoid accidentally selecting it and slowing you down. Go to the Display panel 🔲 and click the Freeze Selected button Freeze Selected . Now you don't have to worry about accidentally selecting the guide.

Take a look at the profile of Head Guide; notice the vertices of Head need to be tweaked so they come as close as possible to conforming to the general shape of Callisto's guideline profile. You're going to do this with a series of scales and moves. This "matching up" of vertices to an outline or guideline is a key technique to accurately model your character. Many of the tweaks like the ones you're about to do happen fast and intuitively as you adjust the volume of the primitive to fit within the confines of the guide.

Step 4: Tweak the Shape of the Geosphere

Now I'm going to try to illustrate on paper what it takes seconds, minutes, or sometimes hours to do based on look, feel, and intuition. This "tweakage," as I like to call it, is hard to explain sometimes, but definitely ties into what you see or rather *don't see* in your mesh. As you move the vertices, you're pulling out the features that you want — when they're not there, you keep tweaking until they are there.

MODELING

Go to the Right viewport and select the vertex 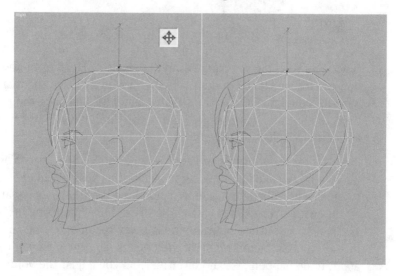 at the top of the head. Pull it down so it touches the guideline.

Next, select the row of vertices in the middle of the forehead, and NU Scale them 93% along the X-axis.

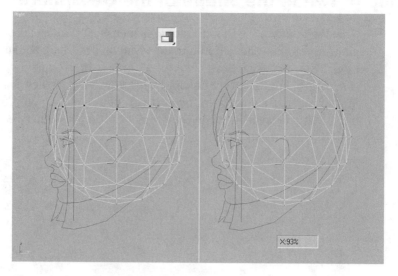

Scaling the vertices almost gets them on the line but you still need to nudge them over a little.

Move the same row of vertices along the X-axis until they rest on the guidelines.

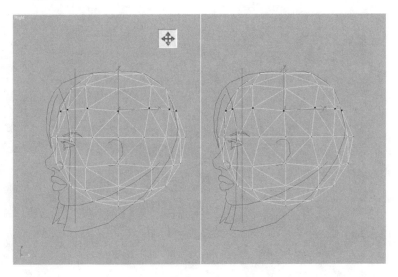

Go down to the next row of vertices and NU Scale them along the X-axis by about 88%.

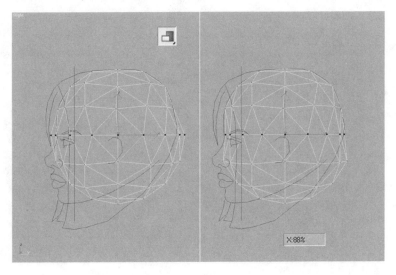

Nudge them a little to the left as well so they're more or less within the lines.

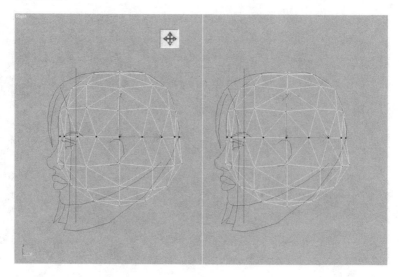

Select all the remaining vertices and slide them to the left so the top row is centered on the line of the nose and back of the head.

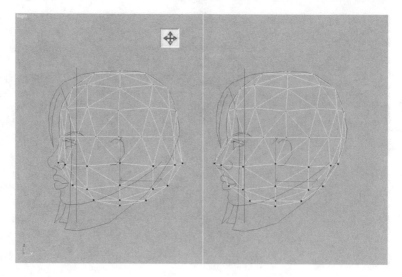

Scale them slightly (about 98%) along the X-axis.

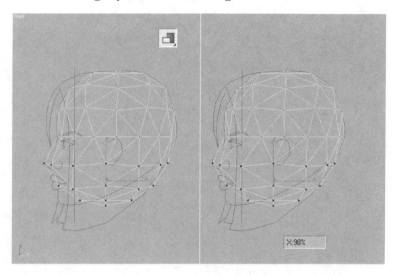

Select just the vertices out of line and slide them even farther to the left so they're more or less centered with the lines.

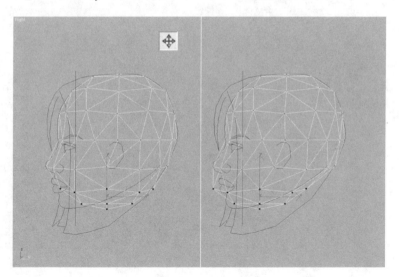

Scale the verts in by 82% along the X-axis.

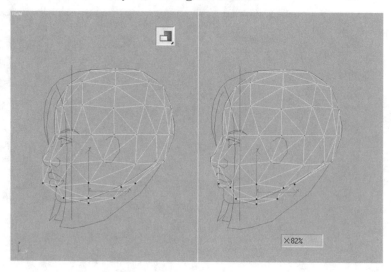

Nudge them over a little to the left.

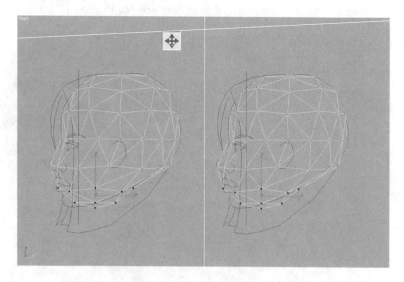

Go down and select the remaining vertices not aligned and slide them over like you did previously.

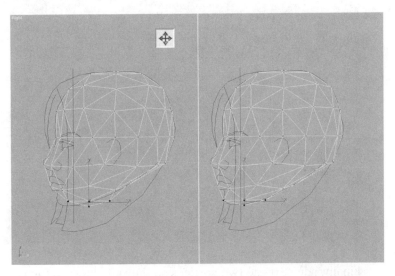

Scale them slightly (90%) along the X-axis to sit on the guidelines.

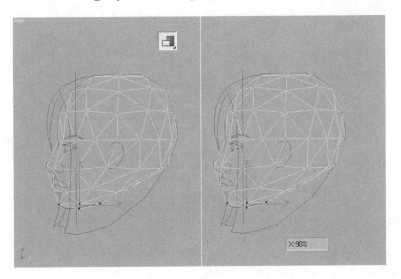

Move the bottom vertex over to define the chin.

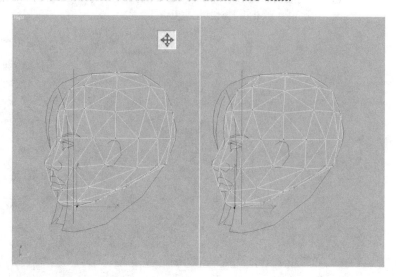

Finally, adjust these two vertices so they sit closer to the guidelines by sliding them to the left.

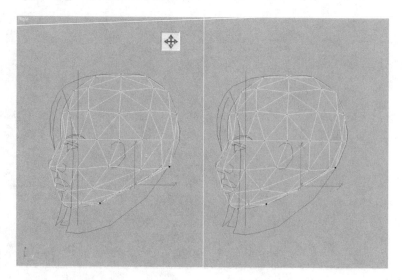

Those tweaks took only a minute to do but show the power of starting with a primitive and then adjusting it to fit your guide. Now you have a rough, basic shape that approximates the head. What you need now are some extra vertices in order to define the head better. You do this by dividing and turning edges.

Step 5: Add Vertices by Dividing Edges

For me, the ability to manipulate edges has always been one of the most compelling reasons to use max as a modeling tool. Starting with a single triangle I can literally model anything using vertex transforms and manipulating edges, *and not create another single triangle*. Dividing edges gives you the ability to add additional triangles and vertices to refine your mesh and add detail where necessary. Turning edges allows you to make sure the surface of your model is nice and convex instead of concave. This simple ideology of making all edges align correctly so the surfaces of your mesh have volume is key to building and animating better-than-average characters.

Use the mesh you've been working on or load Callisto04.max from the CD. Select Head and zoom in to the nose area.

Make sure you're at the Modify panel and hit the Edge button ◁. Check Ignore Backfacing for your own protection…

... so you're only affecting the edges in view and you're ready to start adding geometry to the profile of Callisto's head. But first, to make sure you can see the edges you're about to divide, right-click on Head, slide down, and click on Properties.

Uncheck Edges Only and check Vertex Ticks. This will let you see the new edges you create and always see the vertices whether you're in Vertex Sub-object mode or not.

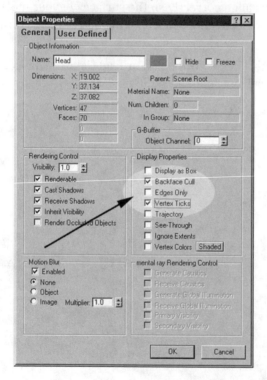

 FYI: *EDGES ONLY SHORTCUT* Since by default, max chooses to check the Edges Only box upon object creation, I use the Visible Edge toggle, Ctrl+E, religiously and immediately to show the edges after I make something. In max 6, however, you need to manually assign this key since by default it's been assigned to Scale Cycle.

Hit OK and go back over to the Modify panel. Press the Divide button 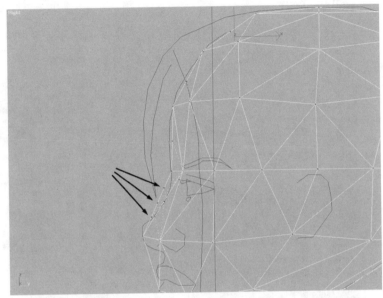 so it's green and active and left-click on the edges around the nose and forehead at the following points:

Go down to the Turn button and click it so it's green . Zoom in even closer to the nose area and turn some of the edges you just created.

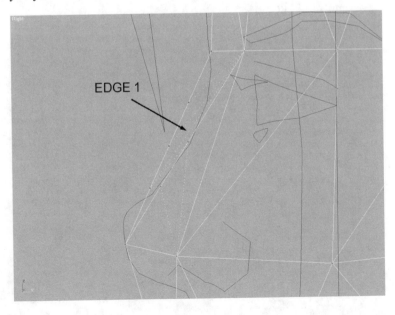

EDGE 1

MODELING

With the Turn button still green ⌈ Turn ⌋, click on the longest diagonal edge that was just created by your edge dividing (edge 1). Click on the long, *undivided* edge a little bit to the right of that one as well (edge 2).

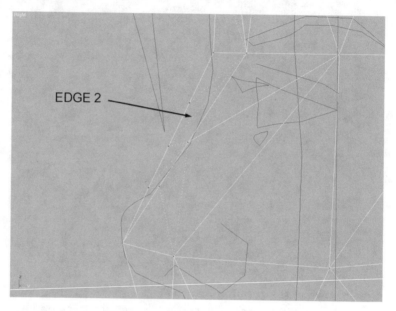

EDGE 2

Click on two of the inner edges to turn them and you end up with something like this:

FYI: *WHY TURN AN EDGE?*   The ability to manipulate edges is very important to me and I'm always on the prowl for one to turn if it needs it. How do I determine whether or not an edge needs to be turned? Look at the following two rectangles.

In rectangle 1 the long diagonal line A just seems out of place and awkward.

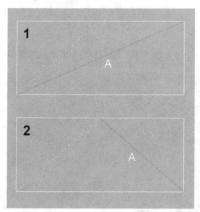

By turning line A, notice in rectangle 2 how it just *looks* better and the lines are more evenly distributed. Now look at two more rectangles with even more edges before and after the edges are turned.

For me, the deciding factor on whether or not to turn an edge is line length. When I look at edges I try to make sure that each line that makes up that edge *is the shortest it can possibly be.* If by turning it I can make it shorter, you bet I turn it. The exception to this rule would be if it makes a crease or something equally unpleasant in the mesh. Even if long, skinny lines are perfectly functional, they're ugly and in some cases cause weird rendering

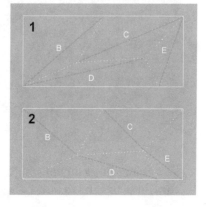

glitches when the mesh is seen in the game engine. Keeping your mesh pretty isn't the main reason you turn edges, though. Shorter lines result in an object that has more evenly distributed faces and adds to the appearance of volume.

MODELING

Step 6: Tweak the Shape Some More

The reason for turning edges after they've been divided is so you can move the new vertices around to match the guideline even closer. Click the Vertex button 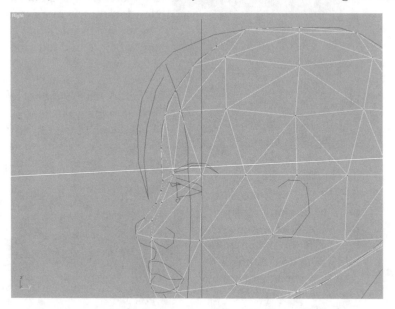 under the sub-object menu. Hit F8 until the axis changes to both X and Y . Then, one by one click on the new vertices by the bridge of the nose and position them so the contour of Head matches the profile of Head Guide better.

When you're done, the Head object should look something like this:

Now things start moving faster with this technique of "Divide, Turn, and Tweak" to shape the profile of the face even further.

Zoom in to the nose and lips area and divide some more edges so you can define the nose and mouth.

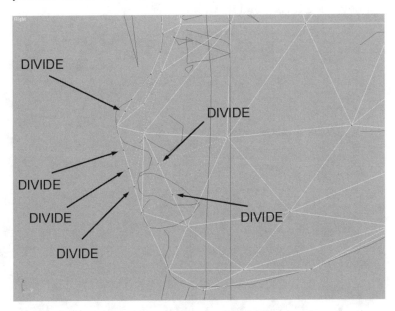

Notice how in addition to the edge of the face you need to add some to the interior as well. This is because you will need them later on, and if nothing else, they should seem necessary for keeping a judicious and evenly distributed number of faces in that region of the head.

 FYI: *BUILD NOW, OPTIMIZE LATER*   It may seem like you're adding a whole lot of faces to the Face for it to be "low-poly." Don't worry about it right now because as you'll see later on, you can always optimize it and use other geometry to get to your target number of polygons. Although I do it occasionally, adding detail to an area once the mesh is "finished" because I have more faces to work with doesn't occur too often!

MODELING

Turn some of the newly created edges so you can move the vertices to match the profile. Compare it to the previous image to see which edges are turned and why.

Now, go back to the vertex sub-object and move the newly created vertices so they match the guide.

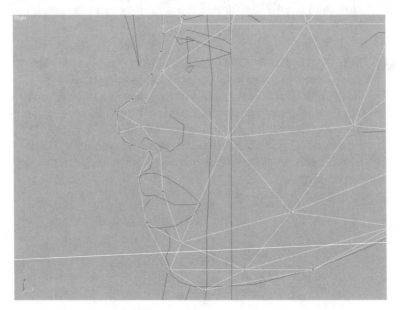

Something that will help you position the vertices better is to visualize the topography and lines of the overall head. These "terrain" lines should describe a definite pattern as the profile line of the head goes inward. The amount of segmentation or detail of each defining line becomes less.

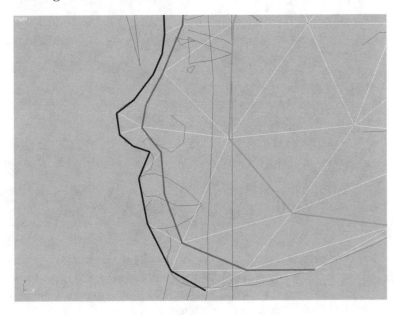

Keeping these concentric lines of the mesh in your head as you work on the object is important. It gives you a "feel" for your work and alerts you to potential problem areas.

Add some more vertices using Divide Edges around the nose.

The power and utility of edge manipulation should be obvious by now. It is a quick and easy way to add vertices and faces to massage the mesh into the correct shape. After some more Tweak and Turn and Turn and Tweak action, take a look at your lines.

They are now better and will support a facial shape more effectively. By the way, don't worry if your mesh isn't exactly like mine at this point. The important thing for you to have understood is the Divide, Turn, and Tweak principle.

Add some more vertices to the lips, mouth, and chin area, and push them into shape. You'll end up with something like this:

Now keep in mind you've only been working in one view and are simply *guessing* at giving yourself enough vertices, edges, and faces to work with to make the head look like you want. However, this is a 3D shape and other planes or views need to get in on the action.

Step 7: Switch Viewports and Tweak Some More

Load Callisto05.max from the CD. Switch to the front view and zoom in so the face fills the screen.

Go back to the Modify panel, activate Vertex Sub-object mode, and select these two vertices that correspond to the nose (when seen in profile):

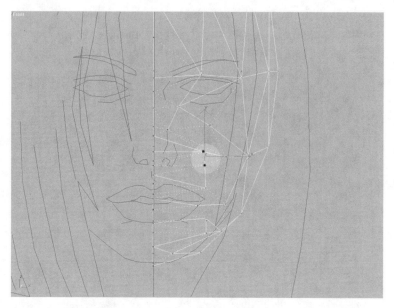

Slide them over so they each correspond to the guide better.

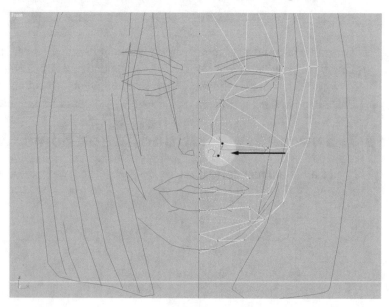

Next select these other vertices...

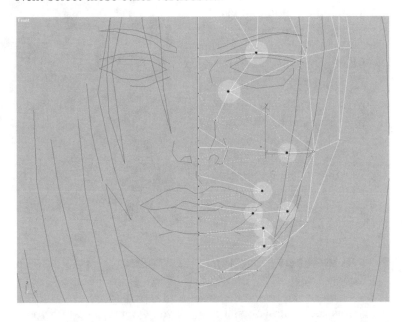

...and move them over as well, positioning them so they match up to the guidelines.

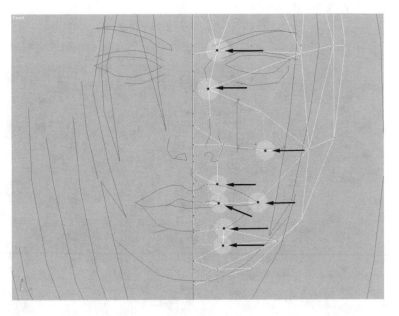

MODELING

Still in the Front viewport, switch the shading to Facets by going up to the viewport name (Front) and right-clicking on it. Change the shading mode from Wireframe to Other|Facets.

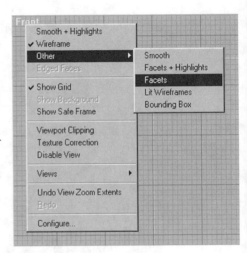

Now hit P to go to the Perspective view and hit the Zoom Extents Selected icon . This centers your mesh "in view" so while in the Perspective window your view will rotate around the object you have selected.

FYI: *VIEWPORT "VIEWING" PATTERNS* Hitting P, Zoom Extents Selected 🔲, and Ctrl+R to rotate around and look at your mesh will be the first and most repeated series of movements you'll find yourself doing if you want to speed up your modeling skills when modeling in one window. Again, this has changed in max 6 so you have to reassign Ctrl+R to activate the rotate view function.

Rotate the view around, using 🔄, so it looks something like this:

FYI: *FACETS MODE*   When building a lower-polygon mesh I always view it in Facets mode when I want to see it shaded. This is because it lets me see the shape more clearly, allowing me to catch any edges that need to be turned, and generally gives a better view of all the faces individually than Smooth + Highlights. It gives a better sense of volume, too. Another way to view your model in a faceted mode, even in Smooth, is to strip any smoothing groups from a mesh manually in the sub-object menu or by simply assigning a Smooth modifier to the mesh and not specifying a smoothing group number.

Ughh! Obviously you still have work to do. Go back into the Right viewport and look at the position of these vertices around the nose where it meets the face.

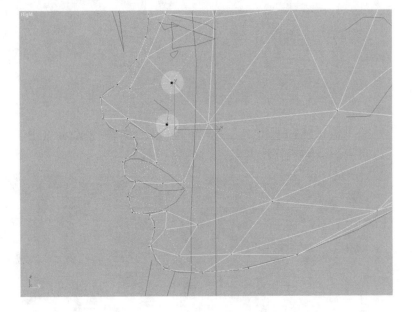

Change the view to Perspective, rotate the view around ⟨⚙⟩, and you'll see that those vertices need to be moved over closer to the middle of the face.

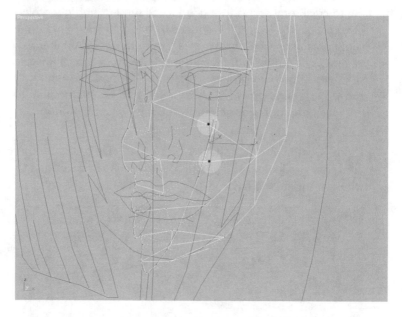

Switch to the Front viewport and move those vertices so they line up better with the guide.

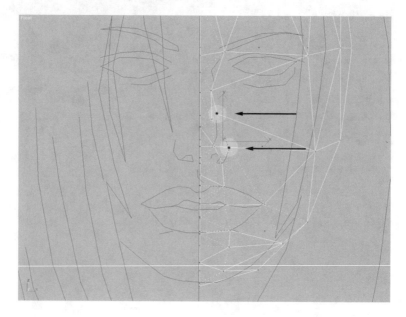

FYI: *ROTATING AROUND A SELECTION SET* Remember that when rotating in view, Zoom Extents Selected  works on sub-objects as well as objects. For example, if you select a face in the Perspective viewport and hit Zoom Extents Selected, the view will center and rotate around that selected face. Same goes for vertices and edges. This is a very useful feature of max.

By going back to the Perspective viewport and turning Facets on again you can see the improvement.

MODELING

Up until now you've been working with just half the face with the knowledge that once it's finished it can be mirrored and attached to the other half. This is the best way to make anything symmetrical: Build half, then mirror it. In max, you don't necessarily have to wait until you're completely finished before you mirror, though. You can work on just one half of an object like the head and have another mirrored half present, dynamically reflecting the changes you make to it.

Step 8: Mirror the Head Half as a Reference Object

Hold the Shift key down and slide the head along the X-axis. When the Clone Options window pops up, click on Reference under Object, accept the default name max gives the new object, and hit OK.

This creates a version of the object called a *reference object* that will reflect any changes made to its "parent," the head object. Now you need to mirror and position the new object so its centerline is flush with the centerline of Head.

Select Tools|Mirror...

...and mirror the object along the X-axis. (You could also have hit the Mirror icon  to get the same menu.) Keep Clone Selection set to No Clone and click OK when the Mirror window pops up.

FYI: *MIRROR CLONE OPTIONS* As you can see by the menu options under Mirror, you could have saved a step by creating a clone and mirroring it at the same time by selecting the Reference option under Clone Selection in the Mirror window.

Now slide the new reference copy over so the two meshes meet.

Click on the new reference copy and look how it shows up on the Modify panel.

Notice how a "dividing" line pops up in the modifier window where normally a modifier name or at least "Editable Mesh" would appear. This just tells you that the object is a referenced copy and any changes made to the original will still affect the mesh. Modifiers still can be applied to it, just as if it was a regular object. Again, the reason for using a reference copy is so any changes made to the parent copy are reflected in its referenced twin. Having both halves onscreen at the same time is more for your mind's eye than anything else and illustrates a very useful tool in max. Once you decide to attach the reference to the original, simply collapse the stack. This severs the link between it and its parent and makes it eligible for being attached.

Step 9: Shape the Mouth

Select the Head mesh again and start shaping it
up by turning some edges. Make sure you're in
the Perspective viewport with Facets shading
turned on. Turn Edged Faces on as well (or hit
F4) so you can see the lines of the mesh better.

Hit the Turn Edges button 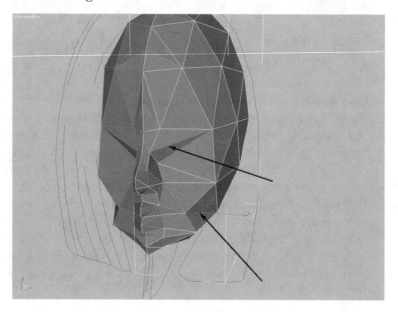 and turn
these two edges.

Now Callisto's face looks a *little* less weird.

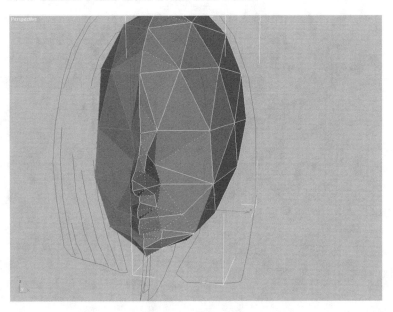

Next, make her chin a little less pointy by moving these vertices...

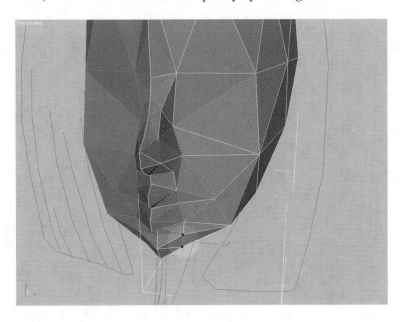

...down and over (X-axis/Z-axis).

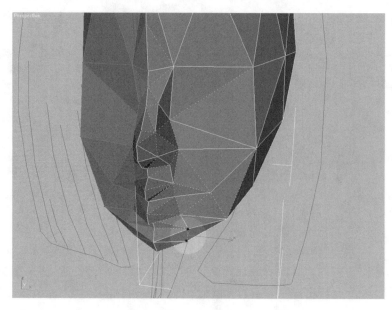

Hit Ctrl+R to rotate the view some more and drag the verts out along the Y-axis.

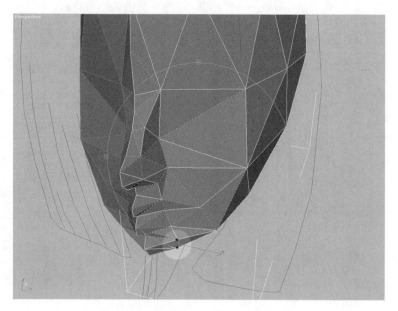

Alternately, you can hit F8 and slide the vertices around on *both* the X- and Y-axes.

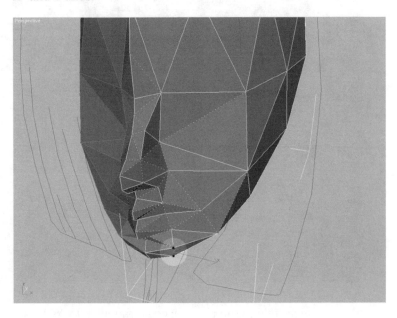

 FYI: *EXPERT MODE* By now you should be comfortable with working in one window, hitting F5, F6, or F7 to switch to the X-, Y-, and Z-axes respectively. Some prefer to work in other viewport configurations and occasionally even I'll need more than one view active at a time. For the most part, I use one window because it gives me more real estate. Lately I've even started using the Expert viewport mode. This is a stripped-down viewport setup where everything drops away but the background and your mesh. You can access most of the commands you normally deal with by simply right-clicking on the object. If you feel daring, give it a try by hitting Ctrl+X and then hitting it again to go back to normal mode.

Rotate the view and select the vertices at the end of the nose.

Slide them around to the right place so the nose looks less pointy.

Next, move on to the lips...

...and make them more rounded.

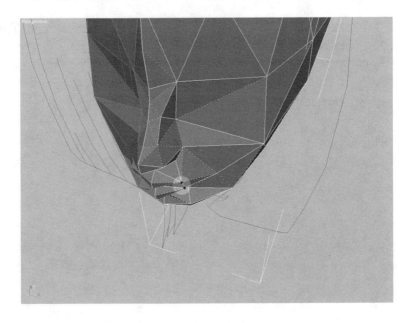

Take some time to shape the mouth and cheek area by dividing/turning edges and moving the vertices around until they look something like this:

The mouth is defined so it will be easier to texture later on. This is a detail that's usually lost in a low-poly head but you can always optimize it later if needed. Time to move on to the eyes and brow.

Step 10: Build the Eye Area

Load Callisto06.max from the CD.

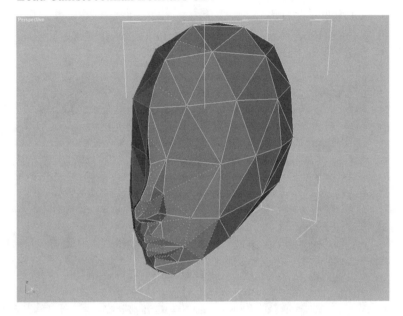

A character's head is basically a blocky, ovoid mass. The eye area can be thought of as the subtraction of areas that define the eye and brow region. Look at the following:

Head 1 represents the basic mass. With a little tweaking, it can work for a *real* low-poly head. Refining the head further to suggest a brow and a nose requires a "subtractive" approach. First, a chunk needs to be cut away for the brow (2) and then nose added (3). Callisto's head has a nose, but the eye and nose bridge area need some of the gross geometry of Head 3. To do this you need to both shape the forehead into a more flat surface area and add vertices to create the brow overhang and eye sockets.

MODELING

The first thing you need to do for Callisto's head is make the fore-head a bit flatter. Select Head (the left half of the head, not the reference copy), go to the Modify panel, and go to the Vertex sub-object menu.

Select the vertex at the bridge of the nose, right of center, and move it forward along the Y-axis.

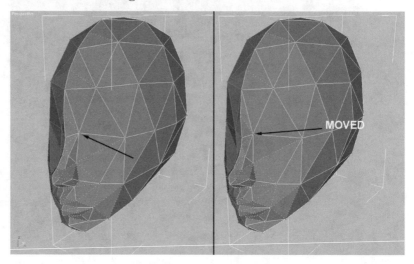

This helps flatten the forehead a little more and prepare the edge of the brow for some vertex additions. Next you need to make the bridge of the nose have more of a distinct shape and add depth to the eye socket. So divide this edge and slide the new vertex back.

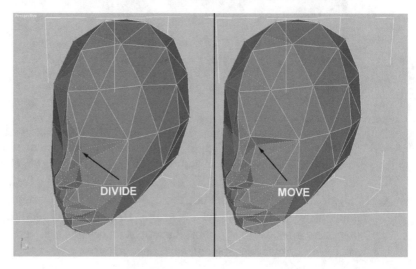

To make the eye more apparent, add more vertices around the upper cheek area by dividing the following edge and turning that resultant new edge.

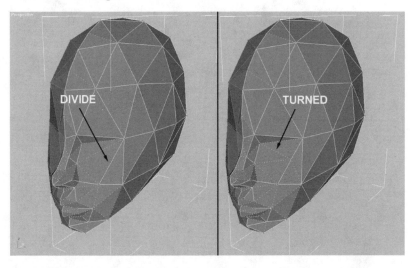

Switch to the Front view and go to wireframe. Define the bridge of the nose even further by adding a vertex using Edge Divide and softening the curve of the bridge by scooting two vertices over.

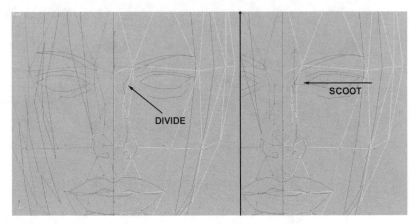

MODELING

Now you need to divide some more edges around the eye area so you can make the eye "geometry" more apparent.

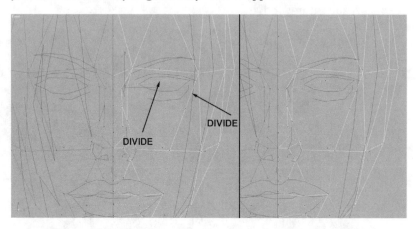

Define the outer brow better by moving this vertex up and turning this edge:

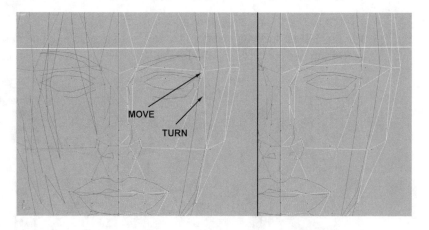

Shape up the cheek area underneath the eye to the right by moving these vertices:

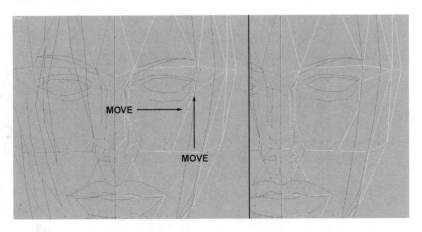

Shape the eye and brow even more by moving some vertices, dividing the edge past the bottom of the eye, and turning the new edge created by the divide:

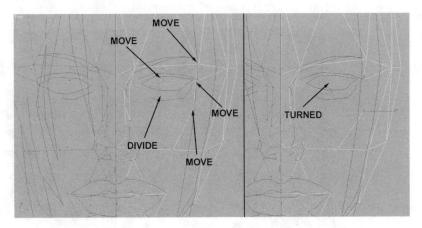

Next, round the eye socket by moving this vertex forward and in slightly:

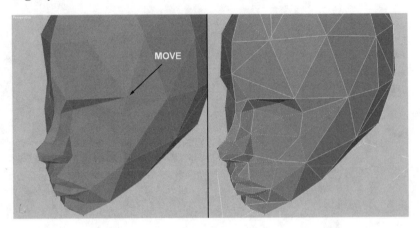

The eyebrow ridge is a little too abrupt, being a straight line going across, so soften it by dividing these two edges, turning the long edge above the brow, and finally moving the new vertex up to make the formerly straight line a little curved.

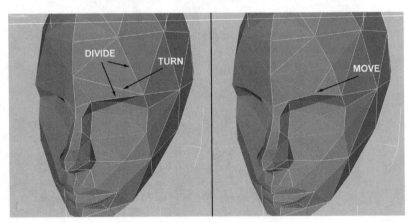

Much better. Now the next tweak is going to be gratuitous, but it will make the eye shape punch out even more.

Divide the edges at the brow, the top of the eye near the nose, and the corner of the eye.

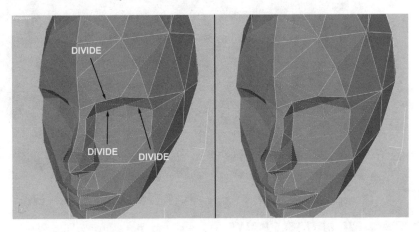

Turn the new edges so the triangles around the eye look more uniform and move the vertices of the brow ridge yet again to be evenly rounded.

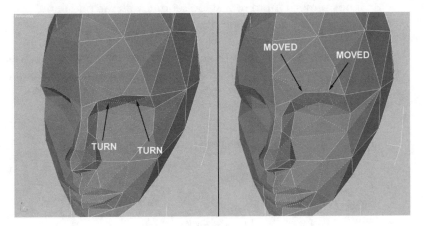

Finally, clean up the surface of the eye area, and impart the best sense of mass by avoiding concavity and turning these edges:

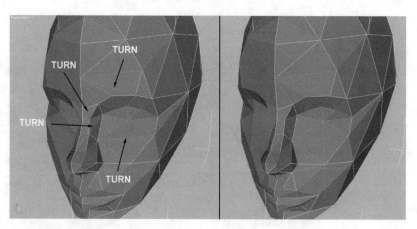

 FYI: *EDITABLE POLYS*   One of the more dramatic additions to the modeling repertoire in max 5 and 6 has been the *editable poly*. It's basically an editable object with five sub-object levels: vertex, edge, border, polygon, and element. It has a much more robust toolset and with the additional sub-objects can give you a quicker way to do things once you get the hang of it. I don't use it because I like to get vertices lodged under my fingernails as my hands get dirty. ;]

However, for the sake of argument and learning I encourage you to try out editable poly. The times I've messed with this new feature have given me the following pros and cons:

Pros:

- Has better selection tools
- Easier to optimize without rebuilding geometry
- UVWs always stay intact when optimizing

Cons:

- Can't be added to a modifier stack
- Turn to Poly/Poly select route isn't useful
- Not a big enough improvement to switch

So that does it for the head and face. Always try to visualize their shape by thinking of the head and its major identifying landmarks and mass composition. Some general rules of thumb as they apply to the distinct elements of the head and face are:

- The forehead is relatively flat with slightly beveled sides.
- The brow is the termination of the forehead and creates a shelf over the eyes.
- The cheekbone region is relatively flat to the front.
- The nose is a continuation of the forehead and frames the eyes at the bridge.
- The mouth area lies on more of a cylinder than a flat plane.
- The lower jaw and chin form a triangular shape.

I encourage you to study the anatomy of the head and face more intensely since it will help you understand the concept of imparting mass with all parts of your models.

MODELING

CHAPTER 5

The Hair

Now comes one of the more challenging parts of a low-poly character — the hair. If you have any, run your fingers through yours. How in the world do you make that in a computer? Sure, there are procedural plug-ins for max that use particle systems to make it *seem* like your rendered character has hair, but that just doesn't work for a real-time, low-poly character. The only thing you can do is try to create the *illusion* of hair by building a convincing mass of polygons and using the opacity map channel to make polygon planes look like wisps of that … wispy stuff.

Before you get started, though, let's talk a little about hairstyles for low-poly characters. Unless you're making Fabio, doing a male character's coif is fairly easy to pull off since most of the time you'll make him bald or with very short hair. When it comes to the female "do," short is okay (butch-short looks a little odd), and ponytails are relatively easy. Molded or more form-fitting styles can work great, too. Here are some "do-able" hairstyles that are variations on buns, bobs, and pinned-up looks:

Unfortunately, long flowing locks are not practical when it comes to real-time characters due to the number of triangles it would take to animate that sort of hairstyle.

Notice from looking at Callisto's reference sketch that I've chosen a "bob" cut with longer bangs that will be mapped onto a curved plane with an opacity channel for transparency to create the illusion of hair hanging down.

This kind of hairstyle works great since it doesn't involve a lot of hair and it can be represented effectively by a solid mass of faces and vertices that *approximate* the shape of the hair. This concept is important to understand because modeling is always about creating the illusion of a real object. Creating a mesh that represents hair is definitely illusory... even for an illusion!

Load up Callisto07.max (or use the version you have now) and compare the mesh as you've built it thus far to the template from the head sketch:

You've built the head essentially bald. There is no hair. If you have the time, it's always better to build the head bald and then add hair. If nothing else, it gives you a basic starting point when building other characters wearing different hairstyles. In Callisto's case, her 'do is a sort of soft helmet that goes over the head. The first thing you'll have to do is literally grow the hair over the existing head shape by using extrusion. At its simplest, "extruding" something means taking a closed outline or shape and pulling it through space, adding depth to that shape by turning lines into faces. This will properly increase the overall mass of the head and add the vertices and faces you need to pull off the design.

I approach modeling with the basic premise that if I have enough raw material, I can tweak and turn the mesh into submission. Just like dividing edges is a quick way to add vertices to a mesh, selecting and extruding faces is another way to quickly add triangles to a mesh. However, it's not the only form of extrusion in max.

Check out the following image:

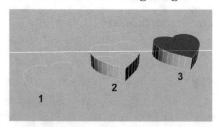

One way to extrude in max is to use an Extrude modifier [Extrude]. Start with a line (1), apply an Extrude modifier, and enter an Amount value in the Parameters selection. You get either an uncapped extrusion of the line (2) or a capped extrusion of the line (3). Using an Extrude modifier to turn a shape into a mesh results in a parametric object in max. "Parametric" just refers to the ability to dynamically adjust parameters at various levels within the object or object stack. This is a basic and powerful modeling tool. The second form of extrusion is at the sub-object level by extruding a face or set of faces.

Step 1: Extrude Faces from the Head

Start in either a Right or Perspective viewport and go into the Face sub-object menu ◢. Go up to the Rectangular Selection Region icon ▭ and hold it down: ▯. Then choose the Fence Selection Region icon ⬚.

Now select all the faces of the back left side of the head (not the reference copy) as illustrated below:

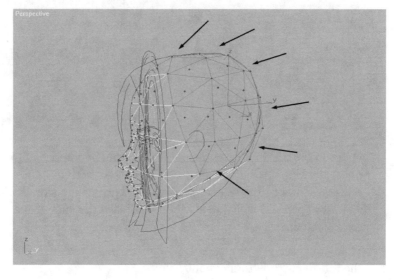

Rotate the view around so you can get a better sense of how much you're going to need to extrude.

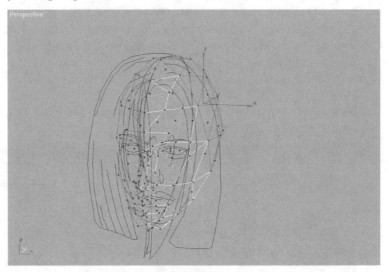

Over on the Modify panel 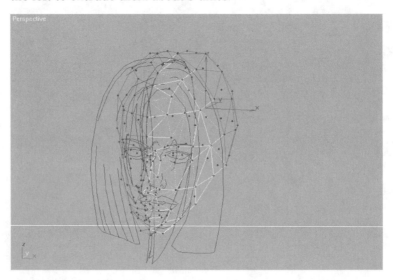 under the Edit Geometry sub-menu, press the Extrude button [Extrude] to make it active [Extrude] and put your cursor over the selected faces. An Extrude icon (looks like a stack of papers) will appear when you place the cursor over extrudable faces.

Hold down the left mouse button over the selected faces and drag to the left to extrude them about 5 units.

Don't worry if the faces don't extrude
exactly 5 units. If you want to be precise,
enter 5 in the Extrude number field rather
than using the extrude mouse-drag icon.

Step 2: Move the Vertices to Match the Guide

Now you need to move the newly created vertices so they line up
with the guide. Change to the Front view so you can see the outline
of the hair. Select the outermost vertices and move them around
until they fit the "drawn" face.

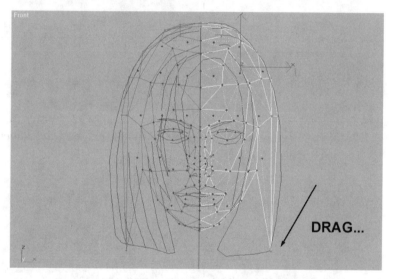

DRAG...

Notice I dragged the bottom vertex all the way down. This is
because, again, I'm just looking for the mass or raw material to
work with. I drag that particular vertex down because I know I can
use Divide Edge ⸻Divide⸻ to add vertices to the "line" and further
refine the shape of the hair.

Go to the Right view and match up the bottom edge vertices to the guideline.

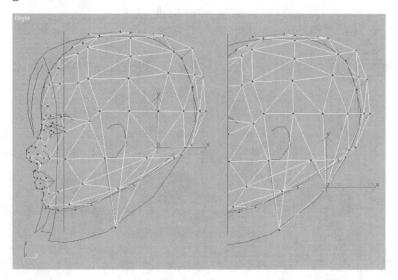

Rotate your view so you can see the top of the head and select the top vertex near the edge of the forehead.

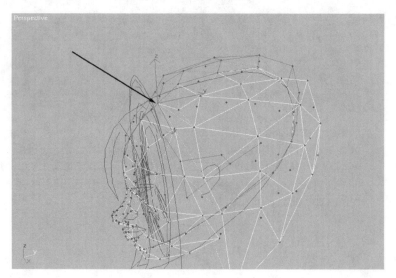

Now drag the forehead vertex forward along the Y-axis to match the template so you can create the beginning of the top of the bangs.

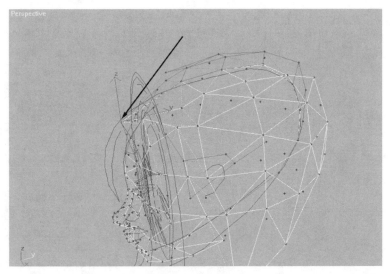

Next you need to continue moving vertices into line, matching them up to your reference object. Select and tweak these verts...

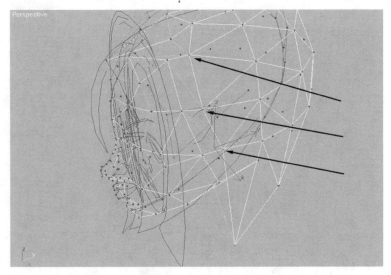

MODELING

...switching between the Right, Front, and Perspective viewports until...

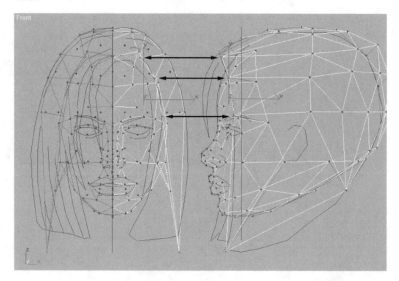

...they match up with the front and side profile of the guidelines.

Switch to Facets and turn on Edged Faces. The shape seems to be coming along.

The trick to making a hairstyle like this work is to avoid making it look like a plastic helmet. You need to add enough segmentation to the hair so that when the character is animated the hair can move subtly around the exposed face, or just have the appearance of a mass of soft hair. The hair needs to imply pliability. Now that you have the rough shape blocked out using just Face Extrude and vertex tweaking, it's time to divide and conquer! Before you slip into this (hopefully) familiar pattern of dividing edges, turning edges, and tweaking vertices, make it easier to see the hair by hiding the face.

Select the faces of the face.

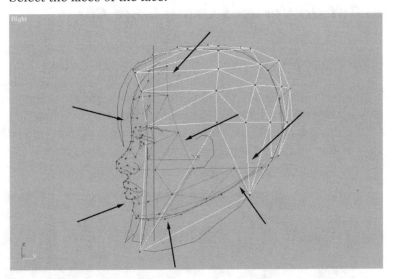

Hit Hide [Hide] in the sub-object menu.

Makes it much easier to see the geometry, doesn't it?

 FYI: *HIDING VERTICES, TOO* A great feature of max is demonstrated when faces are selected and hidden, and the corresponding vertices that define the faces are hidden, too. If you need the vertices back and want the faces to stay hidden, just go into the Vertex sub-object menu and hit the Unhide All button ⌗Unhide All⌗.

Step 3: Add Vertices Using Edge Cut

Now try out a tool unique to the Edge sub-object menu called Cut. This function allows you to click on an edge and drag a dotted line "cut tool" to another edge, dividing the edges it touches. This technique is an easy way to add vertices, edges, and faces and avoids the repetitive pattern of always turning edges after dividing them. Over on the sub-object menu hit your Edge button ⌗ and scroll down to the Cut button ⌗ Cut ⌗ and press it so it turns green ⌗ Cut ⌗.

Rotate ⌗ your view so it looks something like this:

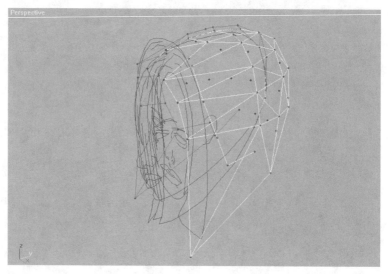

FYI: *"EDGE ON" DIVIDING* I've noticed in max that if you work primarily in the Perspective viewport like I do it behooves you to try to be as perpendicular to an edge as possible before trying to divide it.

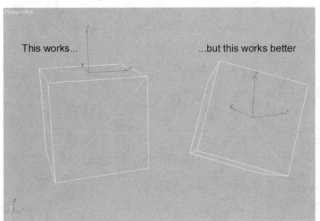

In the second box the face to be divided is perpendicular to your view.

Using the Cut tool [Cut] you are going to "cut" across the geometry, clicking on one edge near the top of the head and then clicking on the bottom edge of the hair here (1) and here (2).

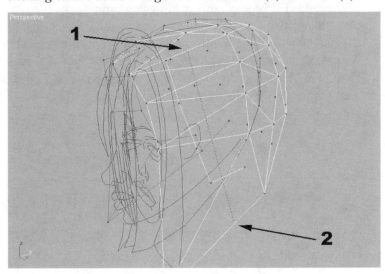

Click at the point mentioned before at the top of the head and you'll see a dashed line stretch down to the second point at the bottom of the hair where a plus sign appears again over the edge. With the Cut button [Cut] active you'll notice that your cursor turns into a thick white plus sign whenever it goes over an edge. This means you can set the beginning point of the cut. Clicking the second [⟁] edge makes the cut…

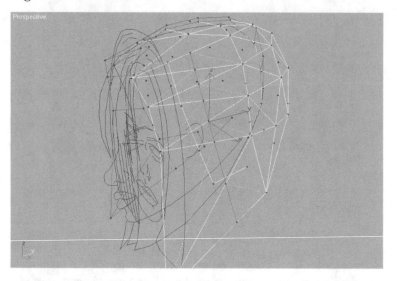

…and adds the new geometry. Now you can push some more verts around and shape the hair into a rounder form. For clarity, get rid of Head Guide by going to the Display panel [▣] and hitting Hide Unselected [Hide Unselected]. Next, select the new line of vertices you just created, change the axis to be in both the Z- and Y-axes, and pull them down and forward simultaneously.

Rotate your view so you can shape the vertices further along the X- and Y-axes, going into Facets mode to help see the impact of your tweaking (sunken or "convex" edges are easier to locate when seen as facets, remember?).

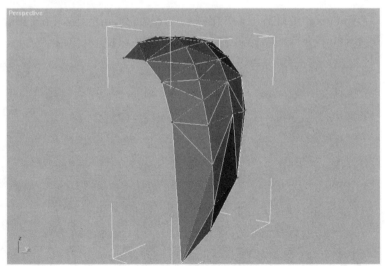

You need to unhide your frozen guide so you can see how close you're matched to it thus far. Since it's frozen you can't unhide it by using Unhide by Name [Unhide by Name...] ; max just doesn't *see* it if it's frozen. No problem, though. Simply do the following. Click on Unhide All [Unhide All] and hit H to bring up your hit list of objects in

MODELING

your scene to select. Click on Invert, click on OK, and then hit Hide Selected [Hide Selected]. Piece of cake!

With your guide back, now you can move the vertices around so they line up with the hair.

You need to also match the curve of the hair in front, but first you need to add some vertices with Divide Edge [Divide].

Go to whatever viewport you feel comfortable in (I start in Perspective and then move to Front) and line up the new verts.

Obviously some edges need to be turned, so take care of those...

...and you're ready to round the front of the hair by adding some more edges using Cut ⌈ Cut ⌉ again.

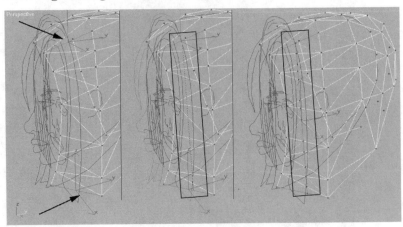

Step 4: Weld Excess Vertices

Sometimes Cut results in too many vertices, edges, and faces. Your last cut did just that so get rid of some of them by using Weld | Selected under the Vertex sub-object menu ⌈∴⌉.

First you need to select these four pairs of vertices...

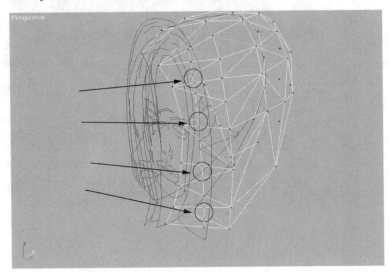

...enter 5 in the box beside Selected...

...and hit Selected. Now, any of the vertices that are selected and within 5 units of each other are welded. In this case it's the series of pairs that you had selected.

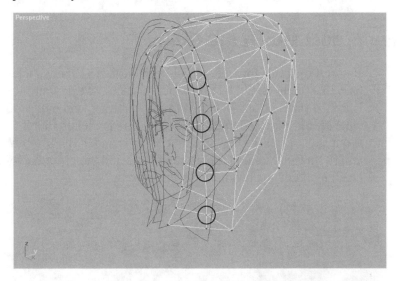

Had you entered a higher number, all the selected vertices would have been merged. A lower number would have resulted in an error message.

This just means any of the selected vertices that could be selected within the tolerance specified *have* been welded. You need to type a bigger number in to get any results.

FYI: *WELD VERTEX SETTINGS*   When welding a group of vertices into a single vertex, most of the time I just enter a big number in the Weld Selected box and hit Enter. This is obviously overkill and after a while it gets pretty intuitive judging how much tolerance the vertices have to collapse, but it makes sure the weld is going to take. Making multiple welds across a bunch of vertices takes trial and error to dial in the right number. This can be a great time-saver and turns into an effective tool for optimizing a high-res mesh, too.

Step 5: Just Match the Guide

Before I turn this into a book solely dedicated to making a head of hair, I'll stop here and let you weld, turn, and tweak your head of hair into shape. Don't be afraid to add, subtract, and move around whatever it takes to match the head to the guideline (don't forget about the area of the hair behind the sides and in the back). When you're through, unhide the missing faces and the other half of the head; it should look something like this:

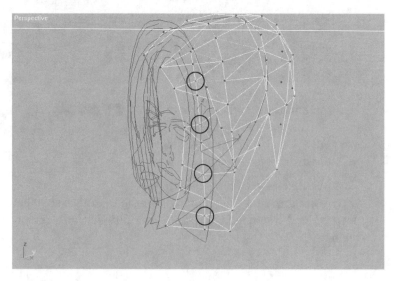

Either save your work or load Callisto08.max from the CD and finally weld the two halves together.

Step 6: Weld the Two Halves Together

Since the right side copy is a reference object, you need to collapse its stack before you can attach it to the left side. Select the reference side and click on the Edit Stack icon  on the Modify Stack panel. When the Edit Modifier Stack dialog pops up, hit Collapse All Collapse All and OK. Go over to the Modify panel, click the Attach button Attach so it turns green Attach , and click on the other half.

Once the two halves are joined into a single object, go to the Front view and select all the vertices in the middle line that bisects the head.

NU Scale them along the X-axis, then go to Vertex | Weld Selected. Make sure the value is set to .01 and hit the Selected button Selected . Of course by now you know that this means any vertices selected that are within 0.1 units of each other will be merged. This is usually the default setting for welding vertices *you know for sure* are lying on top of each other, occupying the same space.

FYI: *SEVEN BUTTONS YOU NEED TO TRY TODAY* There are buttons you tend to skip over on a regular basis until they become part of the scenery. Or, as in the case of max, you may not even see them unless you scroll up and down the menus. Part of the reason they are missed is failing to resize your menus by sliding your border to the right and expanding to two columns. Look at the following object converted to an editable mesh with the Edge sub-object selected.

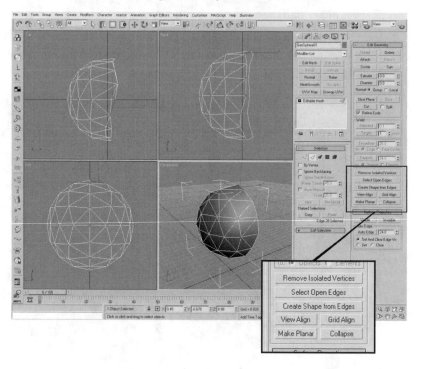

The seven buttons highlighted have been there since version 2.5 and I've never used any of them. However, I know for a fact I've done their job by other means. So take a sec and give them a spin. They might even justify buying that second flat-screen monitor you've had your eye on. ;]

▼

Remove Isolated Vertices is pretty self-explanatory but I
have to confess I've always selected the Element, hidden it,
and selected and deleted any remaining vertices when I suspect there are some free-floating ones hanging around. *Select
Open Edges* and *Create Shape from Edges* seem to work as a
team, giving you the ability to create an object based on missing chunks of your mesh. Hitting the first button, obviously
enough, selects the open edges of the object pictured here (1).
Then hitting the second one creates the new shape (2). Dragging the new shape to the right and selecting both objects
shows the newly created curve more easily (3).

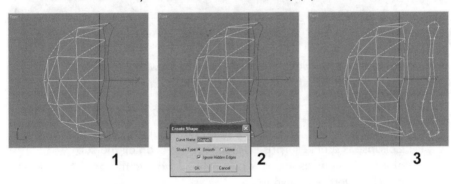

1   2   3

This tandem idea is probably something the engineers at Discreet came up with before the "Cap Holes" modifier was
made.

Of the remaining four buttons, *Grid Align* takes a selection
set (vertex, edge, or face) and flattens it along the construction
grid relative to whatever view you have active when you hit the
button. For example, if you select this jagged row of open vertices in the Top view and hit the Grid Align button, nothing
obvious happens, but in the Front view you can see how the
vertices have all flattened to the construction grid.

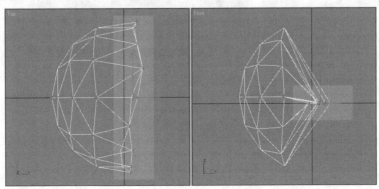

Make Planar seems to work the same whichever viewport is active, but uses the side views or the X-axis to align whatever sub-objects are selected into a planar line based on the volume of the selected object. Notice how the selected edges respond after hitting the Make Planar button.

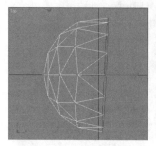 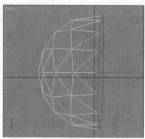 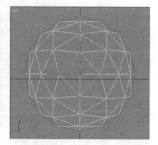

I'm not sure it always orients to the side view, but it could be useful if that didn't matter and you want to quickly line up a sub-object.

The remaining two buttons do prove to be very useful and I encourage you to incorporate them into your bag of tricks. *Collapse* is a nice surprise because it works on all the sub-objects. It replaces the trick I use when I want to merge a bunch of vertices down to zero.

View Align is the winner of this new button beauty pageant. It supplants the trick I use when typing in a 0 scale value to get vertices to line up in a nice little row. Look at the effect on each respective sub-object when selected in the Top view and the View Align button is hit in the Left viewport. Vertices...

 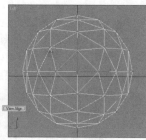 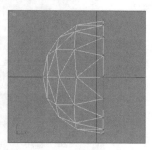

Edges...

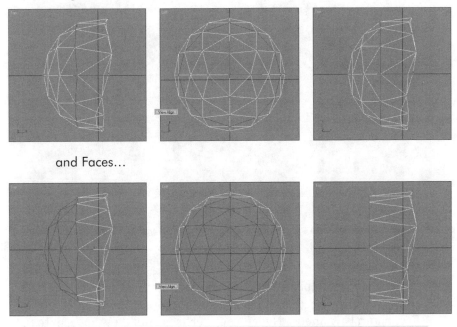

and Faces...

Step 7: Make Final Face Tweaks

All that's left to do is to add the bangs and a little asymmetry to the face and you'll be finished with the head. Bring back the frozen guide by hitting the Unhide All button ▭ Unhide All ▭ under the Display panel ▣. Go to the Front view and zoom in to the face area.

As you can see, the general shape of the mesh is very close to the Head Guide template. However, the eye area and outer areas defining the shape need to be tweaked to be more accurate *and* to avoid unnatural symmetry. Nudge your vertices until they conform to the guide.

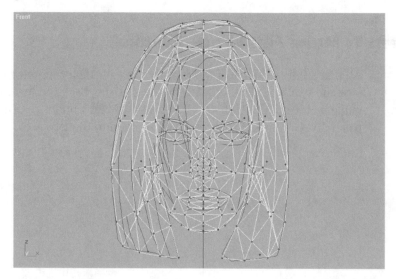

Cool. For the bangs you're going to use a new technique. You're going to create more geometry to shape by Shift-dragging edges.

Step 8: Shift-Drag Edges to Add the Bangs

Hide just the triangles of the face again. (Hint: I did this by selecting all the faces of the hair, going to the pull-down menus, selecting Edit|Select Invert, and hiding the selected faces.) Select these two edges from the Front view:

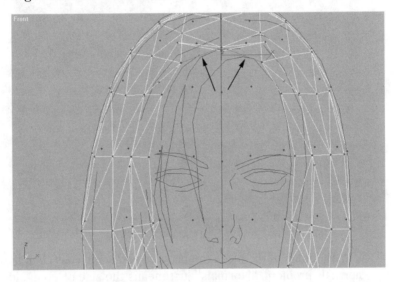

Go to the Left view. Hit F8 until your axes of movement are both X and Y and Shift-drag the edges to fit the shape of the bangs.

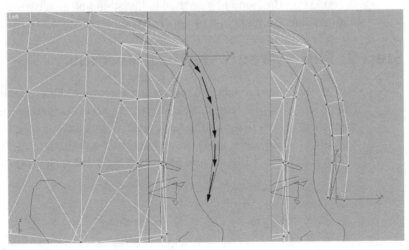

MODELING

As you create each new segment using Shift and drag, rotate the new edge before Shift-dragging it again to match the contour of the guide. Select the new faces of the bangs, rotate the view around, and look at them from the front.

Uh, oh. Some of the faces can be seen and some can't. You have a normals problem. "Normals" just means the side of a one-sided polygon that can be *seen*. In other words, a "normal" is a way of indicating which direction a triangle needs to face in order to be rendered. The other side of a normal is invisible unless a two-sided material has been applied or another triangle has been built.

Step 9: Flip "Wrong" Facing Normals

So half the faces are facing forward and the other half are facing to the back. Not a problem. First thing you need to do is to get at those back-facing faces that need to be flipped. The best way to do that is to hide all those other faces of the hair and head that are in the way. Do an Edit|Select Invert, and hide [Hide] the obscuring faces.

Rotate the view around so you can get at just the backward-facing faces and select them.

Go to the Sub-object area of the Modify panel and scroll down to the bottom Surface Properties section. Click on the Flip button.

The selected triangles are now oriented so their normals face the opposite direction. Rotate around to the front and everything looks cool.

Now you need to shape the bangs to match your reference by giving it some curve.

Looks great. Now, you need to make sure the bangs line up properly with the head.

Step 10: Connect the Bangs to the Head

Rotating ↻ your view and looking at the new faces from the top reveals a slight problem. You need to close *this* gap:

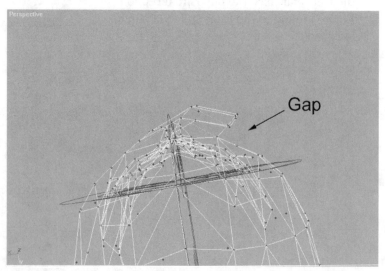

You need some volume for the bangs, so simply welding the vertices to the head or moving them over won't work. You need to add another lateral segment by selecting the edges and using Shift-drag. Select the edges and do just that along the X- and Y-axes with a small Z-axis rotate at the end.

Again, as you've probably noticed I work in one window, usually the Perspective view. For me this feels like the most natural way to work — as if I had the mesh in my hands pushing and pulling vertices. Take a final look at the mesh from the front. Hide Hide all the faces except for those making up the bangs.

I don't like how the far left side doesn't go far enough down, so reshape the bottom to cover that edge. Having the bangs go down to almost the corner of the mouth will turn out cool in the end.

FYI: *BANGS VIA OPACITY CHANNEL*   Now you may be wondering why you've created a big swatch of polygons instead of the individual bangs or strands for the bangs. Two reasons. One, you don't need all those polygons it would take to build the grouped strands of hair because, two, you can use an opacity map to make the strands wispy and hair-like. An "opacity map" is simply a mask used to make portions of an overlying texture map opaque in some areas and transparent in others. You will be learning more about opacity maps in Part III: Texturing.

So that wraps it up for the head for now...

I've detached the bangs for clarity's sake and I've detached the hair from the head and the bangs from the hair. This will make it easier to texture those objects in the future. Remember, when building the hair it's crucial you pick a type of hairstyle that works in a lower polygon situation yet still is an interesting enough 'do.

MODELING

CHAPTER 6
The Torso

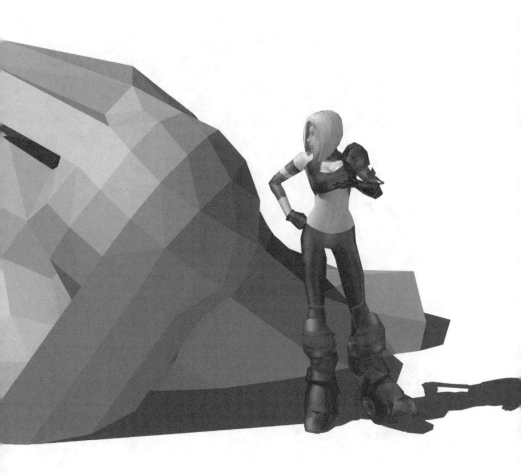

You've built the head of your character using a primitive as a starting point. Then you built the hair using extrusion. These techniques with their sub-object tweaking represent unequivocally the nuts and bolts of polygon modeling. Now you're going to use yet another technique in combination with what you've used so far — a suite of modifiers collectively known as Surface Tools. Normally, these modifiers are used for higher poly, organic shapes that don't worry about face count. However, they're an excellent way to make even low-poly shapes like, say, a female character's torso.

Step 1: Create the Spline Cage Object

Load Callisto09.max from the companion CD.

Note I've made some changes to the guide objects, rearranging the splines of Body Guide to be more effective for building the torso. I've deleted Head Guide since you don't need it any longer, and detached, renamed, and hidden the head objects. I've detached the left arm, and renamed it and hidden it; and I've renamed and hidden the rear leg guide.

Zoom in to the torso area of Body Guide, go to the Create panel  and click on the Shapes icon 🖉. Create a circle `Circle` at about the waist level. Make it about 4.5 units in radius:

```
-        Name and Color
[Circle01]
+           General
-        Creation Method
  C Edge          (• Center
+         Keyboard Entry
-          Parameters
   Radius: [4.5    ]
```

NU Scale 🖉 the circle along the Y-axis approximately 70%.

FYI: *ANGLE SNAP*   Using Angle Snap 🖉 is helpful when rotating an object by a set number of degrees. Just hit A and it becomes active 🖉 ; hit A again to turn it off. Right-click over the icon and you can change the Angle Snap settings.

```
Grid and Snap Settings           _ □ X
Snaps  Options  Home Grid  U ◄ ►
-Marker
 ☑ Display  Size [15   ]  [   ]
-General
   Snap Strength [8    ] Pixels
Angle (deg): [5.0  ] Percent: [10.0 ]
        ☐ Snap to frozen objects
-Translation
        ☑ Use Axis Constraints
```

Rotate the circle along the X-axis 90 degrees and move it up to where it's even with the top of the shoulders.

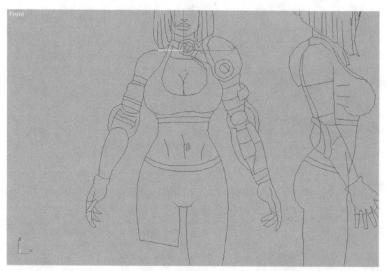

You're now going to use an option in the Clone Options dialog box to make four copies of the circle that are equidistant from each other. With the circle selected, hold down the Shift key and drag the circle down along the Y-axis about 6.7 units. When the Clone Options dialog box comes up, enter 4 in the Number of Copies box.

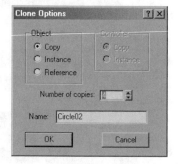

Click OK; there are now five circles.

This works the same as Array , but is limited to the type of transform used with the Shift-Clone function. Now scale and move each circle along the X-axis so they match the Body Guide front view.

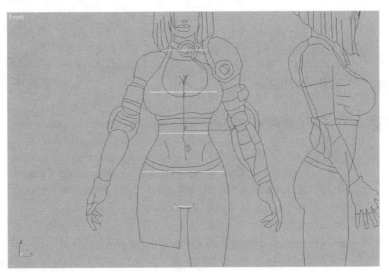

Staying in the Front view, select all the circles, rotate them 90 degrees along the Y-axis, and slide them over to the side profile of the Body Guide. First scale 🔳 , then rotate 🔄 each circle along the Z-axis z so they match the torso side profile lines.

Now that you have your circles in place, you need to make them one object before applying Surface Tools to them. Select just the top circle, click on the Edit Stack icon 🗃 , and convert the shape to an Editable Spline.

 FYI: *EDIT SPLINE MODIFIER* An alternative to collapsing the stack of the circle is to apply an Edit Spline *modifier* `Edit Spline` to its modifier stack. I've always questioned the usefulness of applying an Edit Spline modifier to a simple shape like this and prefer just collapsing the stack because it seems more efficient.

After it's collapsed, attach the other circles to it by hitting the Attach Multiple button `Attach Mult.` , highlighting all the circles that come up in the Attach Multiple dialog box, and hitting Attach.

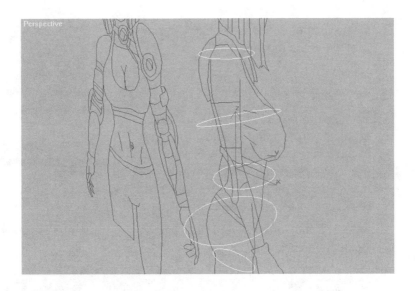

Step 2: Apply Surface Tools

With all the circles now combined to form one object you need to apply one of the two modifiers that make up Surface Tools, Cross-Section. This modifier connects shapes by creating lines between vertices of the existing shape (in this case, concentric circles). It connects the vertices based on the position of the first vertex of each spline and creates a spline cage. This "spline cage" is the precursor to a patch surface and is similar to a polygon mesh without faces — just vertices and lines. However, the vertices and lines of a spline cage are parametric and can be curved as well as linear. The ability to apply as much curve as you want, or need, is what makes Surface Tools and patch surface modeling so useful and powerful.

Hit the More button [More...] to bring up the list of additional modifiers. If you haven't assigned CrossSection to your modifier set, select it.

Check Bezier under the Spline Option parameters when the modifier has been assigned.

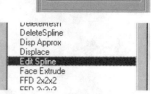

You need to make the vertices Bezier because you're going to adjust the curve of the splines to match up with your reference guide. Again, another way to make sure all the vertices are Bezier is to apply an Edit Spline modifier.

Select all the vertices and right-click on any of them. Slide down to Bezier and click on it.

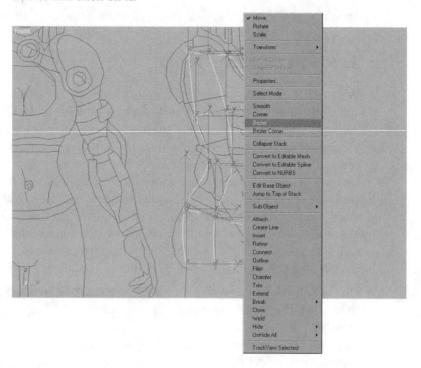

Now all the vertices are Bezier, and spline handles appear.

FYI: *VERTEX TYPES* In max you can right-click on the vertex of a spline and change it to any one of the following four types:

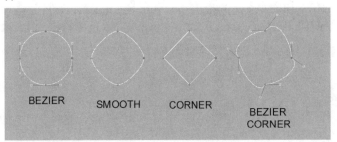

Bezier means the spline handles are locked; moving one handle causes the other to move like a seesaw and the curvature of the vertex is set by the direction and length of the handles. Smooth means the vertex is non-adjustable and curves automatically based on the distance between other vertices. Corner doesn't have any curve and is great for termination points of lines, and Bezier Corner allows you to adjust the spline handles independent of each other.

Step 3: Move and Adjust the Vertices of the Spline

Starting at the top of the shape, go along the outermost vertices, move ⊕ them to their right position, and drag their spline handles to create the proper curve. Make sure you drag the selection marquee ▫ across the vertices instead of just clicking to select them; there are actually two overlapping vertices at each point.

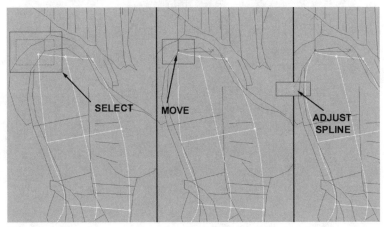

MODELING

Don't forget that because the vertices are Bezier, the spline handles stay locked. Pulling on one handle causes the other to move as well like a seesaw. Don't worry if the curve doesn't match the guide exactly, either. As you move down to the next vertex, it may make up for the lack of curve from the previous vertex adjustment.

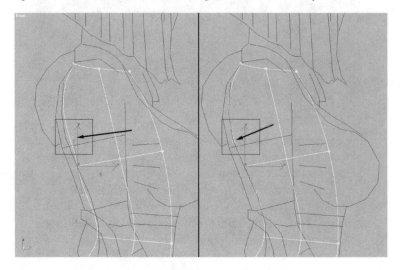

Finish adjusting the other vertices until they match the guide, and you should end up with something like so:

The ability to adjust spline handles makes this modeling technique a great way to make any mesh that has a curved design.

Next, name the spline cage Torso and rotate it –90 degrees along the Y-axis. Move it over to line up with the front portion of Body Guide again. Now tweak the vertices so that the lines of the cage match the guide from the front.

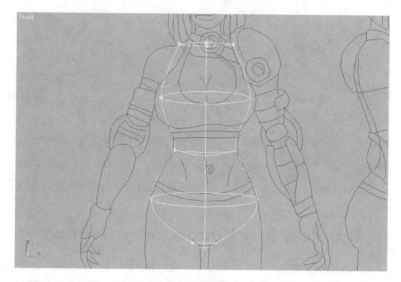

With all the vertices and splines right, you're ready to apply the Surface modifier. Click on the Surface button ⬚Surface⬚ if you've added it to your modifier set. If not, then hit the More button ⬚More...⬚ again and seek it in the list. Once it's applied, set the Patch Topology to 2.

This turns your spline cage into a patch object mesh. However, it causes a problem inside the mesh that you need to fix.

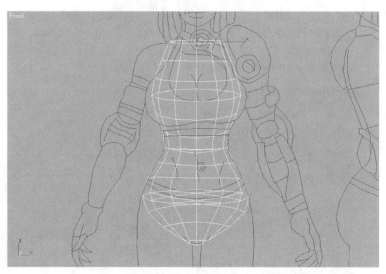

Step 4: Delete Any Unnecessary Geometry

Whenever a Surface modifier is applied to a spline cage it will create a surface or *skin* where the line segments of the spline form a three- or four-sided polygon. Since the circles themselves started out as unique shapes and are four-sided, Surface thinks those circles need a skin *across* their surface. In other words, additional geometry was created *inside* the mesh, geometry you need to delete.

The best way to get at these inner faces is to apply an Edit Mesh modifier [Edit Mesh], rotate your view, use the Rectangular Selection marquee ▢ to select the faces edge-on, hold down the Alt key, and deselect the faces you want to keep. This procedure is shown in the following illustration.

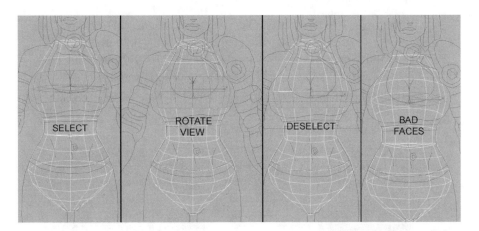

SELECT | ROTATE VIEW | DESELECT | BAD FACES

However you want to do it, select all the extra inner faces and delete them. Hit Yes when you are asked about deleting isolated vertices.

Unfortunately, having to delete inner faces like this makes me suspect there might be overlapping, unwelded vertices where the edges of the deleted segments intersected the body shape.

Using Sub-Object|Element , click on the mesh in a couple of places.

MODELING

If the torso had been one solid mesh (i.e., all the vertices welded), selecting by element should have caused the whole mesh to be selected. Vertices that lie on top of each other without being connected cause problems with smoothing groups and can lead to trouble if they're not intentionally left that way for some reason. Select the vertices where the segments in question meet. Finding them is easy if you look closely at the mesh.

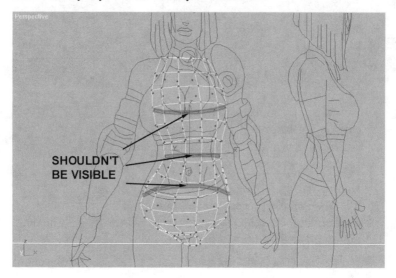

If you rotate your view and see a line that should only be visible from the other side when looking through a mesh, then max is telling you that vertices are lying on top of one another and are not joined. This is easy enough to fix by using Weld Selected. Select all the vertices of the mesh (or just the ones in question) and type in a value of 1 in the Weld Selected spinner.

Hit the Selected button and "poof." The lines disappear, the vertices are welded, and the torso is now one element.

Another way to tell if elements are detached is the appearance of smoothing anomalies. Even if separate elements have the same smoothing group there will be a line or seam where edges formed by unwelded, coincidental vertices meet, breaking up an otherwise smooth surface. If you assign the same smoothing group to an element, then the surface should appear smooth.

FYI: *SMOOTHING GROUPS*   Smoothing groups are simply a way for max to determine whether or not a surface is smooth or faceted. If two faces (or patches) share an edge and share smoothing groups, the edge (and surface) will be smooth. When two surfaces share an edge and have *different* smoothing groups, that edge will be hard, giving the surface a "line" where the two meet. There's no ordering with smoothing group numbers — 1 isn't more important than 2, or 10 more important than 20. They stand for nothing other than giving you 32 different numbers to choose from when creating hard edges. Smoothing groups can also be animated.

MODELING

Step 5: Create the Breast Shape

Continue on with the torso you've been building or load
Callisto10.max. With the general shape of the torso roughed in you
can start on the breast area. Now cup size... er, breast size is sub-
jective to the modeler. In Callisto's case
she is meant to be a voluptuous character
in a Lara Croftian vein. This allows her to
use the distracting advantage of her body
while kicking bad guys' butts. In max I've
found that a great way to make breasts for
female characters is to start with my favorite sphere primitives: geospheres. In the
Front view create an octagonal geosphere
with a radius of 4 and four segments.

Move the object so it lines up with the right breast of the guide.

To make better use of Body Guide, rotate and move the profile like
you did for the Head Guide profile earlier. To do this, (1) hit
Unfreeze All [Unfreeze All], (2) select the Body Guide, (3) select
the splines of the side portion, and (4) rotate those splines –90
degrees along the Y-axis with Use Selection Center 🔲 active, and
slide the splines over so they're beside the front.

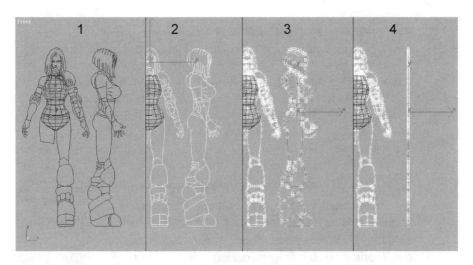

Go to the Left view, scale the geosphere 90% along the X-axis, and position the geosphere so it matches up to the guide. It should look like this from the side and front, respectively:

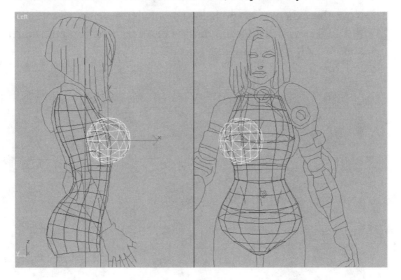

MODELING

FYI: *LIKE A PLASTIC SURGEON* Using geospheres to make breasts on a female character is like performing breast implant surgery. Again, this approach may not lend itself to the reality of a natural breast shape but it does achieve the goal of making a *character* like the kind seen in most games today. Note: This technique does not pose any serious threat to the health of the model and only non-silicone geospheres are used.

When I create a female character I find an area on the geosphere that represents the nipple of the breast and use that as a reference point when turning or shaping the breast mass. Rotate the geosphere along the Y- and X-axes using its local axis instead of the default view axis. Do this by clicking on the small arrow beside View at the top of the screen, sliding down to Local, and clicking on it.

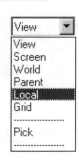

Now, the axis of rotation is based on whatever the pivot is set to for the sphere (by default it's in the center). Once you get it turned it should look something like this:

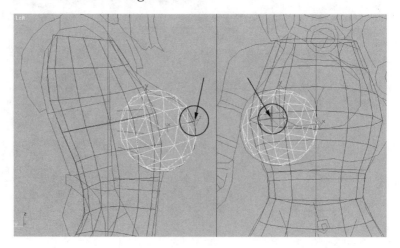

Step 6: Boolean the Breast onto the Torso

Now that you have your "implant" in place you need to merge it with the torso using Boolean. The word "Boolean" comes from the English mathematician George Boole. In the mid-1800s he came up with the logical combination system of modern algebra.

Boolean operations in max form one object by combining two objects in one of three ways: Union, Intersection, or Subtraction.

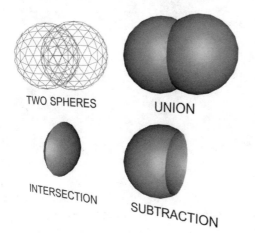

TWO SPHERES   UNION

INTERSECTION   SUBTRACTION

Boolean is a powerful and useful tool in max but I can't say it's the best tool for making low-poly characters. Using it often causes messiness in the form of tiny triangles at the seams of the inter-secting geometry that have to be deleted. It also results in extra, overlapping vertices. For Callisto's torso you're going to use Union to weld the breast onto it, but before you can perform a Boolean operation you need to make sure all the shapes involved are "closed."

Step 7: Cap the Faces of the Torso

Since you deleted the faces from Torso earlier, you need to replace them before doing the Boolean. Trying to Boolean objects that have faces missing causes the resultant mesh to have problems such as flipped normals or extra geometry. You can close an object's open faces by either creating the faces manually in the sub-object menu or adding a Cap Holes modifier to its stack. With the torso selected assign the Cap Holes modifier `Cap Holes` to it. Now, any holes or openings in the mesh caused by deleted faces or vertices will be

MODELING

"capped" by max, creating new faces. In this case, the top and bottom openings get closed (hit Ctrl+E to see the new edges/faces).

FYI: CAP HOLES When using the Cap Holes modifier, keep in mind that it works best on openings that are regular and relatively level. Using it on jagged or irregular "holes" makes for some strange results and often leads to time-consuming edge turns.

Step 8: Perform the Boolean

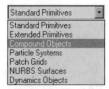

With Torso now capped, you're ready to perform the Boolean operation. Go to the Create panel , click on the small arrow beside Standard Primitives, go to Compound Objects, and click on it.

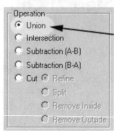

When the new Create menu buttons appear, click on Boolean Boolean . Make sure Union is selected and click the Pick Operand button green Pick Operand B . ("Operand" just means the other object involved in the Boolean operation.)

Click on the geosphere. The two objects are now joined into one.

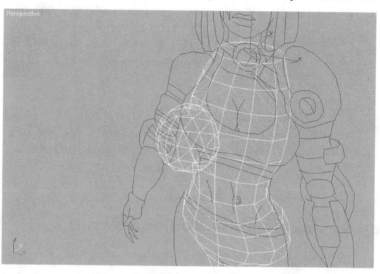

FYI: *NOT CAPPING HOLES*   If you hadn't capped the holes
of Torso earlier,
the result of the
Boolean would
have looked
like the adja-
cent figure.

Instead of
forgetting
about the
intersecting
geometry, max
kept it. You
could manually
delete those
faces and verti-
ces inside the
torso, but why

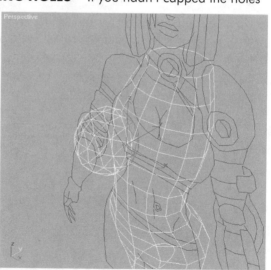

go through the extra work? The best rule of thumb is to make
sure all objects involved in a Boolean are closed.

MODELING

Now it's a matter of cleaning up the Boolean area to get rid of the small triangles and extra vertices. This is a form of optimization, or reduction of extra geometry, to suit the detail level of the mesh. Before you do that, however, you need to go to the Modify panel 🖋 and collapse the mesh into an Editable Mesh.

Convert To:
Editable Mesh
Edit Stack

 FYI: *COLLAPSING THE STACK* I always collapse the stack regularly when I model unless the modifier I'm applying is questionable and there's the potential for going back and removing it. This is just a personal preference, but I recommend it.

Step 9: Clean Up the Boolean Result

Go to the Display panel 🔲 and hit Hide Unselected [Hide Unselected] to hide your frozen Body Guide and make things easier to see. Rotate your view, and zoom in to the area near where the cleavage goes, and start selecting and welding vertices.

Go into Sub-Object|Vertex mode [∵] , check the Ignore Backfacing box [☑ Ignore Backfacing], go down to the Weld Selected area, and enter a value of 10:

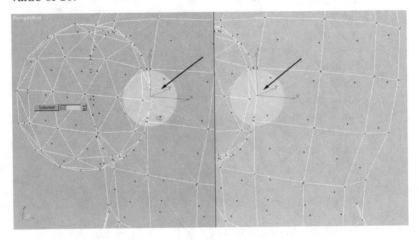

Again, a smaller value probably would have worked, but when welding a bunch of vertices at a time, just pick a big number.

Work your way down to the next vertex cluster, select them, and hit
Selected again:

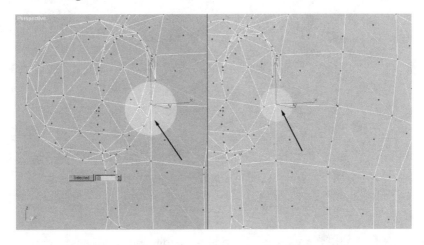

For the next two sets of vertices, enter a value of .5:

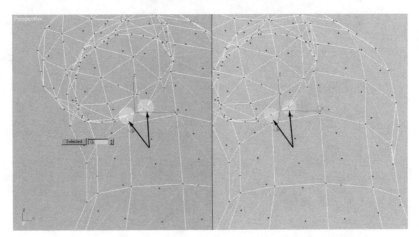

It worked and saved you from stopping at each pair and welding
them individually. After a while, you'll get a feel for dialing in the
values for Weld Selected. You'll recognize an opportunity to weld a
bunch of vertices at one time based on their distances from each
other, so don't be afraid to experiment with it.

MODELING

Enter 10 again and merge the next three verts.

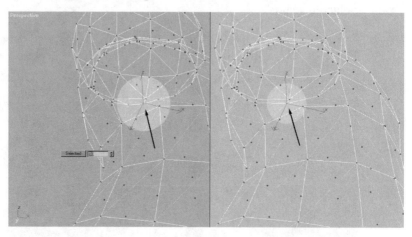

Rotate the view so the side is visible and weld these vertices:

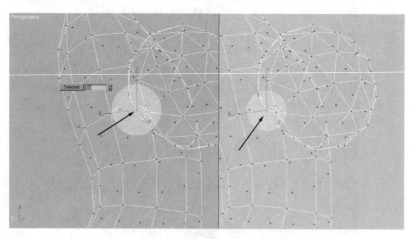

For the next several groups try a value of 1 in Weld Selected and see if it works:

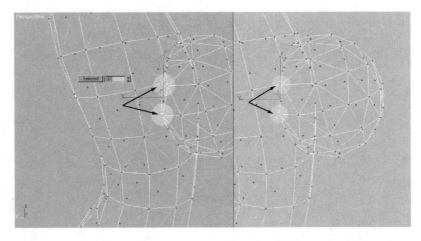

Cool! Now you'll switch tactics and for the next couple of vertices near the top of the breast you'll use Target Weld , selecting multiple vertices. Believe it or not it took me a while to figure out you could weld more than one vertex at a time using this function. With Target Weld green and active, select all these vertices and drag them up to the vertex above:

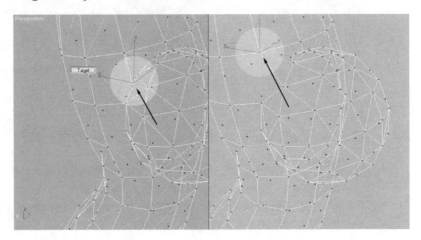

MODELING

Rotate the view so you're looking down at the top of the breast and drag these vertices up to the vertex above:

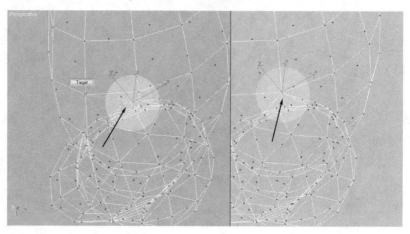

Rotate the view yet again and weld these vertices:

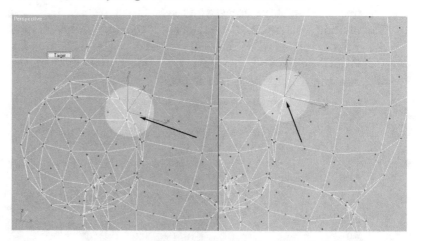

Using Target Weld worked great for those vertices at the top since you're going to have to adjust the shape in that direction later. For the last set of vertices to clean up from the Boolean seam, revert to using Weld Selected with a value of 10.

Select these vertices and hit Selected:

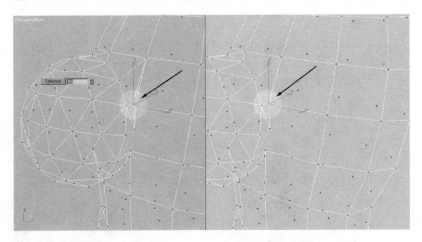

That covers all the seam vertices. Check out your progress in Facets mode to get some ideas of the next set of tweaks you still need to make.

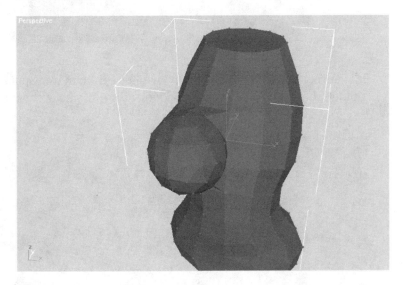

Step 10: Add Some Clothing

To make the chest area look as if Callisto is wearing tight clothing over her breasts, merge the vertices at the side of the breast area to create the illusion of stretched cloth there. You also need to move ⊕ the vertices around on the inner part of the breast to foreshadow the cleavage:

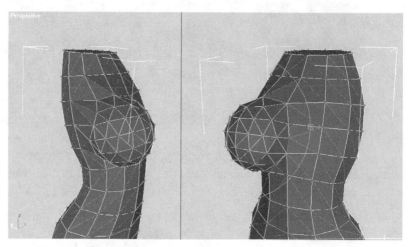

It's getting there, but you need to give her a little more support. Unhide the frozen Body Guide and look at the shoulder/chest area.

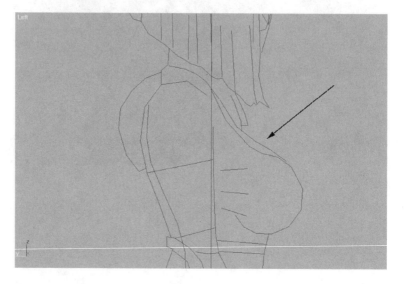

You need to make the geometry reflect a sports bra-looking strap.
That's easiest to do by simply turning some edges and welding a
few vertices:

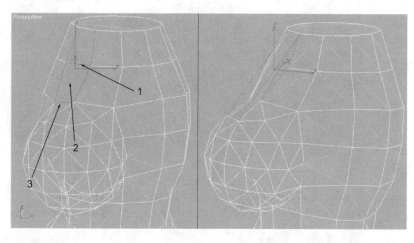

Voilà. Now you've modeled up to a point where you can delete the
undeveloped side of the torso, and copy, mirror, and attach the
developed side. However, before you delete the unwanted half of
the torso, turn your edges at the top and bottom so you keep your
ends capped. Starting with the top, change your view to Perspective, use the Select Polygon ▣ to select the top faces, and then hit
Zoom Extents Selected ▣ to keep your work area centered.

Make sure you have Ignore Backfacing checked and make the following edge turns.

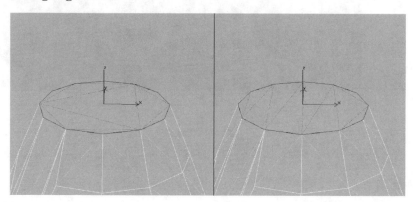

MODELING

Do the same for the bottom:

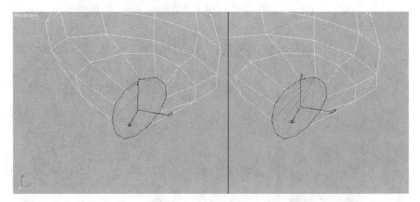

Uncheck Ignore Backfacing, go to the Front view, and select all the vertices of the undeveloped side of the mesh and delete them.

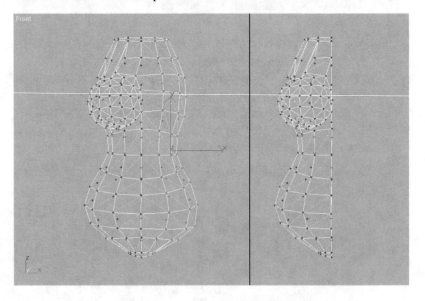

Go up to Tools|Mirror, make sure the X-axis is active, and select Copy instead of Reference. It doesn't matter what the name is since you're going to attach it to Torso anyway.

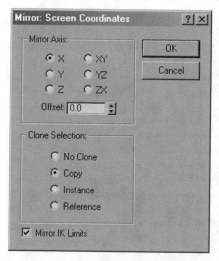

After clicking OK, the new half is created, mirrored, and ready to be lined up with the other half. Select Torso, turn the Attach button green, and click on the object you just created. Select all the vertices of the combined torso *except* for the ones that overlap at the cleavage.

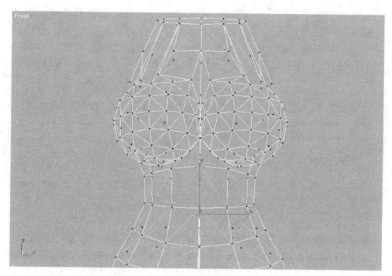

NU Scale 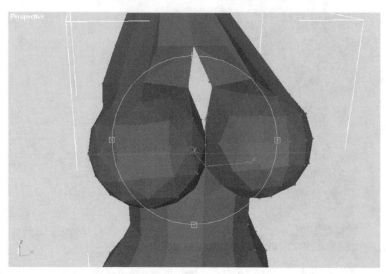 them along the X-axis until they're all in a single line, set the Weld Selected value to .01, and hit Selected. Go to a faceted mode and the torso should look something like this:

Because you're trying to create the look of cleavage, you need to overlap geometry and then join the overlapped faces by dividing those edges and joining the new vertices that represent the point where they intersect.

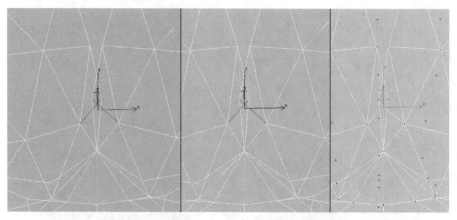

After deleting the extra vertices below the vertices just merged it's time to close the holes. Go to the Face sub-object, click Create [Create], and build the faces by clicking on a vertex and then another two in a counterclockwise order. Repeat this until the holes are filled.

 FYI: *IS IT CLOCKWISE OR COUNTERCLOCKWISE?*
Whenever I build faces in max it never ceases to amaze me
how sometimes building them counterclockwise *does not* work
(i.e., their normals face the opposite direction). This happens
because when you mirror an object and start adding to it, the
direction you create the faces is mirrored as well. Hitting F2
while building triangles is an easy way to see if it's facing the
right direction.

Now finish the cleavage by turning some edges up front to make it
seem like she's actually wearing something stretched taut across
her chest.

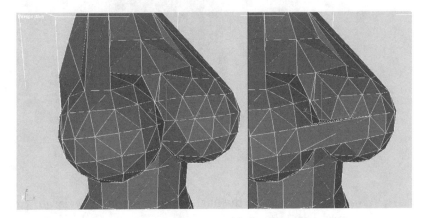

MODELING

Just turning edges won't do the trick, though. Underneath the cleavage in front, you have to Target Weld some vertices and turn some more edges.

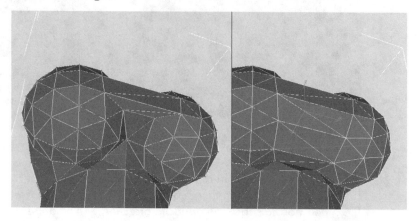

Much better. Rotate the view around to see how the torso looks.

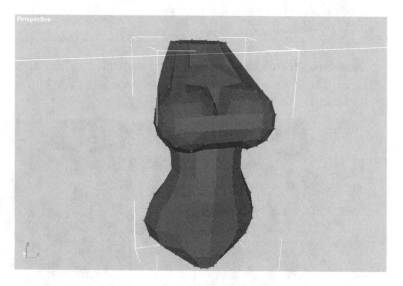

Not bad, but perhaps the bust line is still a little *too* large. Time to perform reductive surgery using a great new tool in max called Soft Selection.

Step 11: Use Soft Selection to Reduce the Chest Size

Using Soft Selection to perform transforms on sub-object selections creates the effect of having a "magnetic field" around the selected sub-objects. Unselected vertices are affected based on their distance and the settings in the rollout menu. A color gradient represents the amount of influence exerted on a vertex going from yellow (most affected) to blue (unaffected).

To use Soft Selection go to the Modify panel and click the vertex sub-object button ⬚ to make it active ⬚. Open the Soft Selection sub-menu, and check the box beside Use Soft Selection to make it active. Leave all settings as they are except change Falloff from 20 to 10.

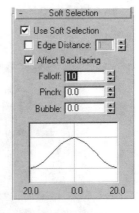

Now, go to the Left view and select the following line of vertices toward the front of the breast.

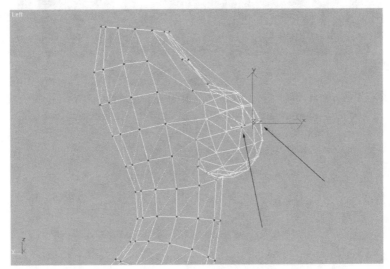

Since selected vertices are red and unselected vertices are blue, max applies this convention to the gradient. Vertices that are under the maximum influence of the selected vertices are yellow; as the distance grows, the vertices under less influence change color toward green and finally blue. Take the time to experiment with the other settings in Soft Selection such as Edge Distance, Pinch, and Bubble.

Go to faceted shading and rotate to a Perspective view. With the same row of vertices selected Uniformly Scale ▣ the vertices by 90% and move them slightly up and back (Z and Y, respectively).

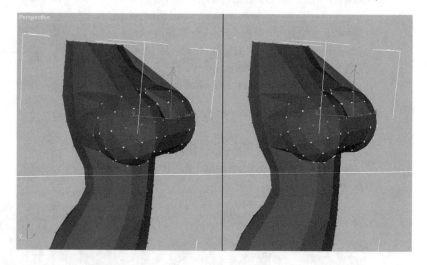

Now, go to the Left view, select the vertex ⋯ above the nip...er, the previously determined spatial orientation point vertex for the breast, change the Falloff to 7, and slide that vertex back along the Y-axis about half a unit.

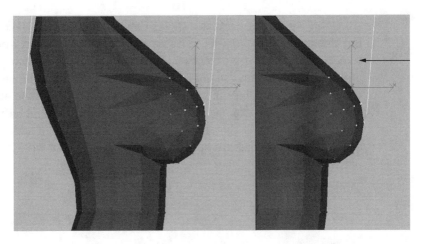

This gives it even more of a "pressed" look, creating the illusion that the clothes are tight. Rotate around to check out the torso yet again:

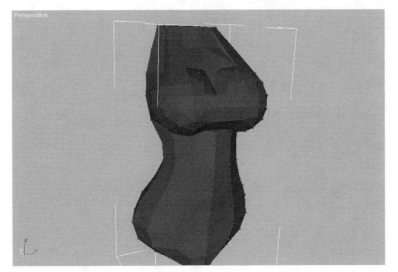

All right. Her breasts are still larger than what's realistic of course, but this is a fantasy character. As an artist it's always your prerogative to make the attributes of your characters mirror life, fantasy, or anything in between. I'm not condoning or condemning the fact that most female characters in games today are products of male adolescent imaginations. The fact is, sexy female characters and buff male characters are larger than life — super-ideal versions of supermen and superwomen that are better suited for the fantasy worlds you put them into.

Time to move on to the next body part — the legs.

CHAPTER 7
The Legs

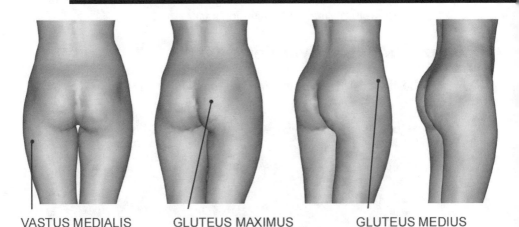

VASTUS MEDIALIS   GLUTEUS MAXIMUS   GLUTEUS MEDIUS

In this chapter you're going to build a leg for Callisto and attach it to her torso. Since you'll be building her boot using a different technique later on, you're just going to concentrate on the waist down to the mid-calf area. You're also going to use a new building technique similar to a Boolean that's more like a manual Boolean: You will shape an object to fit a specific region (in this case the posterior) and attach it to the target mesh (the torso). Of course, there will be lots of edge manipulation and vertex tweaking, as well as raw face creation. First, make the main leg shape.

Step 1: Make a Cylinder

Load Callisto11.max and look at the guide for the leg.

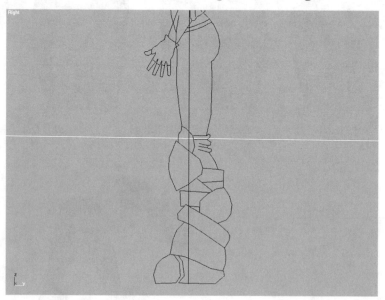

I've hidden everything and zoomed in to the leg profile in the Right view. Like all append-ages, the leg is essentially a cylinder that bends, so it makes sense to start with a Cylinder primitive. Switch to the Top viewport and go to the Create panel 🔧✏️🐎💿⬜𝚼. Hit the Cylinder button ▭Cylinder▭, make a cylinder anywhere close to Body Guide, and set Radius to 3, Height to 20, Height Segments to 5, and Sides to 8.

Parameters	
Radius:	3.0
Height:	20.0
Height Segments:	5
Cap Segments:	1
Sides:	8
☑ Smooth	
☐ Slice On	
Slice From:	0.0
Slice To:	0.0
☐ Generate Mapping Coords.	

You need enough height segments in the cylinder to support matching it to the guide shape, and eight sides makes for a detailed leg that can be optimized later on if necessary. Go to the Right viewport and move the cylinder over and up so it rests within the guidelines.

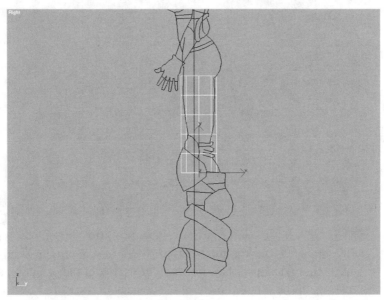

Step 2: Shape the Cylinder to Match the Guide

Now that the cylinder is roughly in place you need to tweak its vertices to match Body Guide. Apply an Edit Mesh modifier Edit Mesh to the stack. Select the top row of vertices ∴ and NU Scale ▣ them 87% along the X-axis. Rotate ↻ them –15 degrees along the Z-axis and move them up a little along the Y-axis so they rest at the point where the curve of the buttock terminates.

 FYI: *COLLAPSING VS. STACKING*   An alternative to adding an Edit Mesh modifier is to simply collapse the stack of the cylinder to an editable mesh. A good rule of thumb? If you don't think you'll be accessing the modifiers in the stack, collapse it. Many times, the decision to collapse or build a stack is one of those personal preferences that can be argued both ways. However, using an Edit Mesh modifier in the stack can also be like an "undo." For example, if you know a series of changes to an object may or may not turn out you could blanket them under an Edit Mesh modifier.

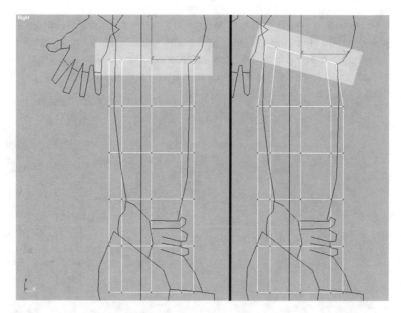

Next, grab the second row of vertices from the bottom, scale them 65% along the X-axis, rotate them 20 degrees along the Z-axis, and move them down so that the far right vertex of the selection set is resting on the top of the curve of the back of the calf.

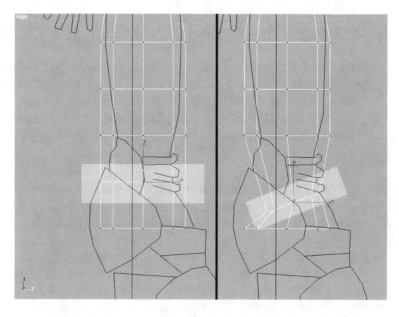

Select the bottom row of vertices, scale 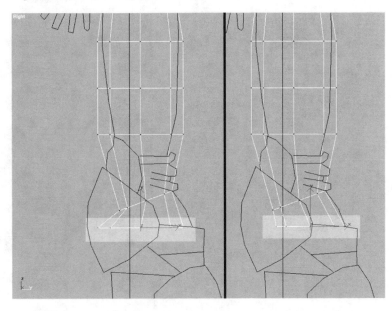 them by 80% along the X-axis, and move them over so the far right vertex is resting on the top of the boot and about mid-calf.

Select the third row of vertices from the bottom, scale them by 80% along the X-axis, and move them down to be at about the middle of the kneepad area.

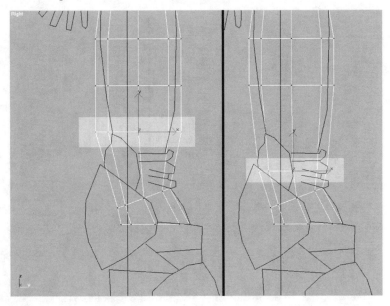

Select the fourth row of vertices from the bottom, scale them by 65% along the X-axis, rotate them by 20 degrees along the Z-axis, and move them down into place at the top of the kneepad.

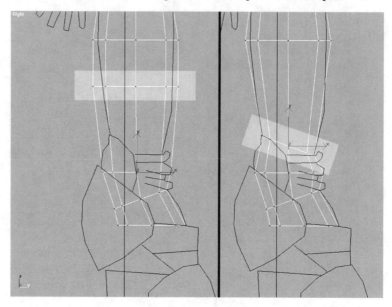

Next, go to the second row down, select the vertices, scale them by 85% in the X-axis, rotate them −10 degrees along the Z-axis, and move them down along the Z-axis to about mid-thigh.

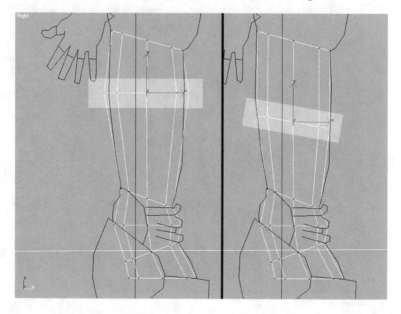

Notice you didn't try to add the folds at the back of the knee area or add enough geometry to match the guide *precisely*. This is because it would add too much geometry and definitely require optimizing later. Details such as small folds that don't add hugely to the design are the first to get reduced if the polygon count goes over your 1,500-triangle limit. Details like this are also easy enough to add if the face count is lower than the target.

Switch to the Front viewport and move the cylinder over so it rests approximately within the guidelines.

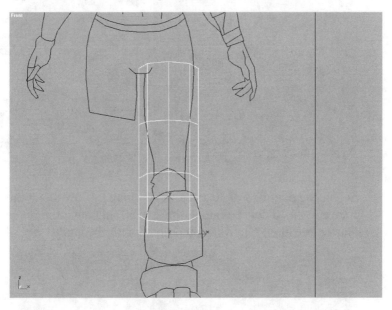

The shape still looks like a featureless cylinder in the Front view, but you know it looks correct in profile. Thus, when making tweaks in the Front view you need to restrict moving or scaling vertices to the X-axis (or side-to-side). You also need to keep in mind the impact that rotating a group of vertices will have on the profile you've already established.

Select the top row of vertices, scale them 85% along the X-axis, and
rotate them 15 degrees along the Z-axis.

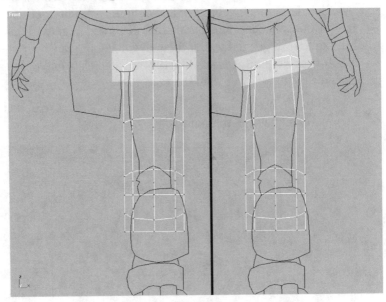

Select the next row of vertices, scale them by 75% along the X-axis,
rotate them 10 degrees along the Z-axis, and move them over just a
hair or two along the X-axis to line up with the guide.

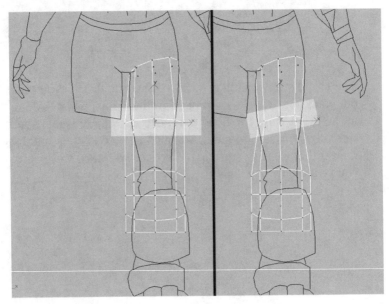

Next, select the remaining vertices and scale them all along the X-axis by 50%. Move them over to line up on Body Guide.

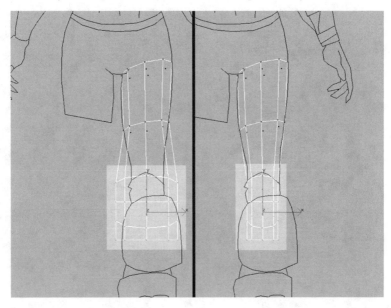

Finally, select the bottom row *and* the third row of verts from the bottom and scale them back out by 120% along the X-axis to give the kneepad and the calf some thickness and shape.

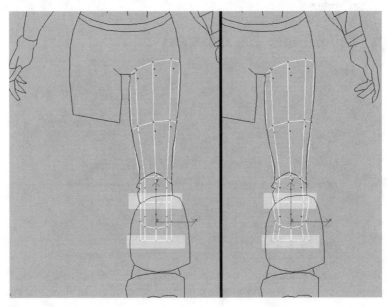

MODELING

Hit P to go to a Perspective viewport, zoom and pan until the leg is in view, and hit Ctrl+E to show the hidden edges of the mesh.

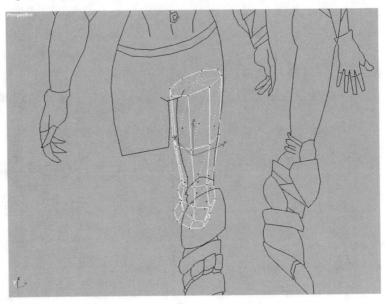

Notice how there is an extra vertex at the top and bottom caps of the cylinder. This is so additional cap segments can be added if necessary both at the time of creation and at the base parameters of the cylinder.

FYI: *CYLINDER CAP SEGMENTS*

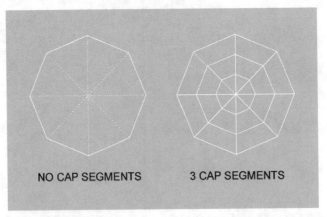

I haven't yet found the need to add cap segments to a cylinder, but that doesn't mean it isn't a useful feature! If you need

them, they're easy enough to add. Just enter the number of segments you want in the Cap Segments box under Parameters.

Normally when it comes to cylinders, I collapse it to an editable mesh once I have the right number of segments and Target Weld or delete the center cap vertices. In this case, however, you need those end vertices to extend the geometry and create better connecting points from the leg into the rest of the body.

Still in the Perspective viewport, select those two end cap vertices and scale them along the Z-axis by 125%.

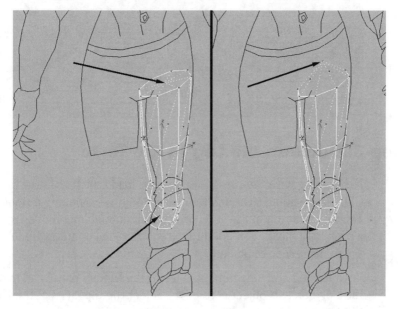

MODELING

Rename the cylinder Leg...

...and switch to a Front view. Unhide Torso.

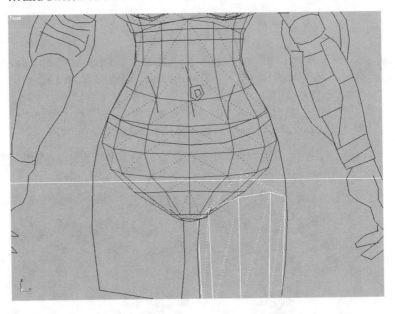

Step 3: Boolean the Leg to the Torso

Keep going with the mesh you have or load Callisto12.max from the CD. You're going to attach the leg to the torso by using a Boolean Union operation, but first, give yourself enough mesh overlap to get a proper Boolean. You need to extend the leg geometry up into Torso using face extrude.

With the leg still selected, go over to the Modify panel and make the Polygon sub-object active ▣ . Select the top faces of the leg, hit the Extrude button [Extrude], and Extrude-drag another set of faces up toward the torso by about 3 units. Notice the small Extrude icon when you place your cursor over eligible faces.

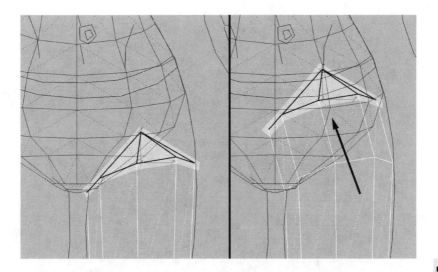

After extruding them, move the conveniently selected faces slightly up and to the right so they correspond with the guide and fully penetrate the torso mesh. Do this for both the Front view and the Right profile view.

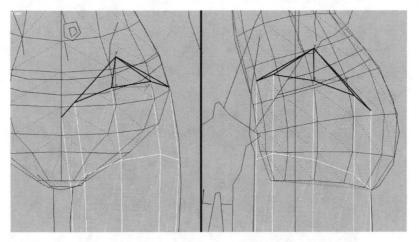

Now you need to prep the torso as well as the leg before performing the Boolean. Start by reducing the faces of the lower region of the torso to make a cleaner Boolean (too many faces make for just that much more cleanup after the Boolean).

MODELING

Take the second row of vertices from the bottom of Torso, and one by one Target Weld 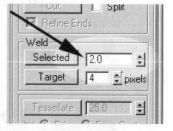 each of them to the vertex on the row directly above it.

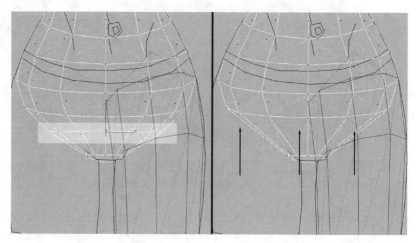

Next, go to a Perspective view and select the following two sets of vertices at the bottom of the torso. Enter a value of 2 in the Weld Selected box and hit the Selected button 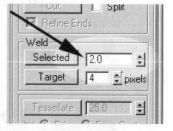, thus welding the vertices and reducing the faces even more.

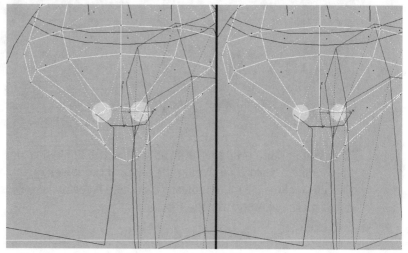

Alternately weld the following two sets of vertices using a value of 10 in the Weld Selected box and hitting the Selected button.

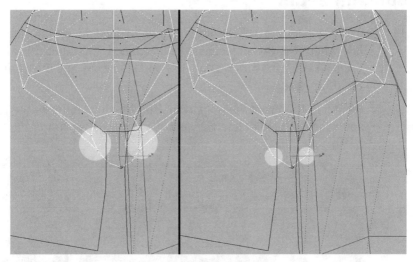

Now the torso is in better shape to be Booleaned. With it still selected, go to the Create panel, go to the Compound Objects menu, and hit the Boolean button Boolean . Click the Pick Operand B button Pick Operand B and check Union under Operation. Rotate the view so you can see what you're doing and click on the leg object as shown in the following illustration.

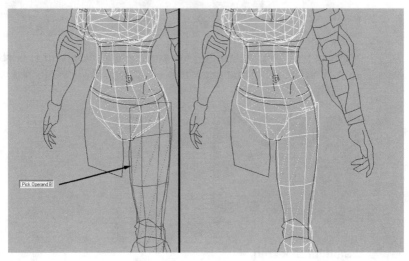

The leg is now joined to the torso.

MODELING

Step 4: Clean Up the Vertices of the Boolean Seam

The leg is now attached, but you need to do some cleanup along the line where the two objects have been joined. First, get rid of half the torso so you can work on one side and later copy and mirror it to the other side.

Switch to the Front view, apply an Edit Mesh modifier to the mesh, and select ▣ and delete the vertices mid to lower left of the torso mesh.

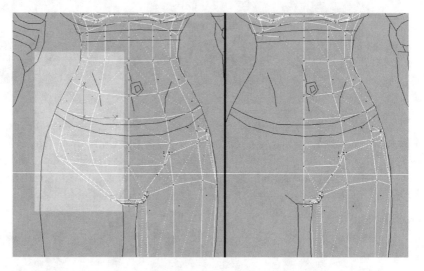

Starting with the front of the hip area, select the group of vertices shown on the following page, make sure your Weld Selected value is still 10...

...and hit Selected.

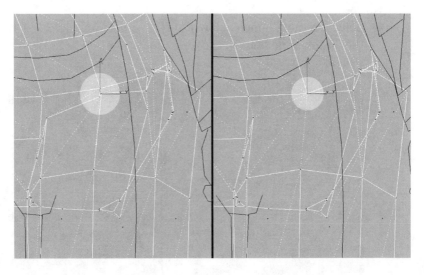

Rotate your view to the right, select the next group to the *left* of the first, and hit Selected.

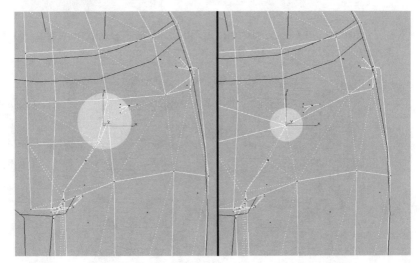

Select the next bunch below where you just Weld Selected, turn on the Target Weld button, and drag the vertices up to those vertices you just merged.

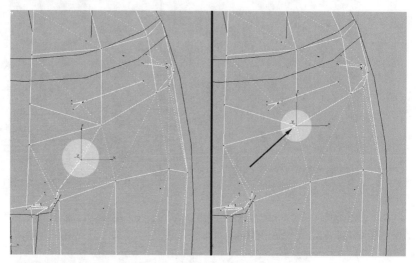

Rotate your view so you can see the next group near the groin area, select them, and hit the Selected button again.

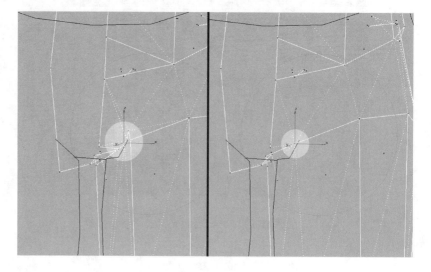

Continuing to rotate your view so you're now looking at the inner thigh, Target Weld the next vertex to the one above it.

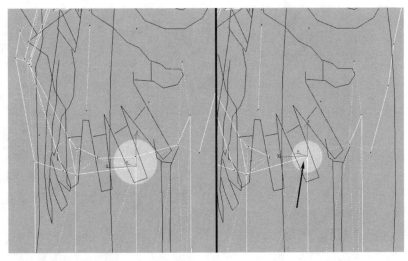

Rotate your view so you're looking at the back of the character. Select this ugly group of excess vertices and merge them into a single vertex using Weld Selected.

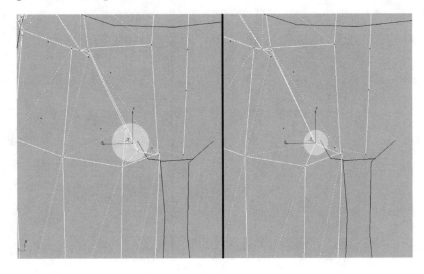

Keep rotating around to the next clump of vertices at the side of the hip and collapse them into one.

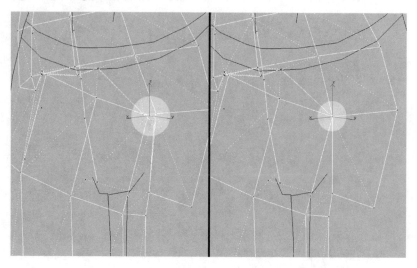

Now zoom in and select these two groups and Target Weld them to this vertex above them.

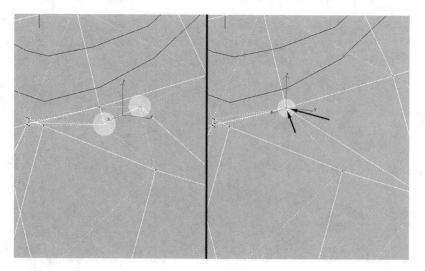

Rotate your view toward the front and merge this mess of jumbled verts.

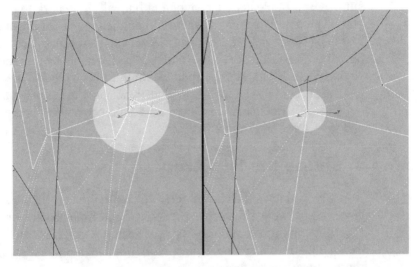

Finally, rotate back around to the rear, grab this vertex, and Target Weld it to the vertex above it. It doesn't do much in the way of suggesting a nice rear shape, but it cleans the geometry up, prepping it for when you build the butt.

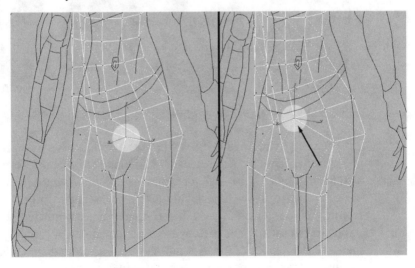

MODELING

The previous welds were designed to simply "clean" the mesh up. The shape is important, but it's always important to keep your work surface tidy. Booleans are convenient but will come back to haunt you if you don't go over the seam and do the type of optimizing you just did. Merging clumps of unattractive vertices after a Boolean operation is par for the course and expected but can be lessened by paying close attention to the points where the two objects meet. As in all aspects of modeling, using your mind's eye to visualize the outcome of a Boolean helps you prepare the two objects beforehand and save some time and effort.

Step 5: Shape the Hip Area

Now that you have the raw material to create the leg and hip area you need to tweak the shape so it looks right. Emphasizing once again the importance of knowing your anatomy, check out the following illustration created from a render of a high-poly mesh that represents a typical female figure:

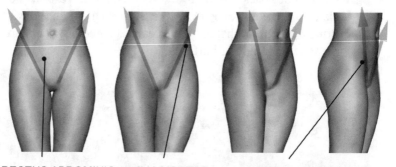

RECTUS ABDOMINIS   ILIAC CREST   TENSOR FASCIAE LATAE

There are definite lines formed where the stomach Vs down to the groin area made from the rectus abdominis muscles, but they are also formed by the protrusion of the iliac crest portion of the pelvic bone and the tensor fasciae latae muscle of the upper thigh. Even in low-poly character creation this sort of anatomical knowledge is important. If these lines are apparent in your mesh, it can only increase the quality of it and reinforce the illusion that this piece of computer graphics represents a humanoid character.

FYI: *MASS MODELING* Hopefully you've come to realize that my main modus operandi when it comes to modeling is to give myself enough mass to work with and then spend time refining it to meet the shape I'm after. Using this technique, it's up to you and your deadline to decide just how much refining or tweaking you do to a mesh, but keep in mind the differences you see in other artists' models are largely due to the time they spent or didn't spend tweaking it. As you gain more experience, your speed will increase and you'll make these sorts of changes intuitively and more quickly. However, you need to always stop and ask yourself when you massage your model into shape, "Does this look right?" Does it look like a leg or an arm or a properly proportioned figure? Many times I critique art by asking the artist, "Does this look right to you?" This is why you need to fill up sketchbook after sketchbook with drawings of the human body and as many poses and anatomical diagrams as you can make time for. If you want to make great characters it starts with the foundation of knowing your subject matter: anatomy and relative proportions.

Load Callisto13.max from the CD. I've detached and hidden the arm so it's easier to see the lower body profile.

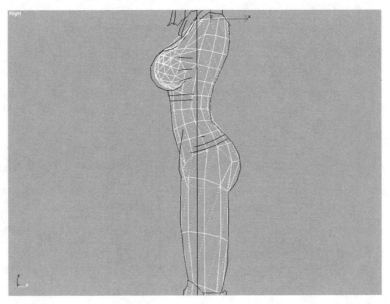

MODELING

You have the raw material for the front hip area; you just need to shape it up. Start with these five vertices and move them over to form the sweep of the tensor fasciae latae muscle.

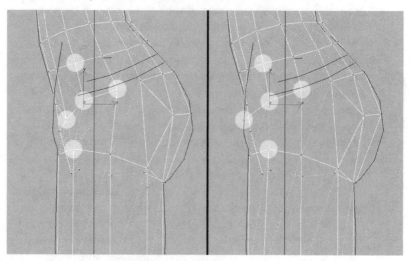

If you compare the mesh before and after the moves, notice how in addition to better defining the hip area, the longitudinal lines of the mesh that run up the side of the hip and torso are now smoother, as shown here.

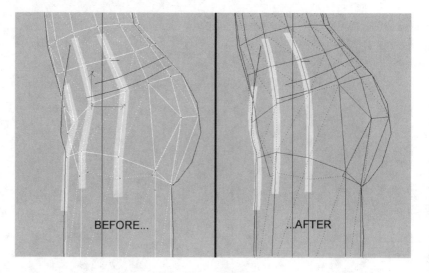

BEFORE...   ...AFTER

FYI: *MESH LINES* Seeing your mesh in terms of lines is an important modeling concept. It allows your brain to look for influence lines and patterns in your mesh like evenly distributed faces. When those lines and patterns are "off" you know it intuitively and make minor adjustments to get the mesh where you want it to be.

Before you go to the Front view and make more tweaks, zoom in and turn ⌐ Turn ⌐ this edge:

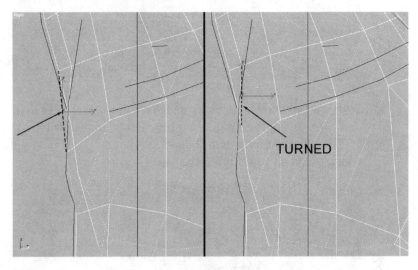

That way it tucks back in along the abdomen and matches the guide even better. Go to the Front view and weld vertex 1 to vertex 2 (this keeps the number of lateral lines even and the faces evenly distributed) and move the other vertices over into the following position.

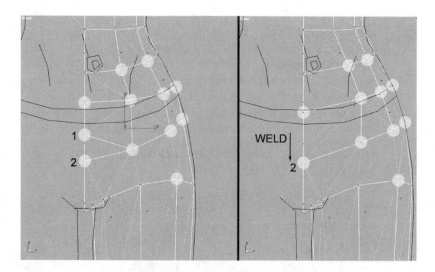

What you've done is basically match the lines of the mesh to the natural shape of the torso. Now, hide Body Guide, switch to a faceted Perspective view with Edged Faces turned on, and rotate your view around so you can see the mesh better.

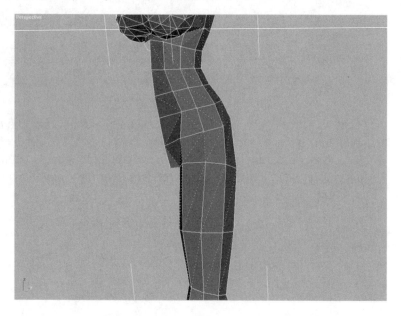

Although it looked right from the side, the front of the mesh still needs work. The upper thigh muscle needs to go further toward the edge of the hip and not the abdominal area.

You need to adjust the thigh and add a vertex using Edge Divide 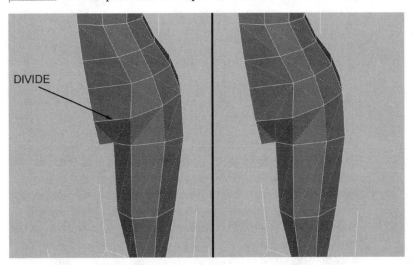 to complete the sweep of the tensor fasciae latae muscle.

DIVIDE

Next, turn these edges so that when you move the vertices to create the leg shape at the top, all the edges are convex, or "non-dented."

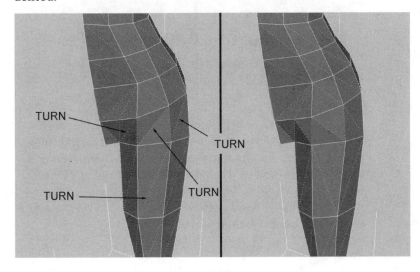

TURN

TURN

TURN

TURN

FYI: *WHY TURN AN EDGE...PART 2* I went into detail in
an earlier FYI about why I decide which edge to turn...

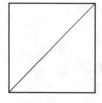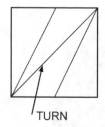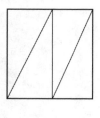

TURN

I concentrated on making all edges *as short as they can be.*
Doing this keeps the faces evenly distributed and the overall
detail of the mesh proportionate. Another reason for turning
an edge that is just as important is to *maintain its volume.* By
this I mean that during the modeling process I find myself
arc-rotating my view in a faceted view to find any divot or dent
caught by the default lighting (or custom lights). As soon as I
find an edge that is an unnatural crease or divot, I turn it.
Turning concave edges like this ensures a nice smooth surface
on the mesh as well as giving the mesh optimal *volume.*

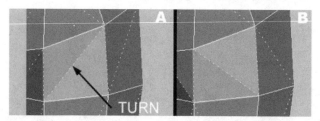

In render A notice how the upper triangle of the edge indicated is slightly *darker* than the one below it. This indicates a
concave edge. Turning it makes the surface more even and
adds to the illusion of volume to the mesh (render B). An
uneven surface caused by edges in need of turning are one of
the most frequent flaws I see when critiquing someone else's
model and detract from the quality.

Now move these vertices to smooth the curve of the lower abs and upper leg/hip.

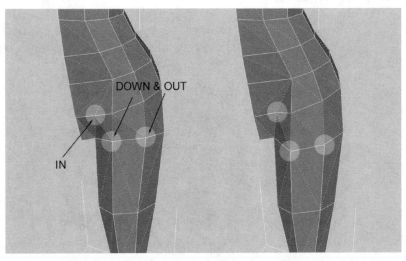

Finally, do some minor tweaks in the abs area to create better lines. Turn these edges and move these vertices.

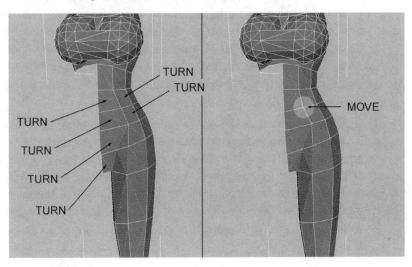

Step 6: Shape and Position the Rear for Attachment

Now that the front of the torso looks cool, it's time to work on the backside. Look at the following illustration. It's also from a render of a high-res mesh of a typical female figure:

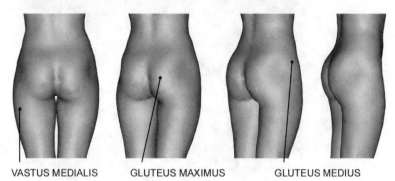

VASTUS MEDIALIS   GLUTEUS MAXIMUS   GLUTEUS MEDIUS

I've identified the major muscles that define the buttock area. Of course there are many muscles that define the leg, but in Callisto's case her boots obscure most of her calf and foot area so the focus is on her butt. In a female figure the shape of the bottom is rounder than a typical male's due to more fat storage. Terms like "hour-glass" figure and "curvaceous" when applied to the female form come from the fact that it has more curves than the more angular male form.

To create the rear of the character, first you're going to build and shape a geosphere to approximate the gluteus maximus and gluteus medius muscles and then use Face|Create to attach it to the torso. This is similar to using a geosphere for the rounded surface and Boolean Union to attach it, but this time you'll avoid the messy results and subsequent cleanup of a Boolean operation by prepping and manually attaching the shape.

Load Callisto14.max from the CD.

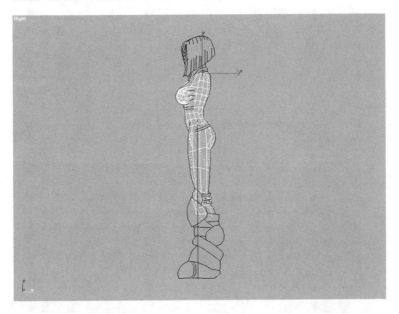

I've detached the profile from Body Guide and unhidden the back leg reference so you can match the mesh to it. The first thing you need to do is delete the vertices and faces that currently make up Callisto's posterior. Select these five vertices of the rear and delete them:

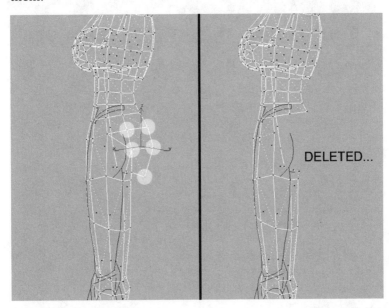

Go to the Back viewport by hitting the K key, make a geosphere with a radius of 3.1 and segments of 4, select Octa for Geodesic Base Type, and check Hemisphere.

Line the sphere up with the curve of the rear leg guide.

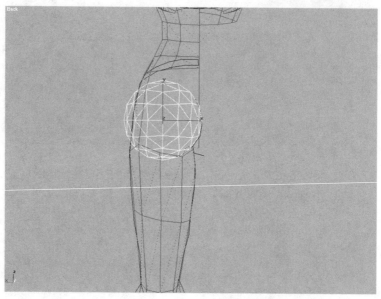

Go to the Right viewport, and move the geosphere over along the X-axis so it matches the curve of the guide.

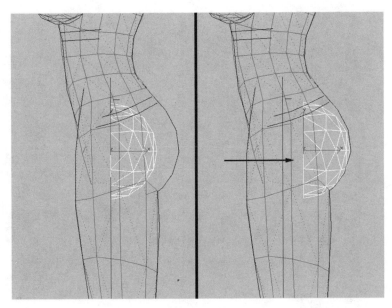

Next, apply an Edit Mesh modifier to the geosphere, go to Vertex, turn on Use Soft Selection, and enter a value of 5 for Falloff.

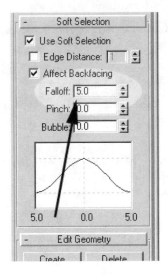

Select the top group of vertices and move them up exactly one unit along the Y-axis.

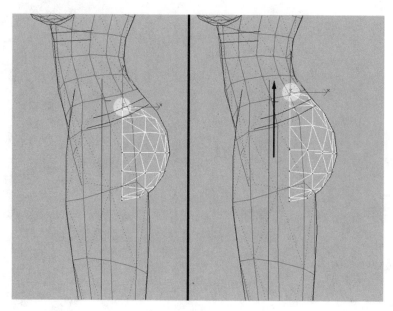

 FYI: MOVE TRANSFORM TYPE-IN Right-clicking on any of the transform icons brings up the Transform Type-In window. To move something one unit along the Y-axis, make sure Move is the transform type. Right-click on the icon and enter 1 in the Y-axis field under Offset: Screen.

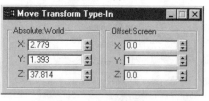

Go back to the Back viewport, rotate the geosphere –10 degrees along the Y-axis, and move it to the right until the left edge rests flush with Torso's left edge.

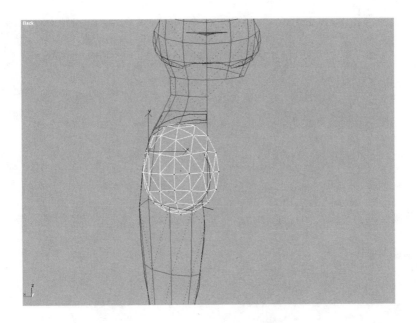

Rotating the geosphere matches the flow lines better to the torso. Moving it causes the right side of the geosphere to overlap the line of the curve and break the dividing plane of the torso half. The overlap is because that line of the rear leg guide showing the curve of the butt cheek is actually caused by the *intersection* of the two cheeks. Overlapping the geometry ensures the two cheeks will intersect and results in that same line seen in the guide.

Now you need to create the dented look on the outside of the cheek using Soft Selection again. Go to the Vertex sub-object menu; Use Soft Selection should still be checked. Leave the Falloff at 5, select the vertex in the following figure, and move it over about half a unit to the right along the X-axis.

MODELING

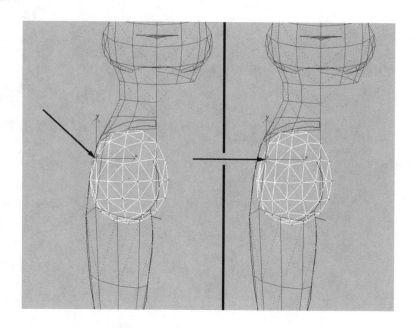

Now that the rear is shaped and roughly in place, you need to make a couple of tweaks to Torso before attaching the butt shape to it. Hide [Hide by Name...] the guide objects and select Torso.

Go to the Modify panel [ ] and hit Edge [ ]. Divide this edge and turn the new edge.

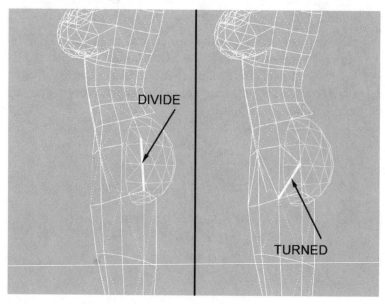

These changes to Torso align the vertices about to be joined when the geosphere is attached. It's easier to do these kinds of tweaks before attaching since the two meshes overlap but are still separate.

Preparing two objects for attachment in this "manual Boolean" method entails one of two things (or both): moving the vertices of each shape into the proper position using Snap  and deleting unnecessary vertices. Deciding which vertices to either move or delete relies on the same decision: Which part of each respective object is more important? In this case, the bottom and rear half of the geosphere is crucial in suggesting the roundness of the buttock shape. The vertices of the lower back on the torso take priority over the top vertices of the geosphere since they are more aligned with the guide and define the torso better than the top of the geosphere.

Right-click on the 3D Snap Toggle icon to bring up the Grid and Snap Settings window and check Vertex if it isn't already checked. Uncheck Grid Points and check Endpoint.

Close the window and hit S to make Snap active. Go to a Perspective viewport, select the geosphere, and hit Zoom Extents Selected to make sure viewport rotation occurs around the selected geosphere. Zoom out a little, open the Vertex sub-object menu, and turn off Use Soft Selection.

Select and move this vertex so it snaps to the vertex of the torso above it.

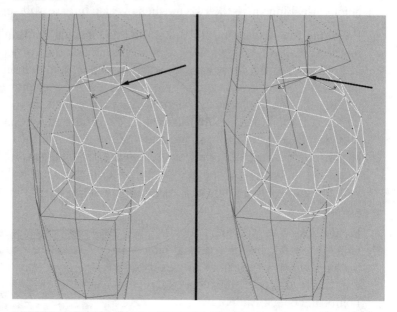

FYI: *AXIS CONSTRAINTS*

max gives you the option of using the Snap tool with or without normal axis constraints. Typically it's a good idea to keep the Use Axis Constraints box unchecked, keeping in mind axis constraints are turned off if Snap is on.

Now you are faced with the choice of further identifying key vertices integral to the shape you're trying to achieve, snapping more vertices in place based on those key vertices and turning edges accordingly to make each mesh look right before attaching them, *or* deleting useless vertices of each mesh with the knowledge you'll be manually building faces to fill in the gaps later. The first approach is great because it keeps manual face creation to a minimum, but it requires a lot more thought. The second is an easier solution because deleting vertices — well, that doesn't take much brainpower at all.

Select these vertices at the top of the geosphere and delete them:

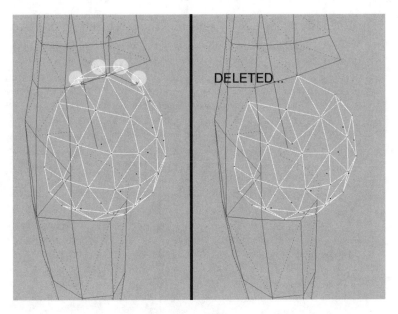

Rotate the view to see the front of the geosphere and delete these vertices as well:

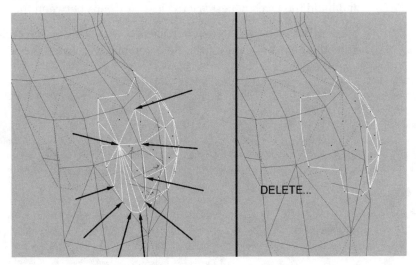

Now you have a floating piece of "cheek" that can be attached to the torso.

Step 7: Attach the Rear and Complete the Shape

Attach the geosphere by selecting the torso, hitting the Attach button [Attach] so it turns green [Attach], and clicking on the geosphere.

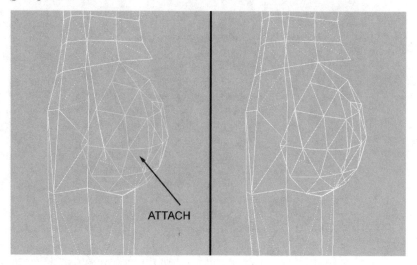

ATTACH

Now merge the appropriate vertices of the combined Torso and rear and build the faces necessary to close any gaps between the two.

Start with these two pairs of vertices by entering 2 in the Weld Selected field and then hit the Selected button to weld them simultaneously.

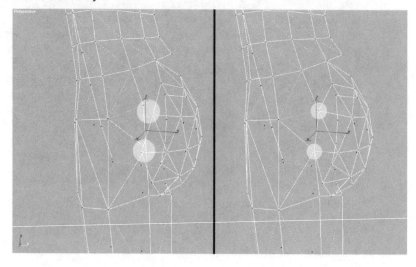

Rotate the view, select these two vertices, and Target Weld them to the vertex of the upper leg.

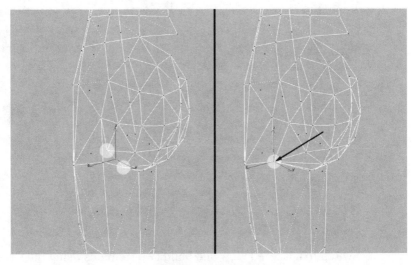

Rotate the view again and Target Weld this vertex.

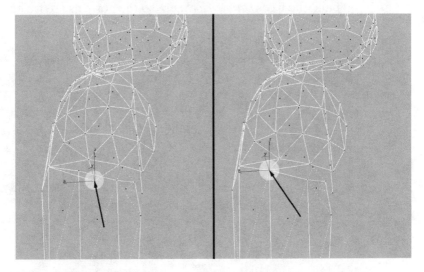

Weld this one as well.

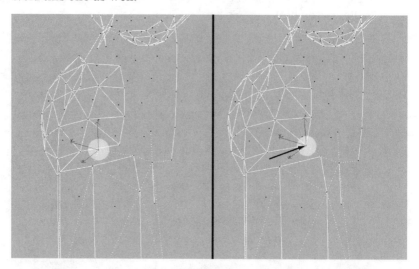

Switch to a faceted view and build two triangles using the Create button ⌷ Create ⌷ under the Face sub-object menu ◄ . Make sure you build the faces *counterclockwise* so the normals are facing the right direction.

FYI: *CREATING FACES IN FACETED MODE AND F2*

Creating faces on a mesh in a faceted or even smooth shaded mode allows you to quickly see whether or not the normals are facing the right direction when you make the face.

An alternative is to hit F2. Any selected or freshly built triangle turns a nearly opaque, more solid red, making it easier to identify.

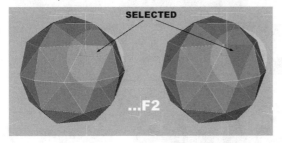

Rotate the view and build the appropriate faces on the top of the buttock.

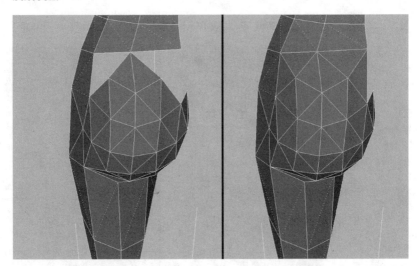

MODELING

Refine the mesh by Weld Selecting these two vertices (change the distance value to 10 instead of 2):

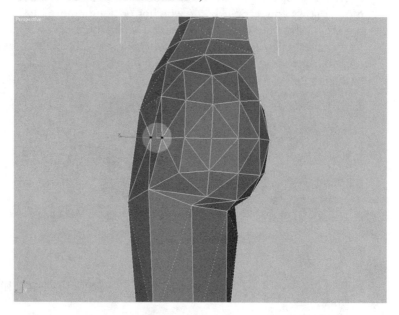

Next, delete these two vertices and Target Weld this vertex:

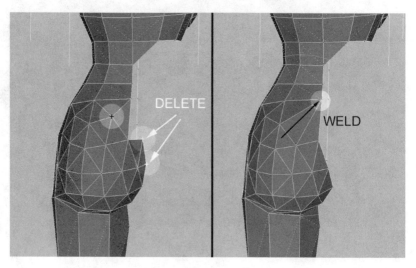

Delete this face so you can mirror the lower torso and leg you just created.

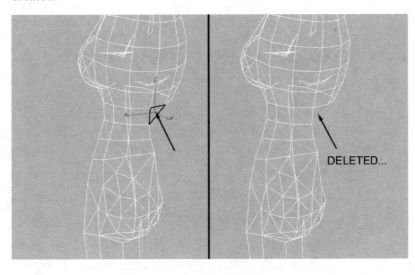

DELETED...

Step 8: Copy and Mirror the Lower Torso and Leg

To get a better feel for the progress thus far, collapse the stack of Torso, select the faces of the lower torso and leg, and Shift-drag to the left, detaching them to a new object.

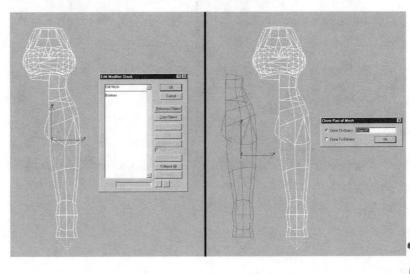

Mirror the new object using the Tools | Mirror command and slide it over to meet the torso.

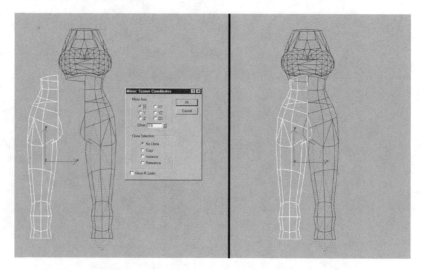

Attach the mirrored object to the torso, select *just* these overlapping vertices, enter a value of 1 in the Weld Selected box, and hit Selected.

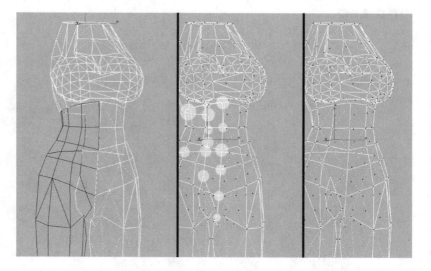

Rotate your view, go to the bottom two sets of vertices at the rear, select them, choose a Non Uniform Scale transform, right-click on it to bring up the Scale Transform Type-In window, type 10000 in the X-axis box under Offset: World, and hit your Enter key.

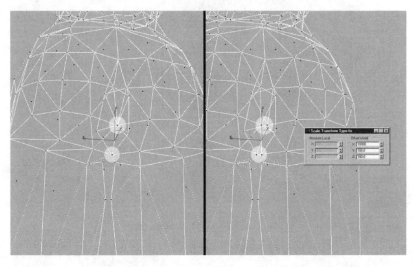

This obviously over-scales the vertices but separates them so you can get at the close vertices individually. Leave the top set "as is" and move the bottom set away from each other so they *don't* cross.

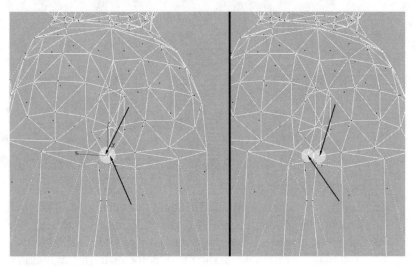

Now close the mesh by building these faces:

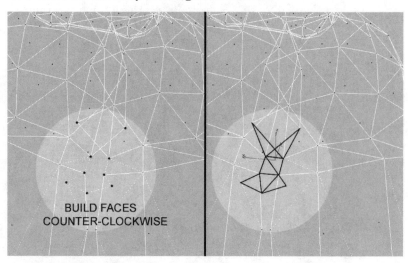

Divide this edge and turn these edges:

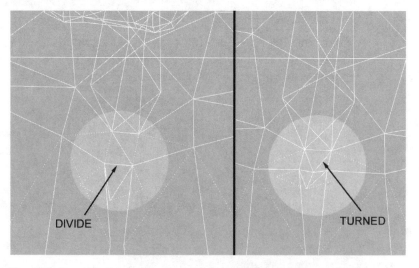

You didn't weld the vertices near the bottom of the rear for a very specific reason: animation. Bringing the vertices to a single line around the groin area makes it very difficult to work with when animating a character. Leaving a space or gap keeps the groin intact and makes certain when the mesh deforms during animation that it looks right and maintains the shape of the leg. The intersecting geometry of the rear supports better leg animation because the legs can move with the rear cheeks sliding against each other as they do in real life. A few more tweaks and the torso and legs are good to go.

Select this vertex at the back and slide it away from the torso just a bit (about half a unit).

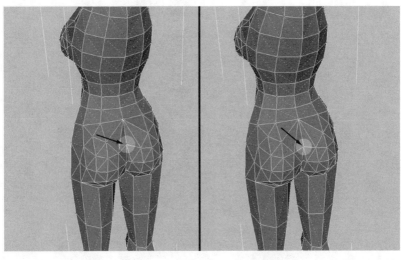

And turn these edges of the bottom:

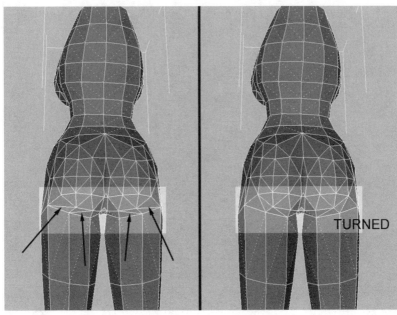

Looking at her from the front, you can see that Callisto's body is coming along nicely.

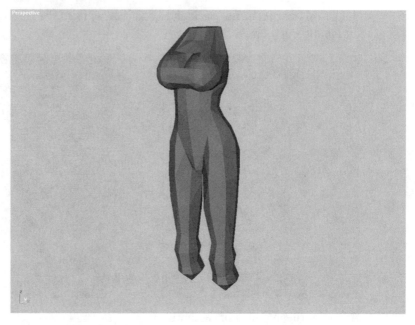

Now it's time to move on to the back, neck, and shoulders.

CHAPTER 8
The Back, Neck & Shoulders

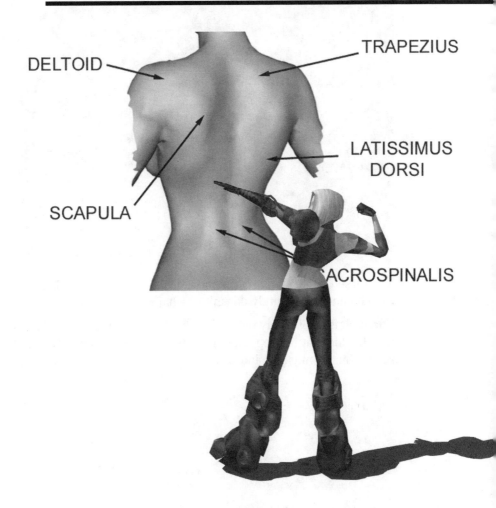

DELTOID

TRAPEZIUS

LATISSIMUS DORSI

SCAPULA

ACROSPINALIS

The reason I didn't have you spend much time on the back when you did the torso earlier is because I wanted to wait until you got to the shoulders and neck geometry. The upper back, neck, and shoulders are closely linked in both structure and function. Load Callisto15.max from the CD.

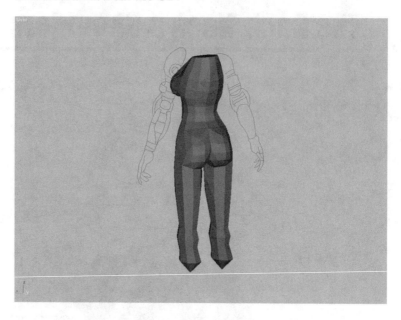

The torso matches up great in the side view but if you look at it from behind, it definitely doesn't fit what a back should look like.

The back is a relatively flat region that broadens into and includes the shoulders at the top, tapers down to the waist, and is defined by several major muscles and bones.

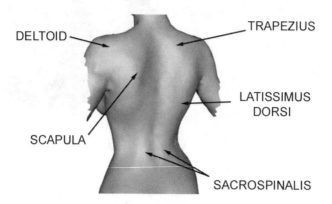

Of course, the spine is the main landmark, but the trapezius, deltoid, and latissimus dorsi (lats) muscles along with the scapula, or shoulder blades, make major landmarks for the mid/upper back as well. The smaller sacrospinalis muscles of the lower back are also good points to suggest — even in a low-poly mesh.

Step 1: Shape the Back

For Callisto, broaden her back at the top, flatten it, and then suggest the scapula and lower sacrospinalis muscles, creating a crease down the middle for her spine. First, make your work a little easier to see by hiding the faces you don't need.

Select the faces ✔ of the back, go up to Edit|Select Invert, and hit the Hide button ▭ Hide ▭ under the Face sub-object menu.

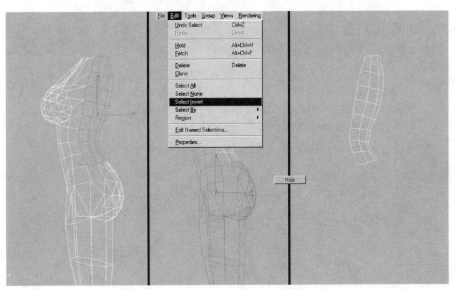

Next, optimize the mesh a little by dropping the second line of vertices down to the row just below it. Use Target Weld 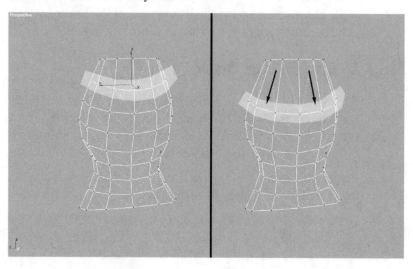 to weld the vertices one by one.

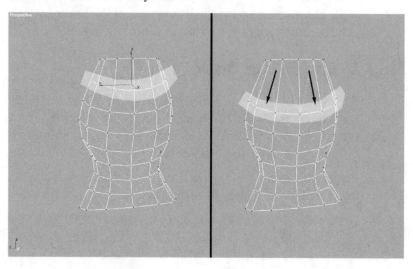

Select all the vertices in the middle of the back except the top and bottom ones and drag them in along the Y-axis [Y] (in a Perspective viewport) about .9 units.

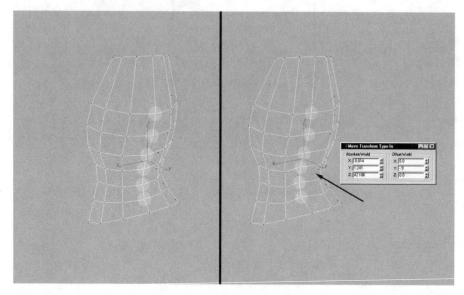

Now even out the face distribution so you can widen the back at the top. Select the middle three vertices of the second row you merged earlier and turn on Use Soft Selection, setting the Falloff to 7.5:

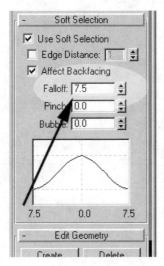

Move them about 1.3 units up along the Z-axis.

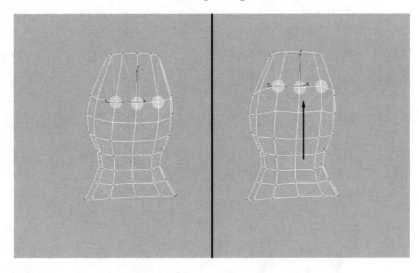

MODELING

With Soft Selection still on, select just these four vertices and NU Scale them out along the X-axis ⊠ by 125%.

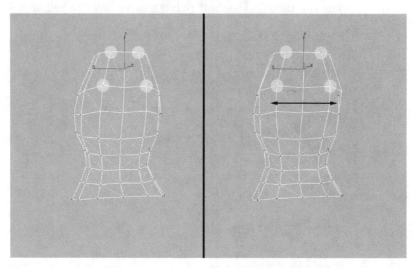

Turn off Use Soft Selection and optimize the back a little more by merging the third and fourth row of vertices from the bottom. Do this by setting the Weld Selected value to 10 and alternately selecting pairs of vertices, one from each row, and hitting Selected ⌊ Selected ⌋. *Don't* weld the vertices at the forward edge of the vertex rows.

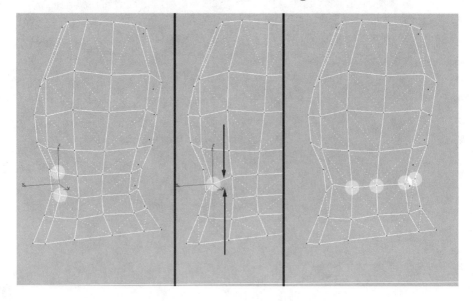

Next, turn these two edges on each side:

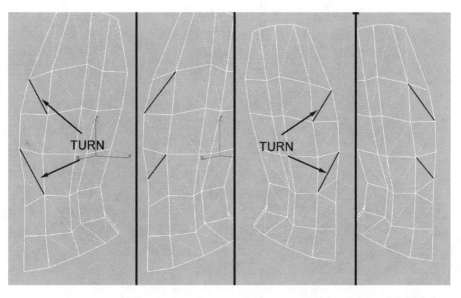

While still in the Perspective viewport, switch to a faceted view to see the tweaks you're about to make more clearly. Select these four vertices and NU Scale ⬚ them 115% along the X-axis:

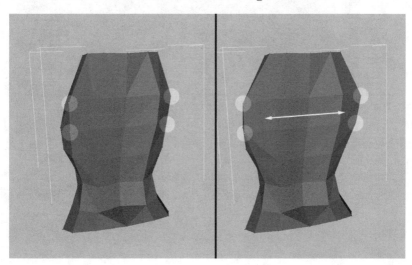

With those vertices still selected, select these four as well and drag them toward you along the Y-axis by about .3 units:

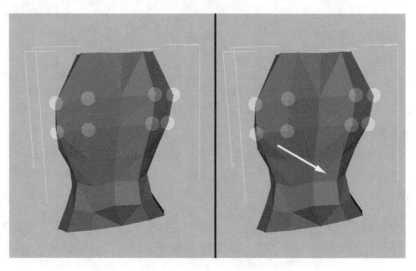

Select these four vertices in the mid to lower part of the back and scale them by 90% along the X-axis:

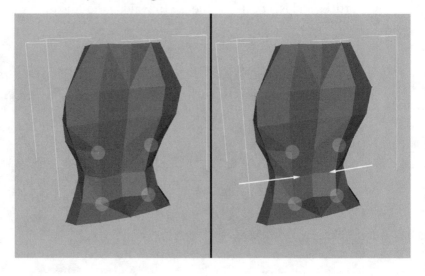

Select these two vertices and scale them in by an additional 85%:

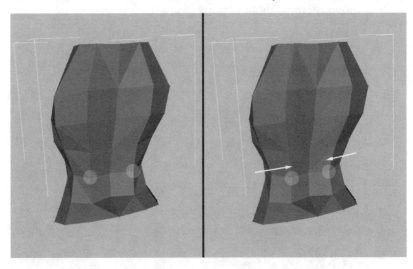

This gives more shape to the lower back and suggests a more athletic build. Go up to the top middle vertex and move it in by about .7 units along the Y-axis.

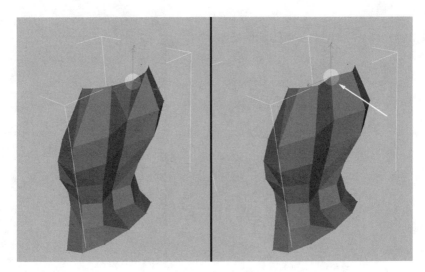

Grab the two vertices on either side of the one you just moved and move them in about .3 units along the Y-axis.

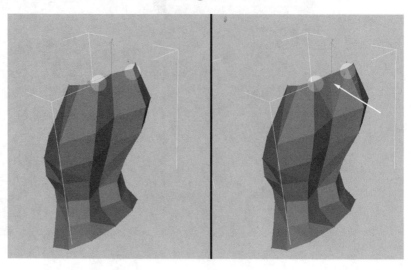

Switch back to wireframe mode and turn these two sets of edges to get rid of some slight concavity in the surface:

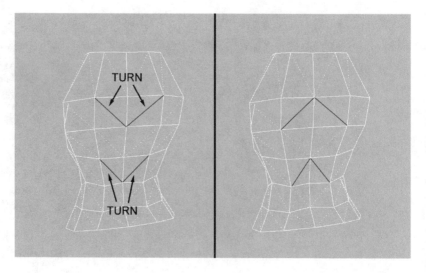

Unhide all the hidden faces of Torso and compare the old back to the new. A definite improvement!

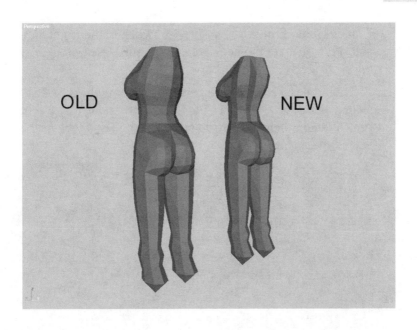

OLD   NEW

Step 2: Create the Neck Mass Using Face Extrude

Load Callisto16.max or continue with your current mesh. Now you need to make the neck. Select the faces ■ at the top of the torso.

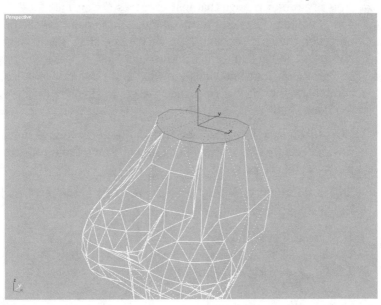

Unhide Guide Profile 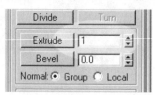, switch to the Right viewport, and zoom 🔍 in to the neck area. Make sure Use Soft Selection is *unchecked*.

Position the top faces a little better by rotating them 5 degrees along the Z-axis ⌷z⌷, NU scaling them 120% along the X-axis, and repositioning them slightly down and to the left so the farthest right vertex rests on the guide.

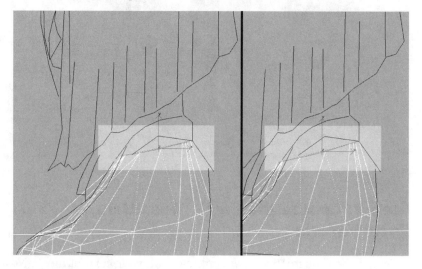

This is a minor change that just prepares the surface for extrusion and gets it a little closer to the guide. At this point for the neck, however, the guide doesn't help very much since the design obscures the neck underneath the hair. This is a case where you'll be relying on your knowledge of what a neck should look like in combination with what reference the guidelines *do* provide to make the neck shape.

Now, using Face Extrude ⌷ Extrude ⌷ you're going to give yourself the raw material to shape into a neck, moving and scaling the extruded faces as you create them.

Still in the Right viewport, enter a value of 1 in the box beside Extrude on the Face sub-object menu:

Divide	Turn
Extrude	1
Bevel	0.0
Normal: ⦿ Group ◯ Local	

Hit Enter and rotate the new faces 10 degrees along the Z-axis.

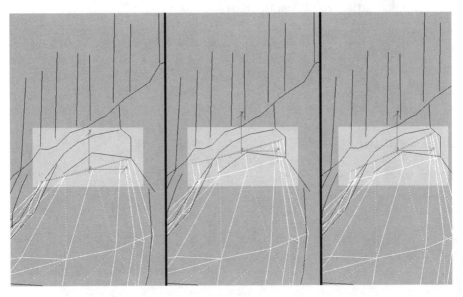

With the extruded faces still selected, switch to the Front viewport, hit Zoom Extents Selected , and zoom out a little to see what you're doing. Scale the faces along the X-axis by 65%.

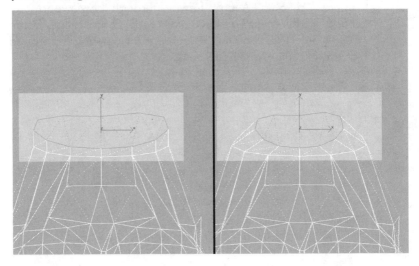

Go back to the Right viewport, hit Zoom Extents Selected, zoom out a little, type 1.5 in the Extrude box, and hit Enter.

 FYI: *VIEWPORT UNDO*   If you find yourself bouncing back and forth between two views like Front and Right viewport, try hitting Shift+Z a couple of times to undo the viewport changes. Hit Shift+A to go forward through the viewport changes. This saves you the tedious repetition of hitting Zoom Extents Selected, zooming 🔍 out, and/or panning 🖑 around to zero in on the same geometry.

Switch to the Front again, get your work in view and scale the new faces in by 80% along the X-axis.

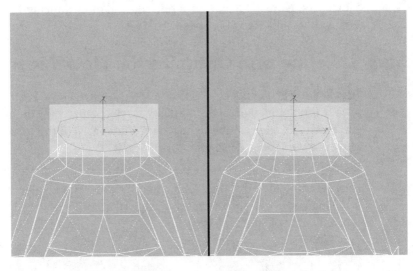

Go yet again to the Right viewport, center your work, and extrude the selected faces by 2 units. Rotate the extruded faces by 10 degrees along the Z-axis and move them back down and to the left about .2 units, respectively.

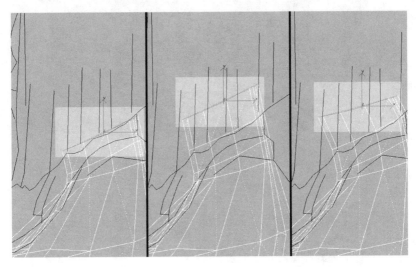

Of course you could have done all those extrusions and adjustments in one window, but in this case it made more sense to switch viewports. Now it's a matter of refining and/or optimizing the geometry you've added to your mesh.

Step 3: Refine and Optimize the Neck Mass

Just looking at the neck area after all those extrusions, I can see the area is too detailed and has too many faces compared to the rest of the mesh and the relative importance of that area of the torso. The neck is a whopping 12 segments at the top!

Switch to a Perspective viewport, select the top neck faces (if they're not selected already), and delete them. Then, select these two vertices at the throat, enter a value of 3 in the Weld Selected box, and hit Selected   Selected .

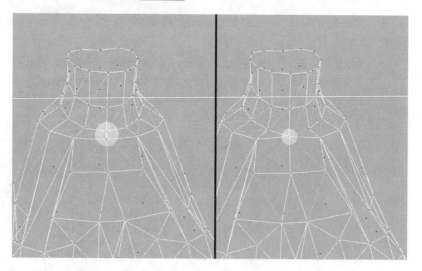

Select these 12 vertices at the front of the neck and, with the same Weld value as before, hit Selected again.

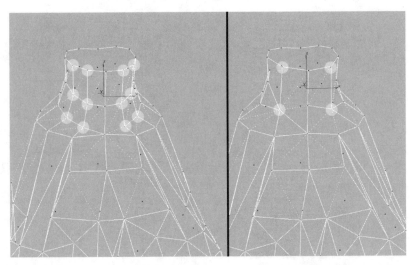

Any time you find yourself duplicating your work on each side of a symmetrical shape like the neck, it should turn a light on in your head: half... copy... mirror. Select all the vertices of the right side of the neck and delete them.

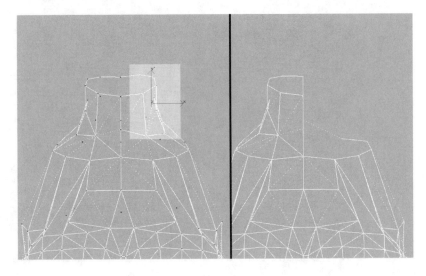

MODELING

Go to the Back view and delete this lone face to keep the demarcation between the halves clean.

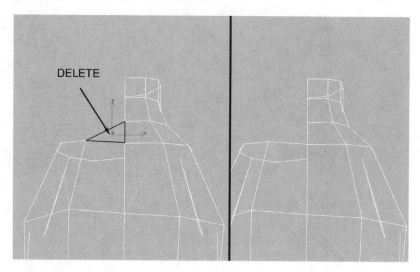

Looking at the neck from the Left viewport you can see the slight indentation at the front. Make this even more apparent by sliding these two vertices up and back just a hair, and turn these two edges to match the lines of the neck.

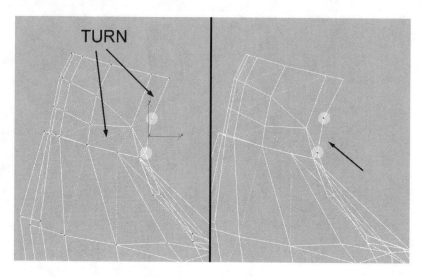

Rotate your view in the Perspective viewport so you can see the back of the neck. Select these two groups of vertices, keeping 3 for a Weld Selected value, and hit Selected:

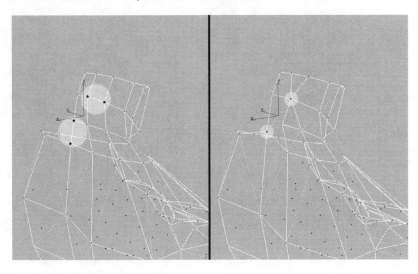

Next, select these two groups of vertices and hit the Weld Selected button:

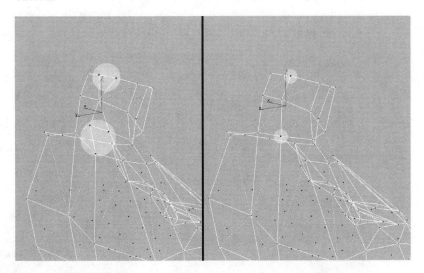

Finally, Target Weld this vertex to the one above it:

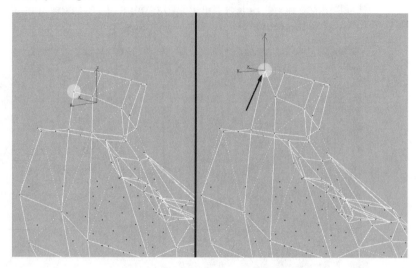

Now that it's optimized from the excess of extruding all those faces, shape the contour of the back of the neck. In the Perspective viewport, make the view faceted and turn on Edged Faces to see the surface and lines of the mesh better. Using arc-rotate (Ctrl+R) and alternating between the different axes, move these vertices slightly to create a more feminine neck shape.

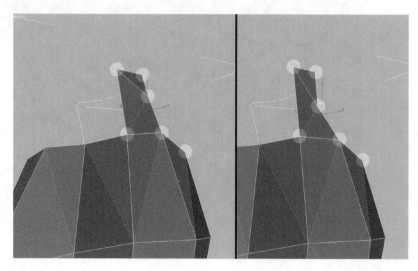

Rotate to the front of the mesh and adjust these vertices to shape the neck further. Again, do whatever it takes: Arc-rotate and switch axes to get at the vertices and move them.

By now you should have an understanding of how to model through mass creation and lots of tweaking. Again, if you're new to modeling, this iterative approach takes time to master so don't worry about your speed...you'll get quicker. If you're experienced, you're probably not even reading this and have already jumped ahead to the next step — the shoulder!

MODELING

Step 4: Prepare the Torso for the Shoulder

With the neck half complete, it's time to make the shoulders. Load Callisto17.max and take a minute to look at the guide again.

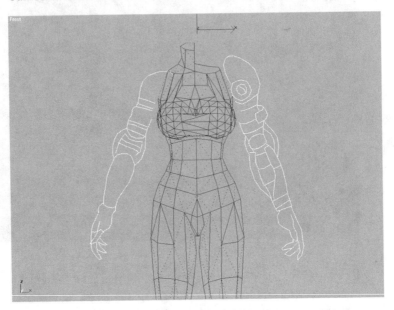

The shoulders are a natural extension of the upper torso. Whether in a low-poly or high-poly character, shoulders are one of the most *difficult* areas to animate so careful attention must be paid when building them. In the case of Callisto, the difficulty is compounded on the right side because her shoulder is bare, making the mesh "contiguous," or one shape. The left shoulder is a typical design for lower polygon characters, and even higher polygon characters, since the arm can be separate and the shoulder pad can hide the seam where arm and torso meet. Detached arms with their joints hidden by a shoulder pad are a common theme for real-time, low-poly characters.

To generate the mass for the shoulder you're going to extrude the faces of the upper side of the torso. First, though, you need to shape the area by moving some vertices around. Switch to a Perspective viewport and hide Guide Arm.

Select this important vertex that is the anchor for the front deltoid and move it .8 units up along the Z-axis, .3 units over away from the body along the X-axis, and .6 units back along the Y-axis.

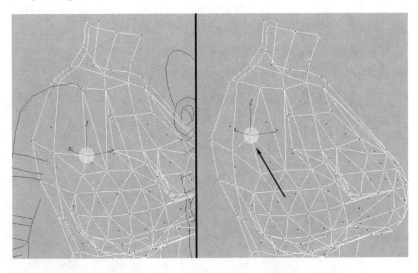

Rotate your view so you can see the back and slide this vertex back about .8 units along the Y-axis.

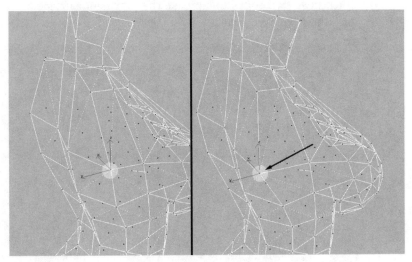

Next, rotate back to the front of the mesh and grab this vertex, moving it down .7 units along the Z-axis, away from the torso .3 units along the X-axis, and then forward in the Y-axis by .7 units. Switch to a faceted, Edged Faces view to see the impact the changes are having on the surface.

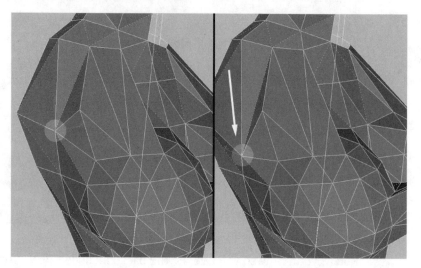

Turn these two edges to increase the extrusion surface and eliminate their concave aspect.

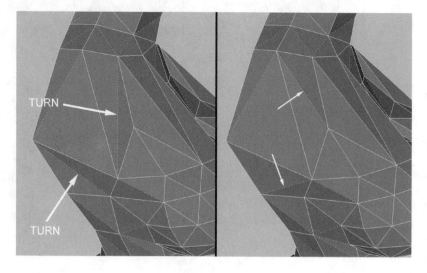

Divide [Divide] the bottom edge where the arm will meet the torso, lower the new vertex about .5 units along the Z-axis, and turn this other edge so it's shorter and the faces are more evenly distributed.

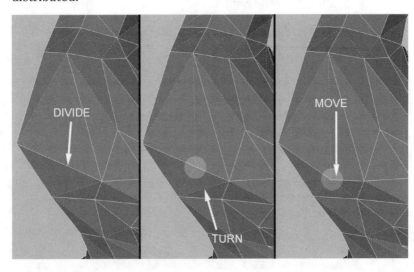

Step 5: Extrude and Shape the Shoulder

Everything you've done with the minor tweaks to the torso has shaped these five triangles so they can be extruded and shaped into the shoulder:

With those faces selected, enter a Face Extrude value of 5.5.

Hit Enter and drop the new faces down by 2.5 units along the Z-axis.

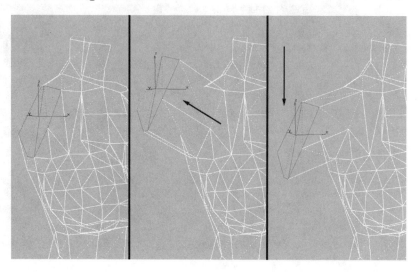

With the mass now there and positioned somewhat where you need it, all you have to do is shape it up. First, Target Weld this vertex upward to the one above it.

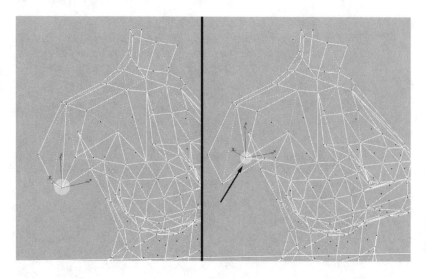

FYI: *TARGET WELD AXIS CONSTRAINTS* If you're trying to Target Weld a vertex in a Perspective view, hit F8 a couple of times to make sure your axis plane is set to XY xy. That way you'll never have a problem merging the vertex in question. If the axis icon turns into a straight line, simply rotate your view a little and the vertex can be moved.

Unhide Guide Arm and freeze Freeze by Hit it. Go to the Front viewport and move the vertices of the shoulder edge so they line up with the guidelines. The lowest lying vertex should end up *behind* the arm.

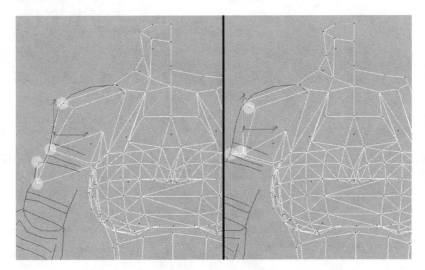

MODELING

Select these three vertices and scale them in along the Y-axis 70%:

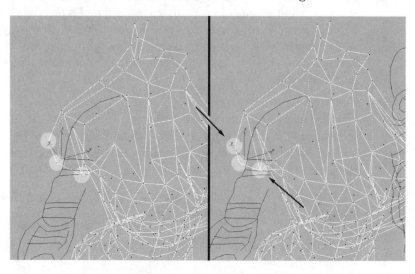

Next, divide these edges and turn the edges the divisions create:

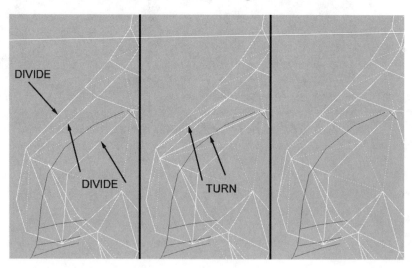

The line of vertices you just created will make up the curve of the top of the shoulder. Go to the Front view and lift them up by .3 units and over by .3 units so they match the guidelines.

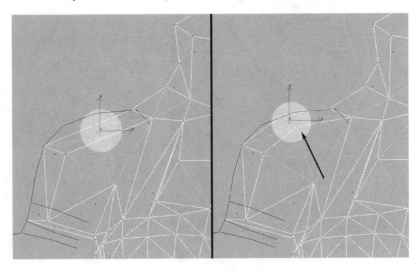

Rotate your view and turn the edges at the rear of the shoulder so they look better.

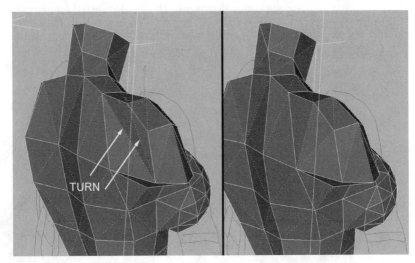

Rotate the view again. You can see, as the shadows point out at the top of the shoulder, that some edges need to be turned due to the concave surfaces they're creating.

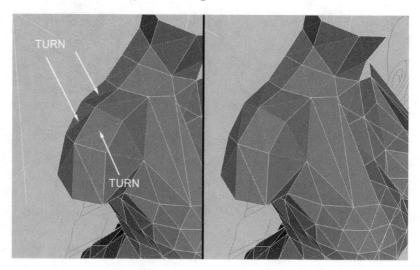

Rotate your view so you're looking up underneath the shoulder, and turn these two edges so that the surface is flat and can be extruded to extend the shoulder down into the beginning of an arm shape.

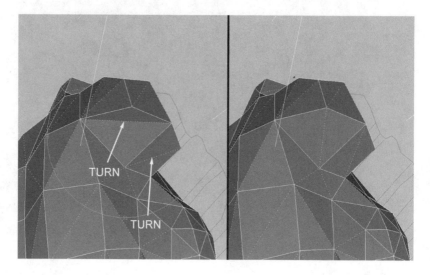

Select the faces of the arm "stump" and extrude them 4 units.

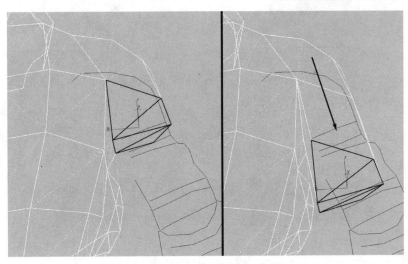

Go back to the Front viewport and with the faces still selected, slide them over to correspond to the guide and rotate them –7 degrees along the Z-axis.

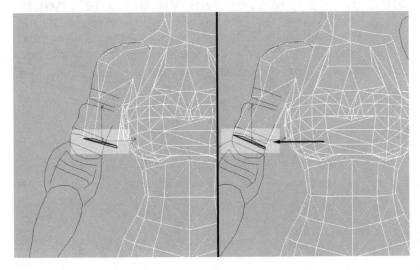

Rotate around to the back and turn these edges that are slightly concave.

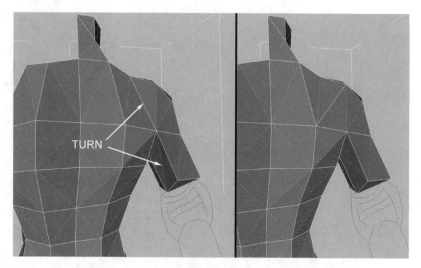

That's good enough for now. Next, you're going to copy the faces that make up the shoulder, mirror the detached mesh, and attach it back to the torso.

Step 6: Copy, Mirror, and Attach the Shoulder

When you deleted half the neck, you left the shoulder area on the left side. That's fine since I want to show you how you can use copied and mirrored geometry as a guide for which vertices and/or faces to delete in the original mesh.

Select these faces on the right side of Torso as seen from the front and back:

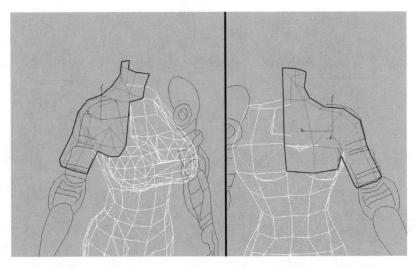

Shift-drag the faces to the right as seen from nearly a Front view and select Clone To Object when the Clone Part of Mesh window pops up.

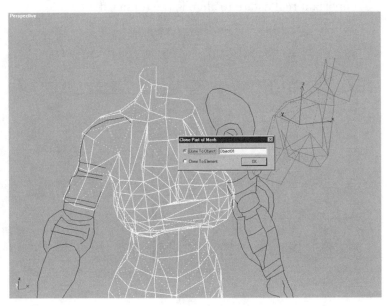

Change Pivot Point Center 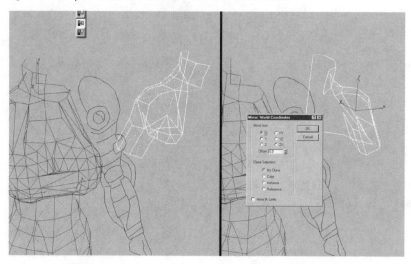 to Pivot Use Selection Center ![icon], go
up to Tools | Mirror, and mirror the shoulder half.

Slide the copied mesh over to the torso, making sure the vertices
line up at point A and not the center. Normally the center is the
point to match, but in this case (as is the case sometimes) the most
important real estate to align is the torso side.

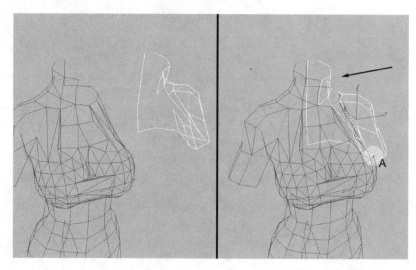

Before attaching the mirrored shoulder, you need to delete the overlapping and now useless geometry of the upper left half of the torso. In a situation like this you have the choice of deleting vertices, faces, or even edges. I usually opt for vertices because when you delete faces max will always annoyingly prompt you to delete isolated vertices. Of course, there are times when you actually would keep those isolated vertices, but most of the time you would want them deleted. Going with vertex deletion, I recommend selecting the vertices that make up the border of the geometry you want to *keep* and then hiding them. This avoids confusion and quickly identifies the vertices that need to be excised.

With that in mind, select all the vertices that correspond to the unattached shoulder half edges and hide them. Select the appropriate vertices inside the area delineated by the hidden vertices and delete them.

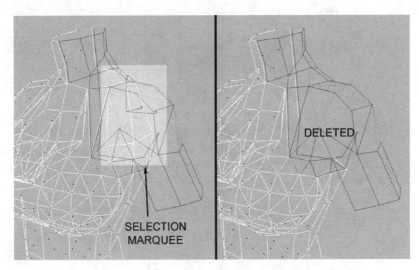

There's a triangle in the back that overlaps and is a possibility whenever you opt for deleting vertices instead of faces. You could simply select and delete this face or select the mirrored shoulder and delete this vertex.

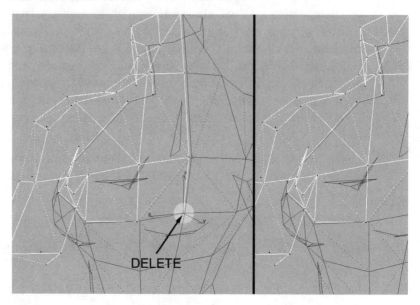

Now, select the torso again and attach the shoulder geometry to it. Merge the overlying and not-so-overlying vertices by selecting all the vertices at the seam where the pieces meet, entering 1 for a Weld Selected value, and hitting the Selected button.

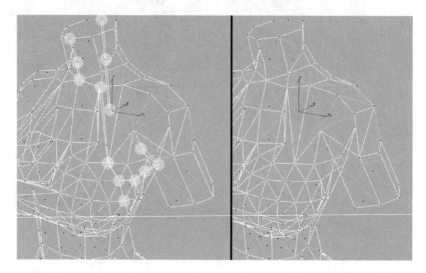

Step 7: Make More Refinements

Murphy's Law states that anything that can go wrong will go wrong. It's not so much that anything is wrong with the mesh; it's just that it needs some tweaks that would have been best done before the shoulder was copied and mirrored.

Unhide Guide Profile and I'll show you what I mean.

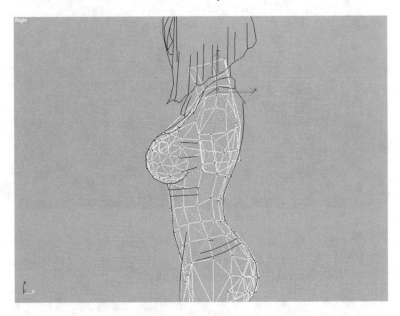

According to the profile of the guide, the mesh is a little off at the back. This is easily fixed, but now must be done for two sides instead of one. Of course, it doesn't have to be like this. I considered redoing this section to reflect a perfectly planned shoulder that was mirrored and then left alone, untouched in its perfection and demonstrating my Jedi-like skills at modeling — but that's not very realistic. In fact, this kind of problem occurs all the time, so get used to it.

As long as I've been doing this I still find myself building up half a mesh, copying and mirroring it, and then *deleting it* a half hour later because I realized I had forgotten some detail. The rule of thumb in a case like this is *time*. If the tweaks are minor and take less time than it would take to copy, mirror, and attach, then go ahead and do double the work. If you find yourself spending more than just a little

MODELING

bit of time and energy working on one half and then the other, delete half, build up the side that's left, and copy/mirror it again.

In the Right viewport, select and move the vertices at the neck and back over to match the guide as best you can.

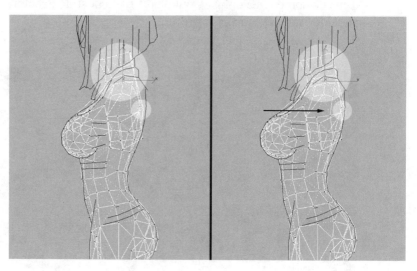

Switch to the Back viewport and add a couple of vertices using Edge Divide. Hit G to bring your grid back so you have some reference to keep the sides symmetrical.

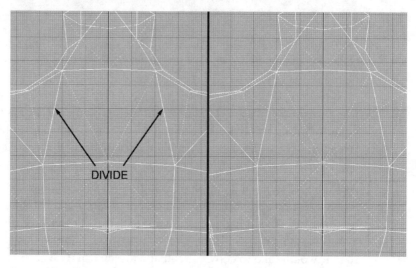

Go back to the Right view and move the vertices appropriately so they line up with the guide.

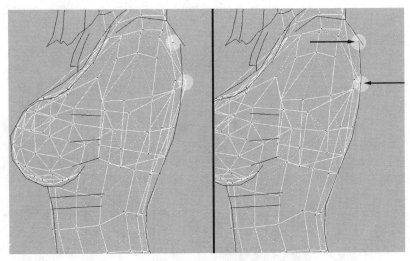

Check it out in a faceted, Edged Faces view.

Even though the back looks a little odd, I see the potential. In fact, the mistake of not checking the profile earlier may have turned into an advantage since it adds more character to the back by suggesting the trapezius more clearly. Turn a couple edges and presto...

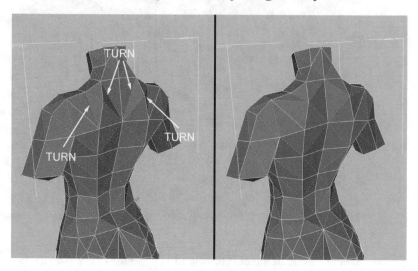

Step 8: Build the Neck/Shoulder Strap

Load Callisto18.max or keep working on the mesh you have. Notice that Callisto has a strap that goes across her front and holds her left shoulder pad on. Unhide Guide Front and you'll see what I mean.

While this small detail can be accomplished with a texture, go ahead and add the geometry (it can always be optimized later). Still in the Front view, create a cylinder 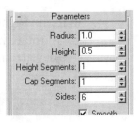 with these settings: Radius of 1, Height of .5, Height Segments 1, Cap Segments 1, and Sides 6.

A six-sided cylinder is about all you can afford for a detail this small. Going with anything more would be disproportionate to the detail of the surrounding geometry; anything less and you risk being too simplified. Rotate it about 50 degrees in the Z-axis and match it to the guidelines.

MODELING

Go to the Right view and position the cylinder at the juncture of the throat; rotate it accordingly (about 21 degrees) along the X-axis. This deviates from the design a little, but that's okay — I designed it!

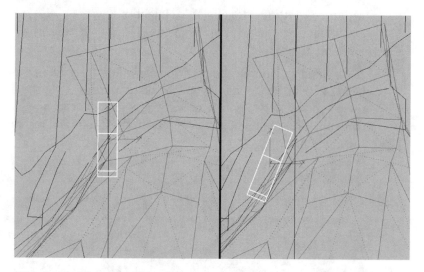

Hide both the guide objects, collapse the cylinder's stack to an Editable Mesh, and click on the Polygon sub-object icon. Select this rectangle of the cylinder, extrude it 1 unit, and pull it in toward the body about .5 units. Take the new extruded faces and extrude them another 1 unit and pull those faces back .5 units as well.

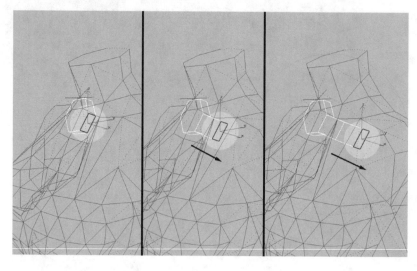

Repeat for the polygon on the opposite side of the cylinder except move the second set of extruded faces up along the Z-axis about .3 units and back half a unit.

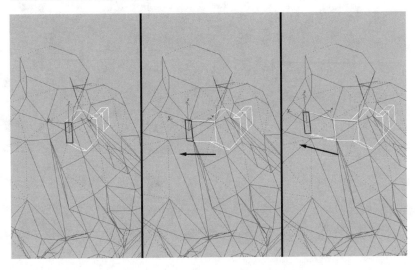

Select these vertices of the strap and rotate them 15 degrees along the X-axis.

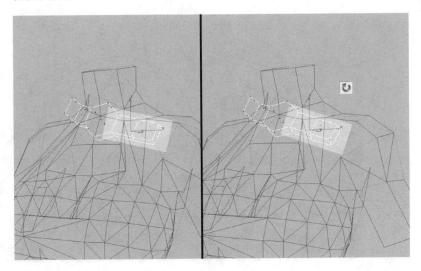

Rotate your view so you can see behind the object, select the back faces, and delete them (delete those isolated vertices, too).

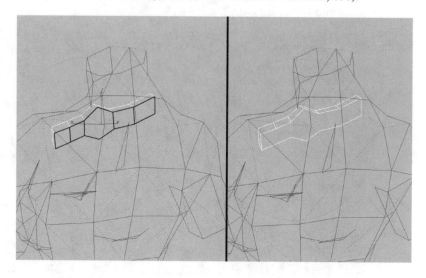

Now, hit Ctrl+E to see all the edges of the mesh, select the end vertices to the left and the middle vertex of the initial cylinder, and pull them back about .3 units along the Y-axis.

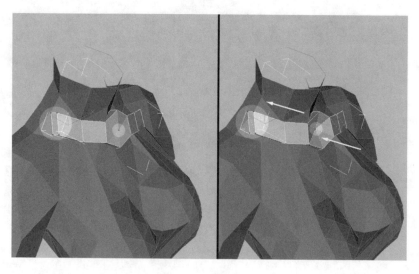

FYI: *OBJECT COLOR* By default, max will assign an arbitrary color to an object when you create it. If the color is too close in luminance or hue to the gray of the viewport background, the object is hard to see. When no material has been assigned to the object, this default creation/wireframe color acts as the material, too. If the mesh is hard to see in wireframe mode, click on the color swatch just to the right of

the object and assign a different color to the mesh.

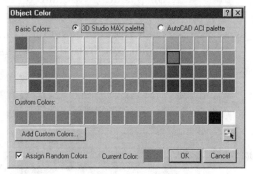

Personally, I favor darker colors, but I know many artists who change their viewport color to black or dark gray so lighter object colors show up better.

Target Weld the front vertices of the left end to the vertices behind them. Then, turn on Snap 🧲 and move the vertices indicated to the torso vertices shown. Turn this edge, too.

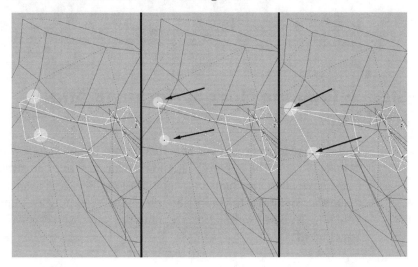

Make sure Snap is off, go around to the other side, and Target Weld
the top vertices at the end of the strap to the vertices behind them.
Move the back vertex up along the Z-and Y-axes .3 units each so the
strap end doesn't penetrate the torso as much.

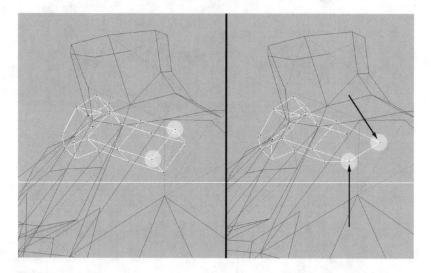

Step 9: Prep the Neck Surface and Attach the Strap

The strap object is ready for attachment, but the torso needs to be
tweaked first in the upper chest and neck area. While the strap
could have been attached at any point before now, it's easier to
make the adjustments you're about to make by simply avoiding
attaching an object until after prepping the surface to receive the
attachment.

Select Torso, rotate your view to see the following edges best, and divide them:

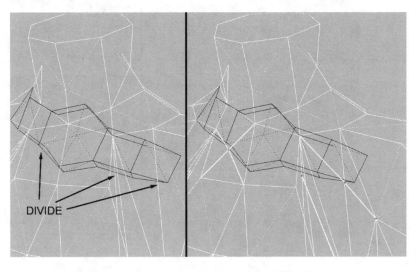

Now turn these edges of the left strap of Callisto's top:

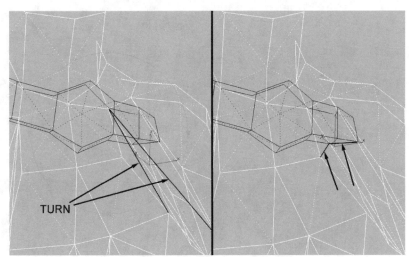

Turn this edge as well:

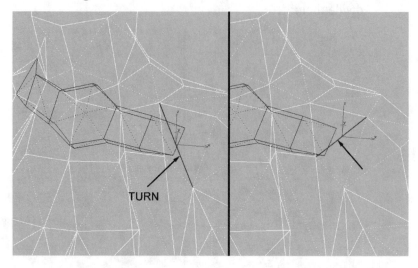

Attach Attach the strap object to Torso and Target Weld these two vertices:

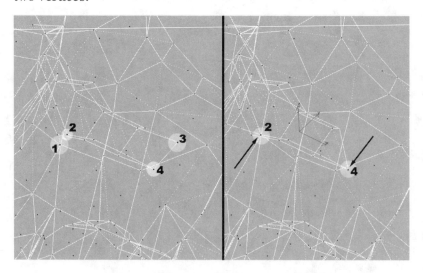

As shown in the following illustration, set the Weld Selected threshold to 1, select these four groups of vertices, and hit the Selected button.

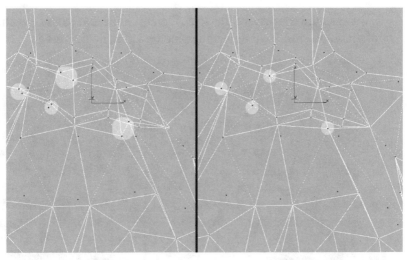

Increase your Target Weld value to 10 instead of the default 4...

...and weld these three vertices to the indicated vertex.

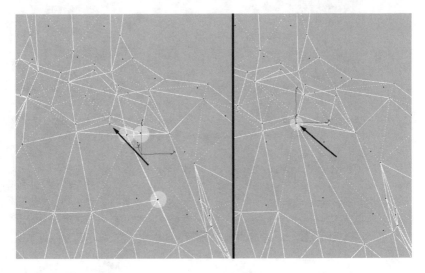

Go to the top area of the strap, select these two pairs of vertices, increase the Weld Selected value to 2, and hit Selected:

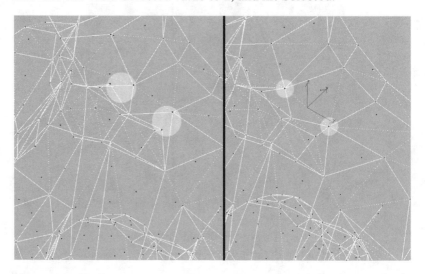

Next, get rid of the faces underneath the strap by selecting these edges and deleting them:

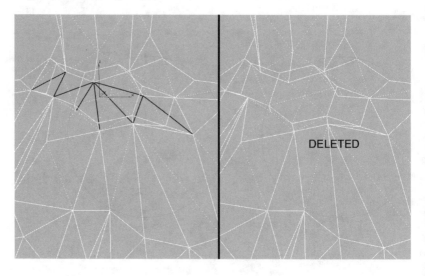

DELETED

FYI: *DELETING COVERED FACES* When you need to delete faces that are behind other faces, selecting and deleting the edges that make up the faces is a quick alternative to selecting faces and hiding them to get at the faces you want to delete.

Rotate your view so you're looking down at the top of the strap and shoulder. Turn the following edges:

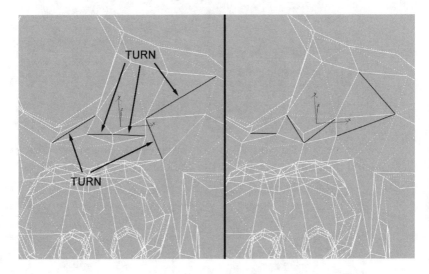

Rotate your view again to get at the following edges and turn them. Also Target Weld this vertex up to the strap "buckle."

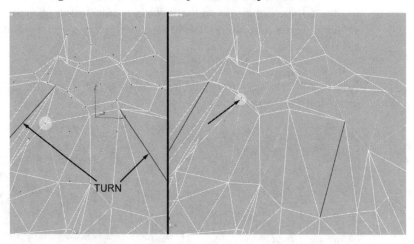

The vertex you welded at the throat needs to be moved back over and up a little to maintain the neck shape more efficiently.

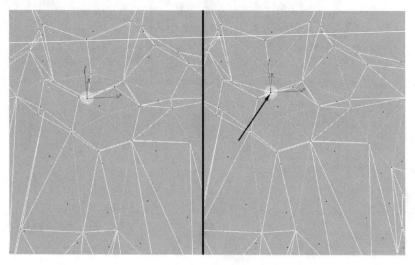

Finally, go back to these four groups of overlapping vertices, enter a Weld Selected value of .1, and merge them. Once they're merged, you can turn this edge to imply that the strap is stretched taut.

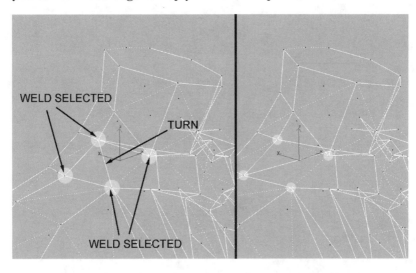

That completes the attachment and upper body for now. Looking at the mesh, it's apparent Callisto's ready to be *armed*.

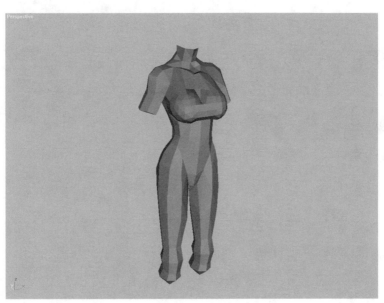

MODELING

CHAPTER 9
The Arms

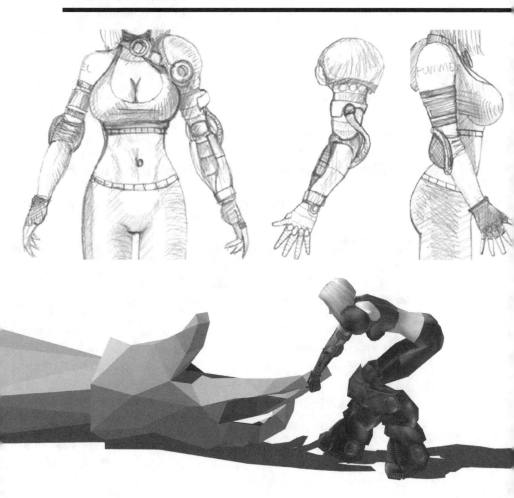

Up until now, I've concentrated on showing you how I model from scratch. I sit down with a blank screen and using primitives, extrusion, and other modeling tools, I make an object. These techniques can be applied every time you want to create a character, but are they always necessary? What I mean is if someone told you that you needed new tires for your car, would you consider *making* the tires? No, you would buy them or pull them out of your garage or basement and put them on your car. In modeling, reinventing the wheel, so to speak, is just as impractical if you have a plethora of models you've already made to choose from and can *cannibalize* from them. Recycling parts of old meshes when building a new model is one of the most common modeling methods but probably the least talked about. Of course, this technique relies on having a stable of models to recycle and a similar figure to choose from. In this case I've provided both for you.

Step 1: Merge an Arm from Another max File

Load Callisto19.max from the CD. Then go to File|Merge, and select Arm.max from the CD.

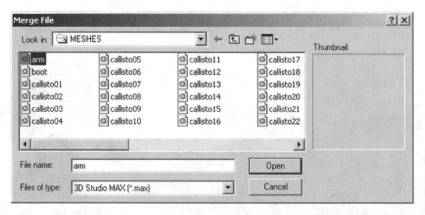

Highlight left arm and hit OK.

With the object merged, you need to fit it to the guide. First, U
Scale 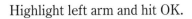 it down by 70%.

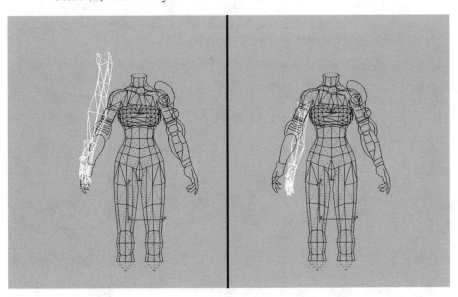

Change your pivot point to Use Selection Center 🔳 , rotate 🔄 the arm 10 degrees along the Z-axis ⊼ , and then move it to the left approximately 2 units along the X-axis ⊼ to match the guide.

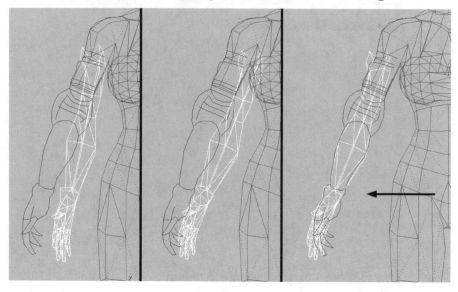

Switch to the Left view, Unhide ⊟Unhide by Name... Side Arm, and align the merged arm with the guide. Rotate it 13 degrees along the Z-axis and move it over to the guide.

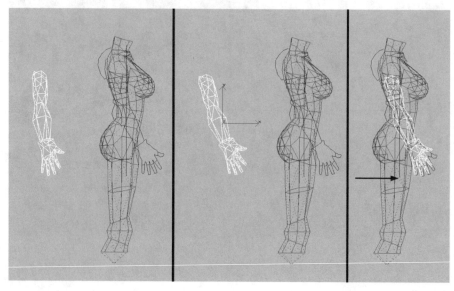

Step 2: Shape and Attach the Arm

Now that you have the arm merged and roughly positioned, you
need to tweak the shape, moving the vertices into the right posi-
tion. Zoom in , rotate, and move the vertices of the hand over so
the mesh fits the guidelines better.

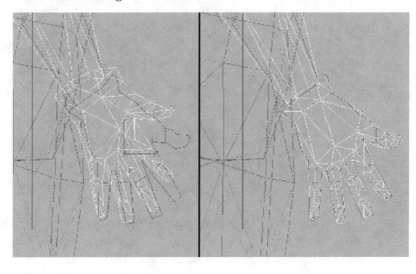

Select all the vertices of the hand, hit P to go to a Perspective
viewport, and rotate around to look at the inside of it.

MODELING

Starting with edge 1 ◁ , turn ⌐⌐⌐Turn⌐⌐⌐ all the edges of the inside palm and the top of the thumb base.

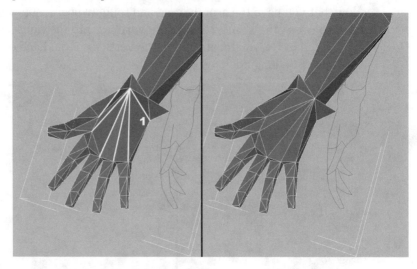

The fingers look a little thin so select the inside middle vertices of the digits, rotate your view to see the hand edge-on, and drag the verts along the X-axis toward the body about .1 units.

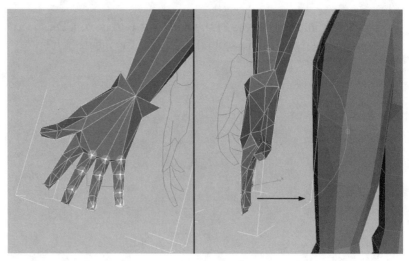

Now drag the tip of the thumb over a little to take out the weird kink in it.

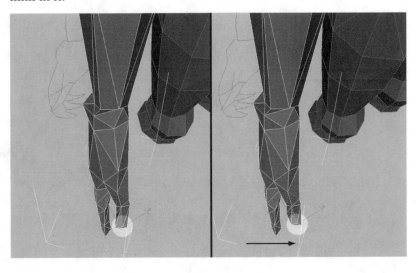

Next, turn a couple of edges at the top of the forefinger:

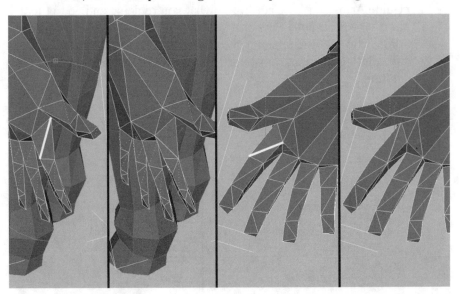

Finally, rotate around to the top of the hand again and turn these edges to give the shape more volume, removing the concave divots.

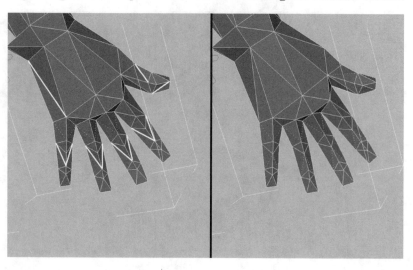

With the hand done, you can move on to the arm. Hide Torso and Guide Arms so it's easier to see what you're doing and go to the Left viewport. Select the arm you've been working on and adjust the vertices of the upper arm so that they match the guide. Begin by deleting the uppermost vertices that make up the merged arm's deltoid.

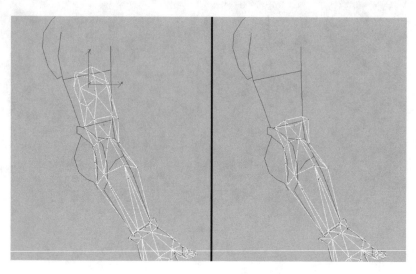

Next, further shape the arm by matching the vertices of the middle arm to the guide.

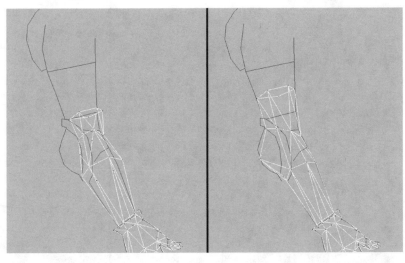

Zoom in  to the elbow area and divide ⌐Divide⌐ and turn these edges:

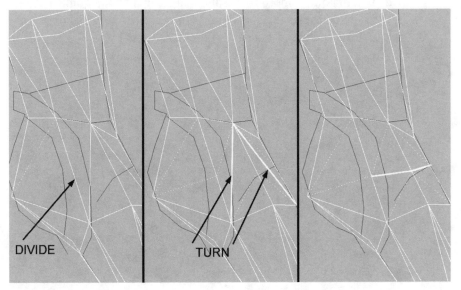

DIVIDE   TURN

MODELING

Rotate your view around to get to the inside edges of the elbow, and divide and turn these as well.

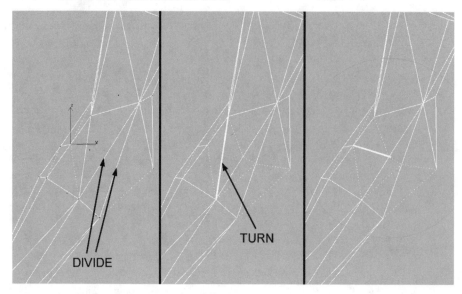

Go back to the Left viewport and add some more faces to the elbow pad area, making it more round and matching it to the guide a little better. Divide these edges and move the vertices that make up the point where the elbow bends.

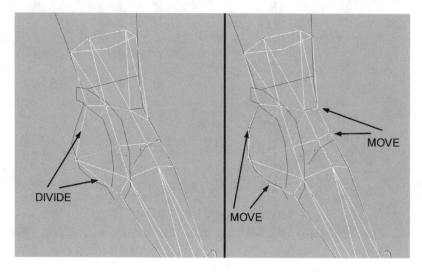

Rotate your view and turn the edges you just created at the back of the elbow. Scale the vertices of the pad out a little.

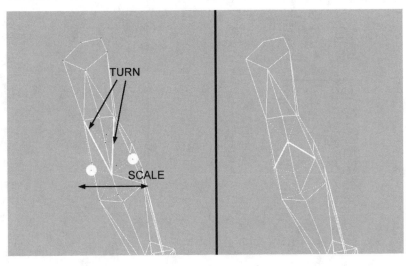

Drag these vertices along the Y-axis  so the elbow isn't so pointy.

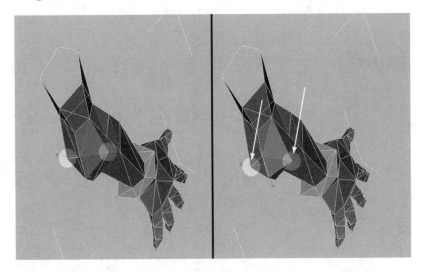

Go to the Left view again and Weld Select Selected these two vertices that make up the crook of the arm:

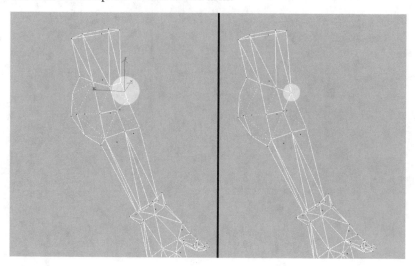

Move this vertex toward the front of the bicep and optimize the
mesh by welding these two vertices:

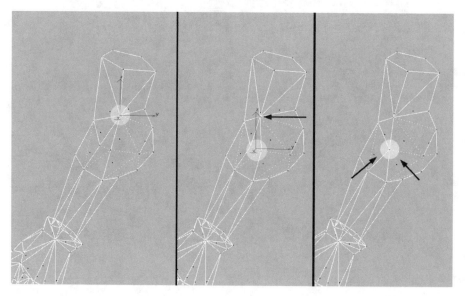

Up until now you've been using the default View coordinate system to make your transforms. Try something different and use Screen for the next transform. Hit Ctrl+R and click *outside* the green circle. Rotate your view until the arm appears upright. Select the vertices of the middle arm and choose NU Scale ▣ for the active transform. Make sure Use Selection Center ▣ is active and hit F5 to make the X-axis active. Now go up to the Reference Coordinate System, click on the small arrow, and select Screen instead of View.

```
View        ▼
View
Screen
World
Parent
Local
Grid
----------
Pick
----------
```

Using Screen as a coordinate system means that the transform is relative to whatever view you have. This means that in a Perspective viewport, rotating your view still causes the axis icon to be perpendicular to the view instead of being constantly aligned in world space as it is under a View coordinate system.

Scale the vertices by 120% along the X-axis:

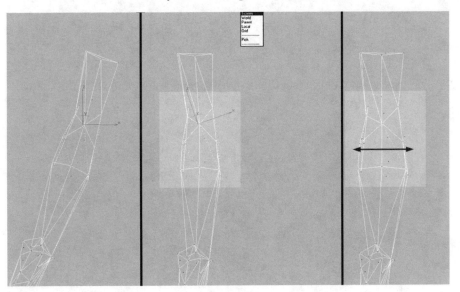

Unhide [Unhide by Name...] the torso and you're ready to join the arm to the body. First, select the torso and delete the end cap faces [◀] on Torso's arm stump. Then hit the Attach button [Attach] and click on the arm.

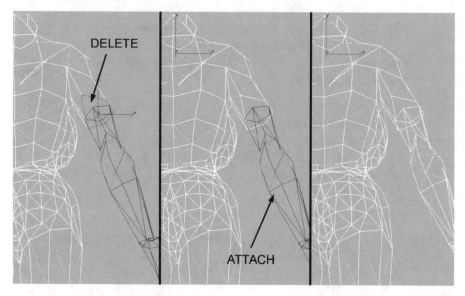

Set your Weld Selected value to 10, and select and weld the following vertices:

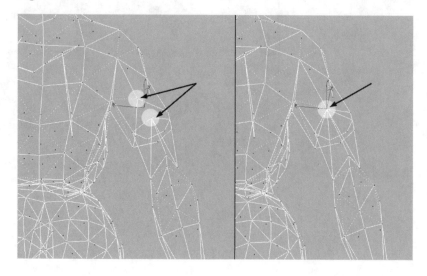

Rotate your view, and select and weld these two vertices:

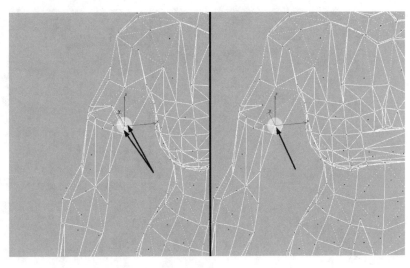

Rotate again and weld these two:

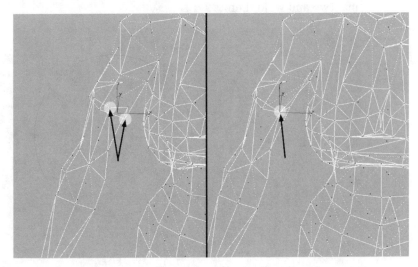

Select these three vertices and weld them:

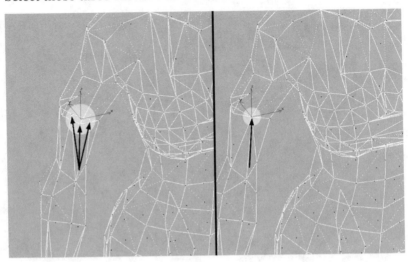

And finally, the moment you've all been waiting for — select the final two and weld them:

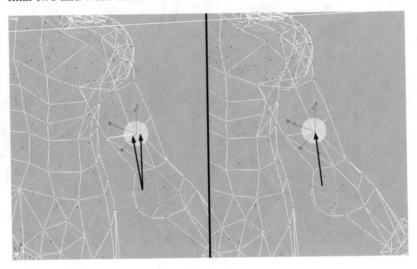

Now that the merged arm is connected, you need to spend some time tweaking the arm shape until it looks right. I could walk you through it, but that'd be a waste of a few good trees and I just made you suffer welding those other five pairs of vertices. Put what I've been showing you into practice and you should end up with the following:

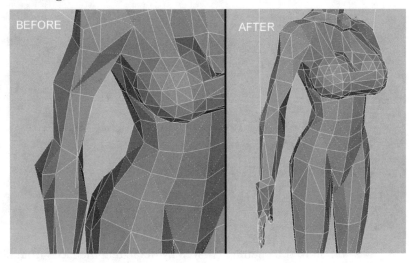

The desired shape was achieved through edge turns and vertex moves. If your results don't look like the picture, load Callisto20.max from the CD.

Make sure the View coordinate system is active again.

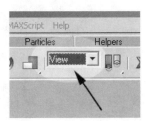

Select the body, and go into the Face sub-object menu.

Select these faces that make up most of the arm, detach [Detach] them to an element, and move those faces to the left along the X-axis:

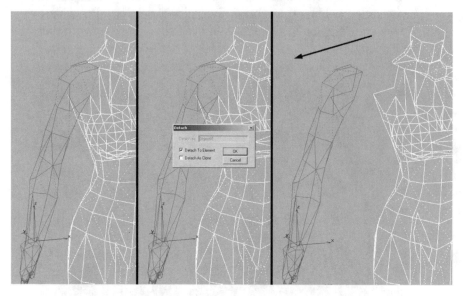

Zoom in to the opening created by detaching the faces from before and build [Create] two faces across the lower half of the hole.

Next, rotate your view and build the same faces on the inside surface of the detached arm, essentially creating an armpit.

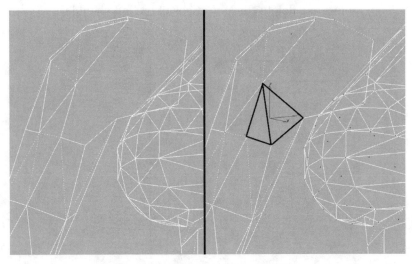

The reason you just did what you did — create an armpit for the character — was purely for animation accommodation reasons. In other words, if Callisto were weighted in Physique, attached to a Biped, and her arm raised without the extra geometry (that will be hidden *most* of the time), the area around the shoulder would crimp and fold and generally look bad. Now she needs another arm...

Step 3: Mirror-Copy the Arm to the Other Side

Select and delete these vertices of the left shoulder:

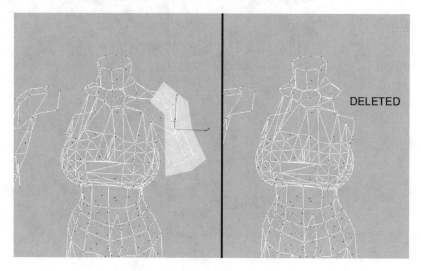

Rotate back around to the right side and ... drat. I don't like that edge on the torso you just made. Go ahead and turn it.

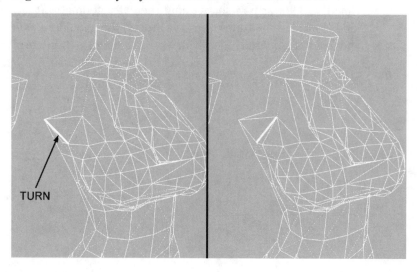

Much better. Grab these two vertices of the inner arm and pull them in about .2 units along the X-axis:

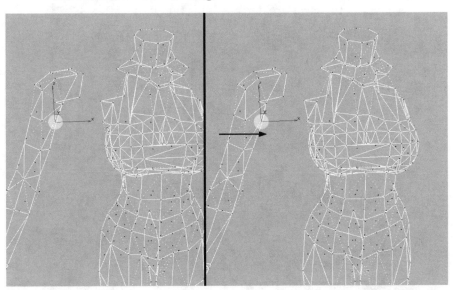

This is so those two vertices of the arm element don't lie *exactly* on the two corresponding vertices of the torso when the other vertices of the arm are welded. Again, this is thinking ahead to make sure the mesh deforms properly when animated in the future. If the vertices lie flush on one another, when you apply the Physique modifier and are weighting the vertices they'll be impossible to distinguish from one another.

Select the faces of the armpit on the torso and the arm itself and Shift-drag them over to the left side of Callisto. Select Clone To Object so the faces are detached this time.

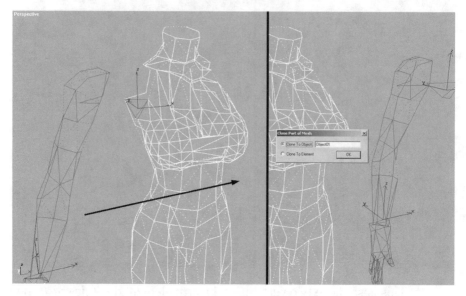

FYI: *MIRROR, MIRROR IN THE STACK...*   You've probably noticed by now that I don't use the Mirror *modifier,* opting instead to detach faces and use Tools|Mirror. This is because in past versions of max that modifier simply didn't work. I got used to doing it this way and it really doesn't seem too much of an advantage to use the modifier instead. The Mirror modifier seems to work fine now, so give it a try and see which method you prefer.

Select the right arm element, turn Snap on (make sure it's set to Vertex), and drag the arm over to the torso. Keep the cursor at the top of the shoulder, over the vertex there, and drag the element to the corresponding vertex on the torso.

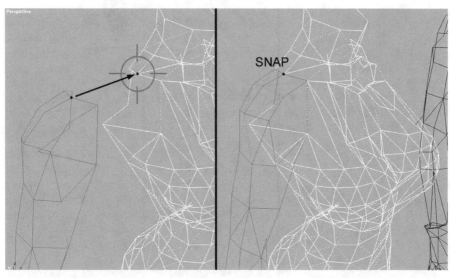

Next, rotate your view, copy the selected right arm, and make sure Use Selection Center is active. Turn it into a right arm by going to Tools|Mirror, making sure Mirror Axis is X and No Clone is selected, and click on the OK button.

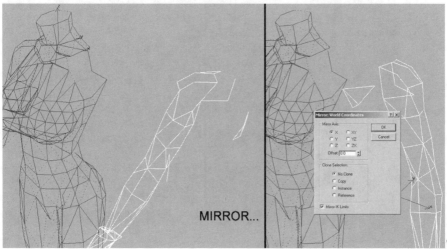

MODELING

Zoom in a little, select just the two-triangle element for the torso's pit area, and drag it over to the torso using Snap to line it up exactly with corresponding vertices. Detach it to an object. Select Torso and attach the two triangles to it.

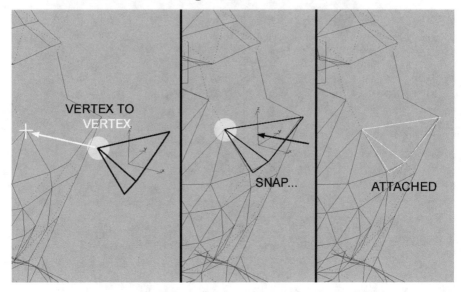

Select the tangent vertices, enter a value of 1 in the Weld Selected box, and weld them.

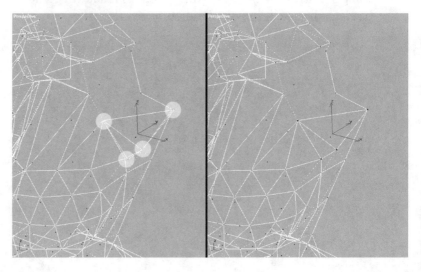

With Snap still on, slide the arm over to Torso, making sure your cursor is again at the top deltoid vertex, and drag it to the top deltoid vertex of the torso.

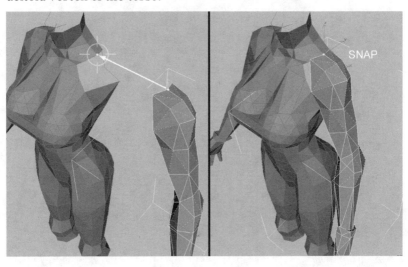

Select the torso, attach the arm to it, select these *three* vertices at the top of the strap, crank your Weld Selected value back up to 10, and hit Selected.

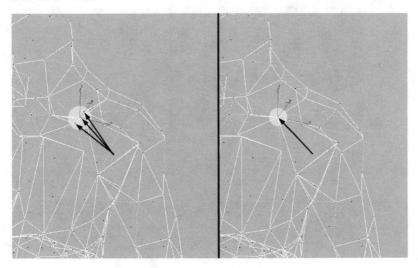

MODELING

Divide this edge on the arm you just attached and Target Weld the new vertex to the one on the torso.

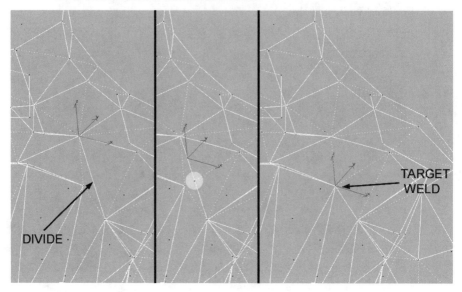

Select all the seam vertices (except the bottom of the armpits) where the arms meet the torso, change the Weld Selected value to .1, and hit Selected.

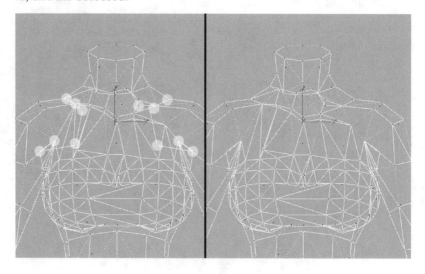

All the vertices lying exactly on top of one another are now merged. Now Callisto really is "armed and dangerous."

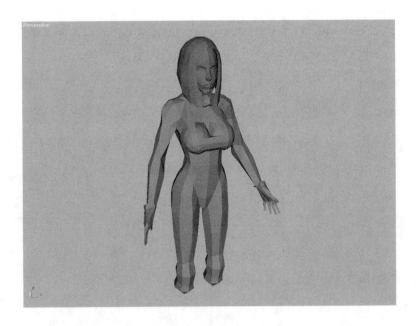

Step 4: Add Detail to the Left Arm

Now that the arms are nice and symmetrical, it's time for you to add the extra details of her cybernetic left arm so it matches the reference. Load Callisto21.max from the CD (or use what you've been working on).

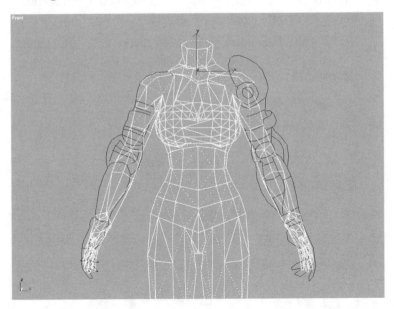

Start with the plating she has on her left forearm. Select these faces and enter 1 beside the Extrude button [Extrude]:

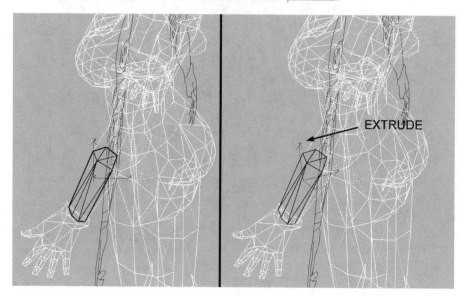

This kind of slight structural detail like armor plating can, of course, be done with a texture. However, as I mentioned before, I like to build out areas like this and then go back and optimize if I can't afford it. It's a time gamble, but better to have to optimize a little later than to build on later. The benefit of doing something like Callisto's forearm plating with geometry is that if it's noticed, it adds a lot of dimension to the model.

Next is the small shroud on her left bicep. Select the six faces (front and back of the arm) and Shift-drag them to the right along the X-axis.

Go ahead and clone the new faces, keeping them as an element of Torso.

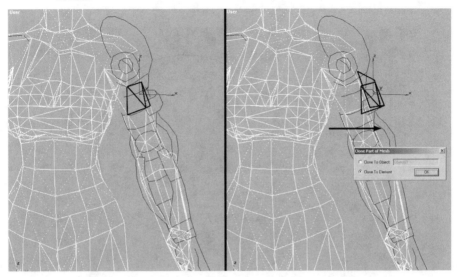

You need to make some minor adjustments to the new shape to conform it to the guide. First, lower it and then lower just the top vertices.

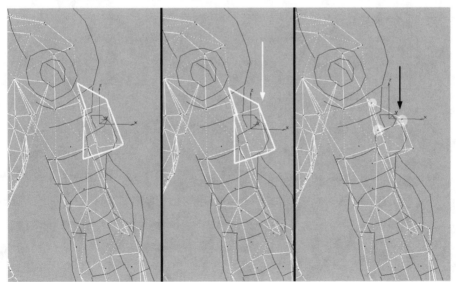

Go to a faceted view and hit F2 to make the faces semi-transparently shaded. Move the element in along the X-axis so it's closer to the arm.

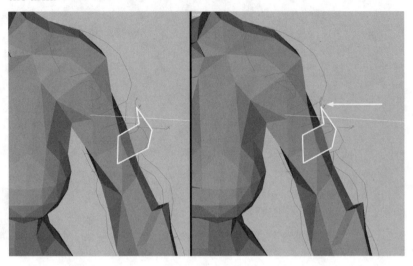

Rotate the view to the back and lower the following vertex in the Z-axis, pushing it in slightly along the Y-axis toward the body.

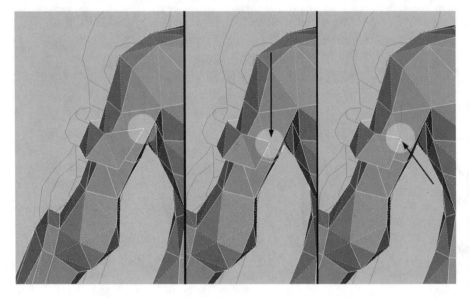

Go back to the Front viewport and push this vertex over to the left a hair:

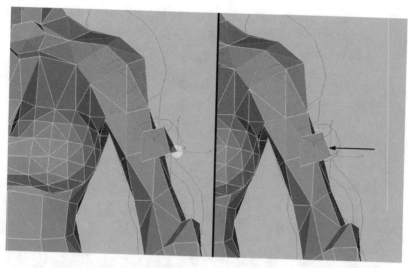

Move this vertex over to the right a hair:

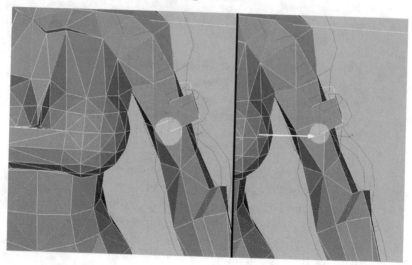

Step 5: Loft the Tubing for the Left Arm

For the tubing that goes from the forearm to up under the geometry you just tweaked, select one of the splines that make up the Arm Guide and detach it.

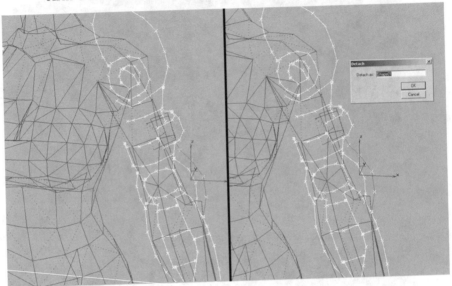

FYI: WHY DETACHING SPLINES IS LOW I have a pet peeve with max in that whenever you want to detach a spline you have to scroll all the way down to the *bottom* of the sub-menu to do it. What would have been wrong with putting it somewhere useful, like an inch down? Sheesh.

The reason you detached this spline was so you could use it as a "path" to loft another shape along. To introduce you to the Outline tool ▢ Outline ▢ under the Spline sub-object menu, you're going to use it to generate the path for the tubing. Simply select the spline, enter a value of .32 in the box beside the Outline button on the Face sub-object menu...

...and hit Enter. Keep the inner line you just created but go to Segment 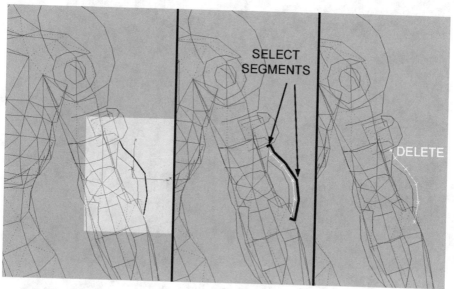, and select and delete the rest of the outer segments you don't need. Now the spline represents the middle of the reference tubing.

Now you're left with a path to loft a three-sided shape along and make the tubing. First, make the spline 3D by moving the vertices around in the XY axes . The spline needs to snake in under the bicep cowling you made earlier and attach at the top of the forearm. This deviates from the design, but again... who designed the thing anyway?

Seriously though, as you model a character sometimes it becomes necessary or desirable to deviate from the reference a little. Unless you're not in a position to change the design, go for it.

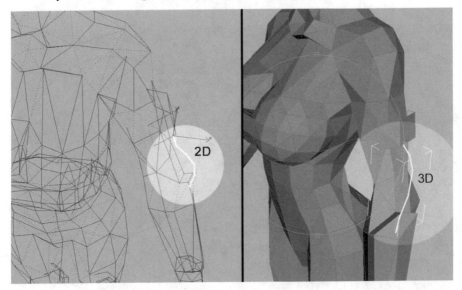

You have the path for the tubing, but you still need the shape to define a cross-section of it and loft along said path.

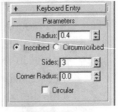

Go to Create|Shapes and make a three-sided NGon NGon approximately .4 in radius. Leave Circular unchecked.

Select the spline path you made earlier, go back to the Create panel , choose Compound Objects from the drop-down, and click on Loft Loft . Hit the Get Shape button Get Shape and click on the NGon triangle.

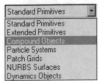

FYI: *LOFTING AN OBJECT* When lofting an object, keep in mind that the object you desire will be created based on which object you pick first and the orientation it's been created in. For example, you could have made the shape by selecting the triangle and choosing Get Path instead of Get Shape. If you had, the object you just made would be over where the triangle is and pointing *at you* instead of being created in the correct position on the character like it's supposed to.

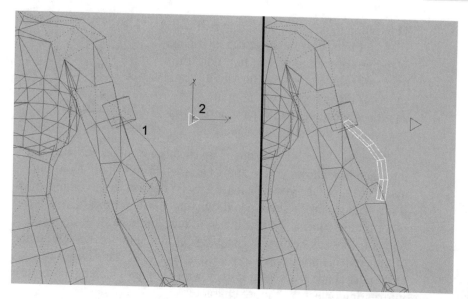

Take a minute to look over the parameters for the lofted object.

Starting at the top, make sure Instance is selected so any backward tweaks you do up the stack of the object (like moving the vertices of the path spline or lofted shape) will reflect on the object. Obviously the resolution of the shape is important and for this small object Shape Steps and Path Steps of 0 are sufficient. Contour and Banking apply if you had tweaked the path, so the vertices were not only positioned in XYZ but had been rotated as well. Finally, under Display check both Skin and Skin in Shaded so you can see the resultant object in wireframe and shaded unless you have a weak system and need to conserve rendering power.

The tubing looks cool, but in the real world an object like this tends to twist as it goes from one connection to another. With the mesh still selected, go to the Modify panel and look at the bottom of the menu, and you'll see a couple of new parameters that are available for the lofted object.

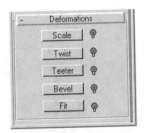

Each one of these buttons opens up to another menu with a graph interface that allows you to apply parametric deformations to the object. In this case you will apply a Twist deform to the tubing since it is a triangle cross-section and twisting it will not only give a little more realistic form, but it will also reduce some of its three-sided polygonal look. Click on Twist [Twist] and slide the far right point of the control spline down to where it says –200. This basically twists the shape twice as it lofts down the spline, making for a more interesting object with more character.

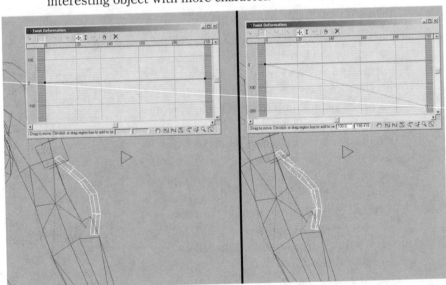

Because the arm will bend at the elbow, the tubing will bend with it. To make sure it deforms correctly, the current number of segments in the shape may not be enough. Go back to the Modify panel and increase the Path Steps to 1.

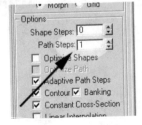

Also *uncheck* Cap Start and Cap End as they're hidden by the arm geometry.

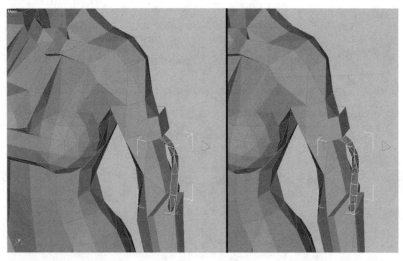

Much better. Again, this may be a gratuitous detail, but stuff like this can add an overall richness to your model — besides, you can always optimize later. Go ahead and attach the tubing to the torso and move on to the shoulder pad.

Step 6: Build the Left Shoulder Pad

Load Callisto22.max from the book's CD.

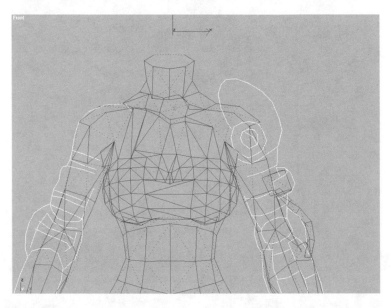

MODELING

The shoulder pad is basically a big rounded shell on her shoulder. Since this is low-poly, the best thing to do is to make it solid. You can get away with doing it this way and still make the pad look like the design. Go to the Right view and start the shape by making a geosphere GeoSphere about 3 units in radius with three segments. Select Octa for Geodesic Base Type.

Go back to the Front view, move it over to the guide, rotate it 30 degrees along the Z-axis, and U scale it by 90%.

Switch to a local coordinate system.

NU Scale ⬚ it along the local Z-axis by 80%. Switch back to the View coordinate system and rotate it 15 degrees along the Z-axis. Reposition it so it rests within the guidelines.

Collapse the geosphere down to an editable mesh.

Convert To:
Editable Mesh
Editable Patch
NURBS
Edit Stack

Select and delete the following vertices:

FYI: *ANOTHER WAY TO CONVERT TO AN EDITABLE MESH*   Instead of going over to the Modify panel and collapsing the stack of an object to an editable mesh, an alternative is to right-click on the object, slide down to Convert to Editable Mesh, and click on it.

In the case of primitives you're given the option of converting to an editable patch or NURBS as well. If an Edit Mesh modifier has been applied, then NURBS won't be an option.

Now shape the object up so it matches the guide even closer by moving these vertices around:

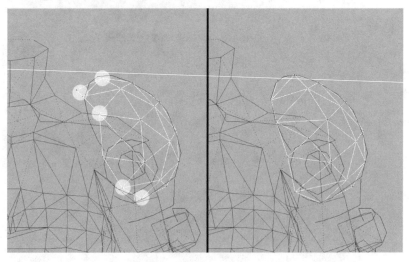

From the side, it looks too much like a ball on her shoulder, so raise these vertices up along the Z-axis:

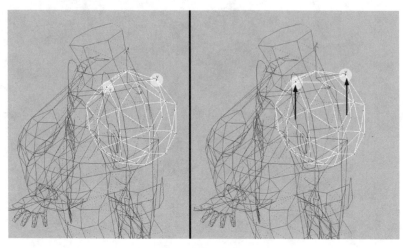

Now to make the shape look less like a sphere, tweak the shape and reduce the face count of the object a little by doing the following adjustments. Take the bottom vertices, Target Weld Target the middle two, and scale the four vertices along the Y-axis by 120%.

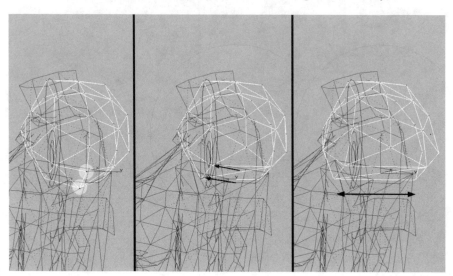

Target Weld this vertex at the back of the pad...

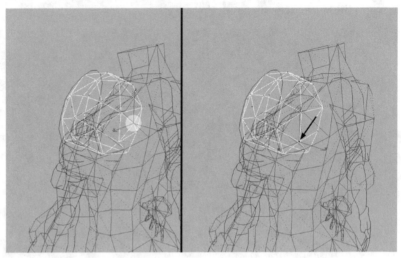

...and Target Weld this vertex at the front of the pad:

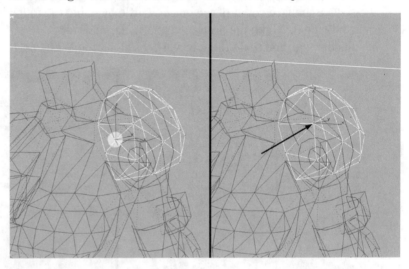

Apply a Cap Holes modifier to the mesh and add an Edit
Mesh modifier to turn the edges prettily:

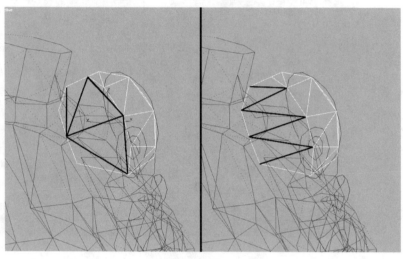

Select these four vertices and scale them along the Y-axis by 120%:

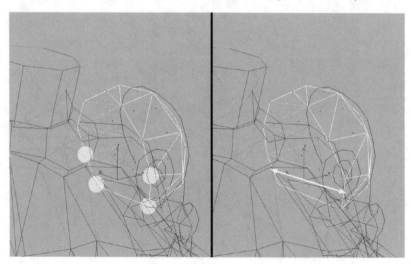

Rotate the view and turn these edges:

Move these vertices around at the front of the shoulder pad to conform to the guide:

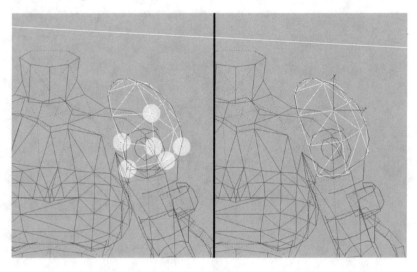

Unhide Left Arm Guide 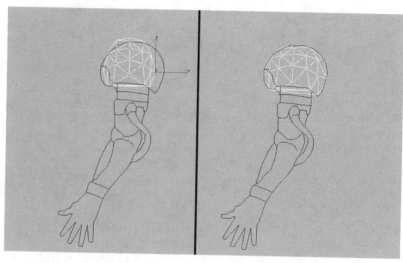 Unhide by Name... and make the final tweaks to the shoulder pad in the Right viewport so it matches the profile reference. Grab and move the appropriate vertices, experimenting with various Use Soft Selection settings to stretch the object into the right shape.

Finally, attach the shoulder pad to the torso. That wraps up the upper body and arms for now. If you want to see the finished, fully baked version, load Callisto23.max and give it a gander.

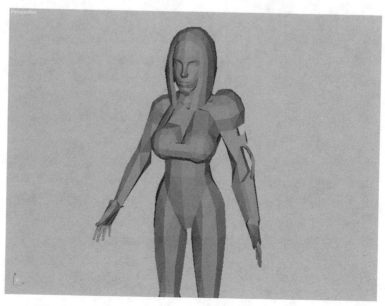

MODELING

Cannibalization is definitely a technique used by more experienced modelers, but even if this is your first attempt at modeling a character, soon you'll find yourself building up a directory full of the little guys (and gals). In time you'll pick and choose bits and pieces of them to start other characters. There are also plenty of places that sell or give away models for anyone to use as they see fit. I visit 3dcafe.com, for example, when I need a weird mesh like a palm tree or pickup truck to use in a scene.

Now you need to hook Callisto up with some walkin' boots!

CHAPTER 10

The Boots

Another way to recycle an old mesh that is less cannibalization and more an advanced optimization technique is using a high-res mesh as a guide for creating a low-res mesh. Selecting just the key vertices of the high-res mesh that define the shape you're going for, you copy this vertex cloud to a new object and play 3D connect-the-dots. This gets a little tricky and requires you to have a good spatial eye. When dealing with an inordinately complex mesh, however, it does save time and gives you more control than using ordinary optimization techniques.

This boot is about 1,442 faces:

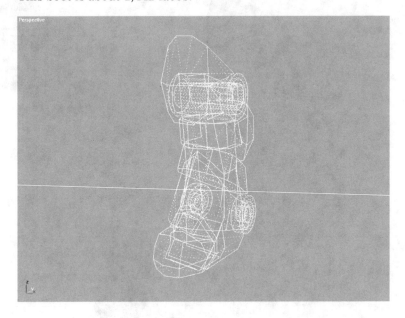

With a budget of 1,500 faces for the entire character, using a mesh like this for even *one* of her boots is, of course, absurd. However, it can be used as a template to build a version that results in a boot that is less than 200 triangles.

Step 1: Merge a High-Res Boot

Load Callisto24.max and merge the boot object from Boot.max on the CD.

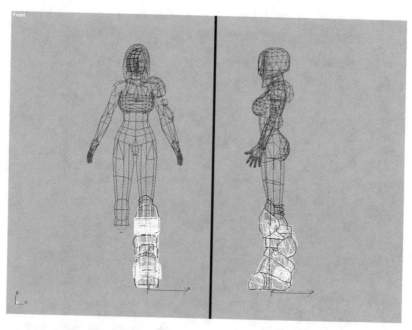

To save time, I've already aligned it with the reference so you don't have to position or scale it. Your job is to identify which vertices to keep and which vertices to hide, leaving a vertex cloud to build the low-poly version of the boot.

Step 2: Identify Key Vertices of the Boot

Go to Customize|Preferences, click on the Viewports tab, and uncheck the Show Vertices as Dots box so the vertices are small crosses, and hit OK.

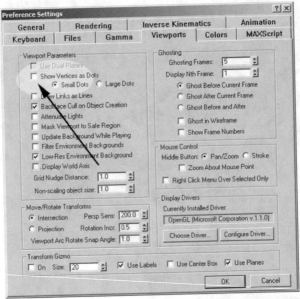

Right-click on the boot, click on Properties, and check the Vertex Ticks box so the vertices of the shape are visible all the time.

Again, the mesh consists of 1,440 faces and 758 vertices. This means the vertices make up approximately 53% of the faces in the shape. Another way to think of it is in a ratio. The faces-to-vertices ratio of the boot is about 2-to-1. Thusly, to create a 200-face boot you want the same 2-to-1 ratio when deciding not only which vertices to keep, *but how many.*

With this in mind you need about 106 vertices (or less) to create the low-poly version of the boot. Go to the Sub-object menu of Boot.

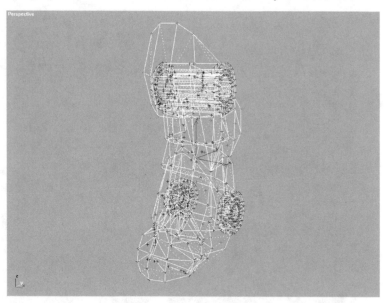

Some vertices are already selected for you and represent the key vertices that I consider integral to maintaining the shape of the boot.

If you look over to the right on the Selection sub-menu of the Vertex sub-object menu you'll see an indicator of how many vertices are currently selected.

This "counter" works for all selected sub-objects and is easy to miss but extremely useful. The 148 vertices indicated are more than the 106 you need, so try to narrow the playing field a bit. Go to Edit|Select Invert and invert the selection.

Hit the Hide button [Hide] on the sub-object menu to get these less important vertices out of the way.

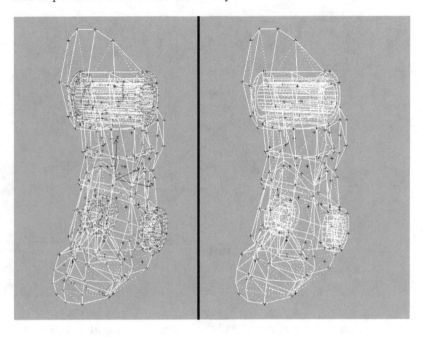

Step 3: Hide *More* Non-Essential Vertices of the Boot

Now that you've narrowed the vertices down to 148, it's time to cut even further. This particular boot design consists of several straps and components. However, these four vertices...

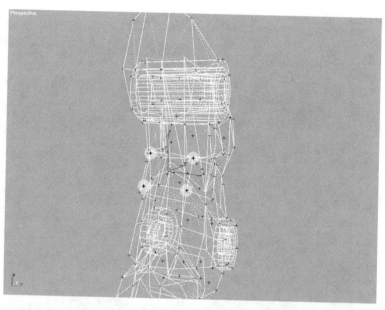

... can go without losing the basic strap structure they help create. Select and hide them, then look at the six vertices highlighted below.

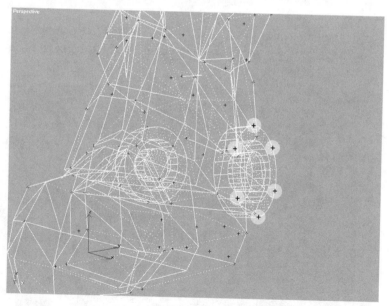

They represent the cylinder structure at either side of the ankle and are a prominent design element. The best thing to do in this case is to view these vertices as anchor points to *suggest* the element they represent and complete the suggestion through a texture map. They have to stay, but with them in mind, select these other two vertices...

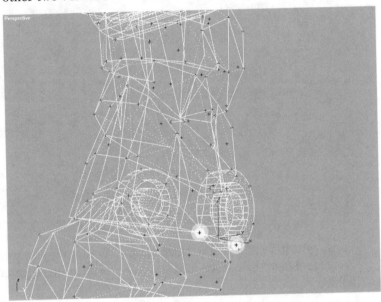

...and hide them since they're close enough to the more important cylinder end vertices to be redundant. At the back of the boot, these two vertices...

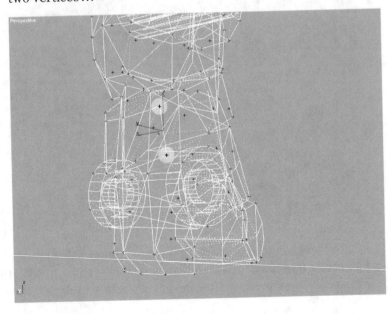

...can be hidden since the edges they help create are in a relatively straight line. Of course, it may be the angle you see the edges in, but that's why you're continually rotating your view in a Perspective view to make sure the angle is shallow. Further to the back, these two vertices...

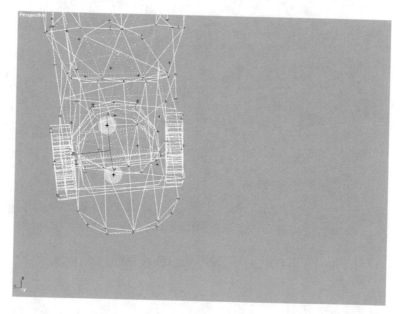

...or even the ones along the same edges to their immediate right can be hidden since the volume at the back can be defined by a single median line coming to a triangular cross-section instead of the squared-off one defined by all four vertices.

These four vertices can be hidden:

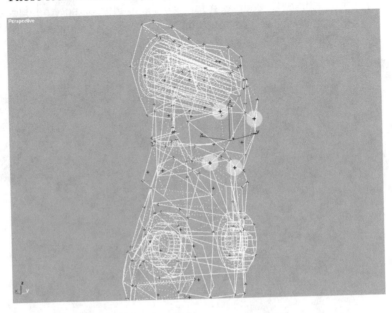

Moving up to the top of the boot, these eight vertices can be hidden…

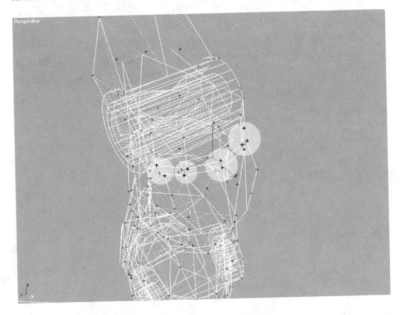

…because the ones immediately above and below them can make a line that with the assistance of the texture can suggest the strap they help shape. The *narrowness* of the space *between* the vertices should also call attention to themselves and beg to be "excused." The following two vertices can be hidden as well:

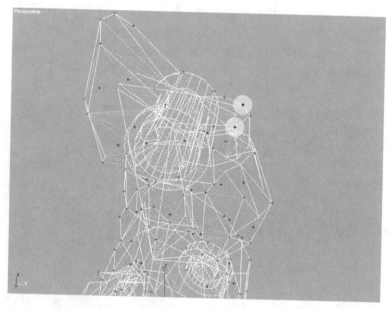

Out of these four vertices...

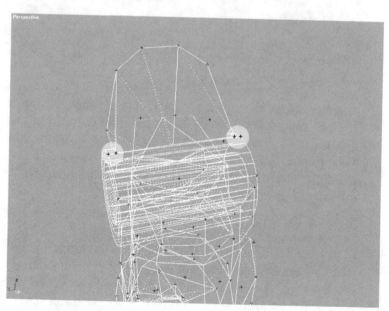

...two of them can be hidden because they're practically overlapping each other — a great reason to get rid of one or the other. Hide the inner vertices since the overall *volume* of the boot is important. The outer vertices represent this volume better than the inner ones.

Sometimes you're faced with a choice of vertices between which it seems impossible to distinguish the most important. Out of the following six vertices at the front of the boot...

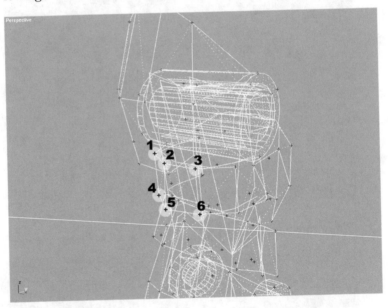

...getting rid of vertices 1, 3, 4, and 6 would take away from the effectiveness of the strong strap element of which they are a part. Hiding vertex 2 and 5 would flatten the front of the strap and maybe give the wrong impression for the strap shape. Hmmm. How about a compromise? Take 2, 4, and 6 away, leave 1, 3, and 5, and make a triangular shape that represents enough volume to maintain the integrity of the strap shape. Perfect solution!

So, covering some of the methodology behind how to choose which vertices go and which vertices stay should give you an idea of what to look for when you use this technique in the future. After looking over the mesh some more, notice I've gotten rid of a few more non-essential ones and further narrowed the vertices to 117. It's not the 106 we were after but is okay since once you start building the mesh, you can always optimize it even more.

Load Callisto25.max so you start the next step with the same vertices I ended up with.

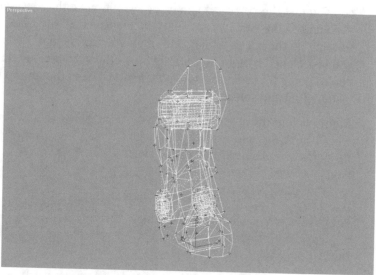

Step 4: Build the Low-Res Boot

Select all 117 vertices that are visible on the boot, right-click on the mesh to select Move, hold the Shift key down, and click on any of the selected vertices (don't actually move them). Clone the vertices to an object and call it "low boot."

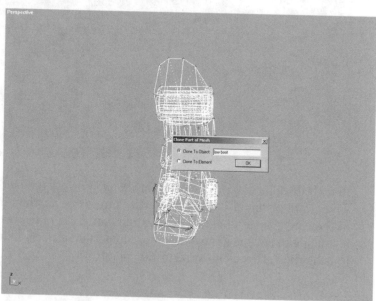

Now, get out of the Sub-object mode for Boot so you can hide it. It now appears that there's nothing in your view. This is because copying just the vertices of an object won't make the new object visible until the vertices are set to be displayed all the time. Hit H to bring up the scene hit list. Although you can't see it, the object you just cloned is right in front of you — the vertex cloud that you're going to turn into a low-poly boot. Choose the low boot you just created and select it.

Right-click in the space in front of you where Boot was a few minutes ago, go to Properties, and check the Vertex Ticks box.

Hit OK. Now you should see that nice big mass of vertices to play "connect-the-3D-dots" with:

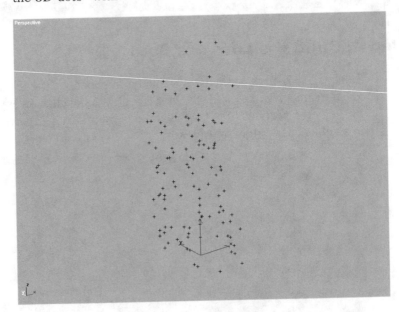

In a 2D medium like the pages of this book, it's very difficult to convey how to distinguish different vertices from one another. Instead of showing you step-by-step how to build the faces of the boot, I'm just going to key on some of the more important aspects of building it using the vertex cloud as a starting point.

Bring back Boot by unhiding it, bring up its Properties to uncheck the Vertex Ticks box (so it doesn't conflict with the mesh you're about to build), and freeze [Freeze Selected] it.

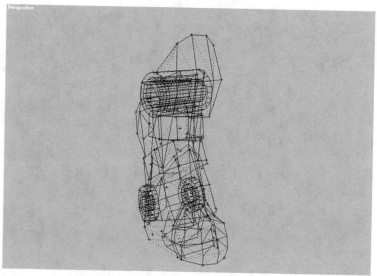

It looks a little confusing here, but having the original mesh in view as reference will help you. Hit H again to choose and select low boot (dragging a selection marquee won't cut it).

Start with the front top of the kneepad and build a few faces there:

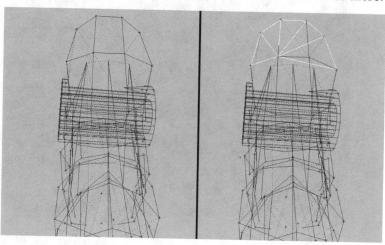

Move this vertex just left of center of the kneepad over to the *real* center. This helps keep the mass distributed correctly and attempts to approximate the volume of the original mesh.

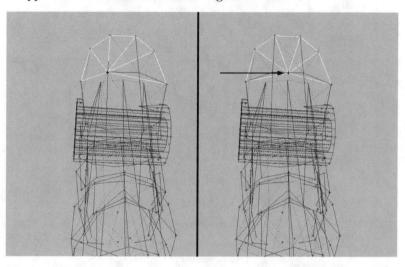

Rotate your view as much as you need to get the right angle and build the rest of the kneepad front:

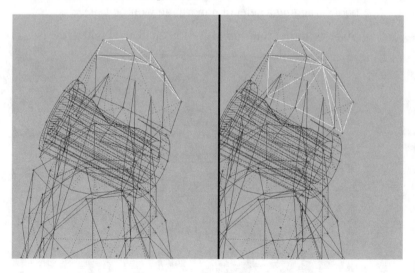

I've hidden the frozen high-res reference boot for the next several illustrations in order to more clearly show you how to approach building the rest of the low-res boot. As you build the faces, turn [Turn] any bad edges ☑ as they appear.

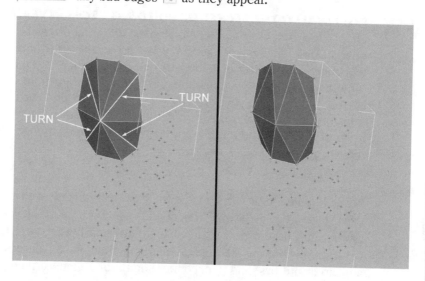

Use F2 to highlight the faces red and semi-transparent if it helps, remembering it's a way to distinguish *selected* faces only.

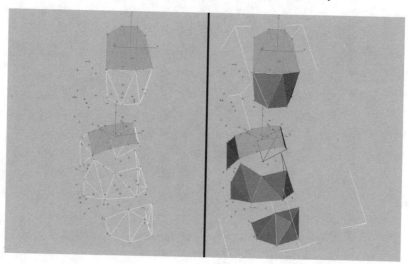

Since I mirrored the object previously and didn't reset the xform on this mesh, you must build the faces in a *clockwise* direction instead of the usual counterclockwise.

 FYI: *FINALLY! THE SECRET OF BUILDING FACES REVEALED*
I finally found out through a helpful guest at a Game Developer's Conference talk the reason why 95 percent of the time you build faces in max in a counterclockwise direction and the other odd 5 percent you build them in a clockwise direction: Mirror. If at any time your object has been mirrored and the transform hasn't been reset in some way, you will build the faces of that mirrored mesh in the opposite direction you normally would: clockwise. Very cool!

While building your faces, match the frozen "template" as best you can. Make areas in "strips" if necessary and then fill in the gaps (sometimes it helps to see the shape more clearly that way). Concentrate on creating the implied elements, building small recognizable areas out first and then connecting them. Again, turn edges and optimize as you feel necessary.

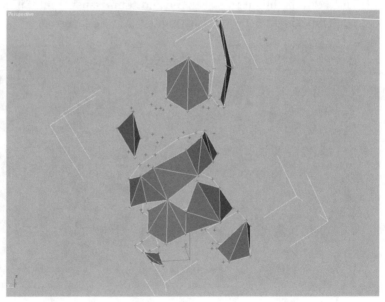

Once you've built the stronger elements and filled in all the holes, you'll hopefully end up with something like this:

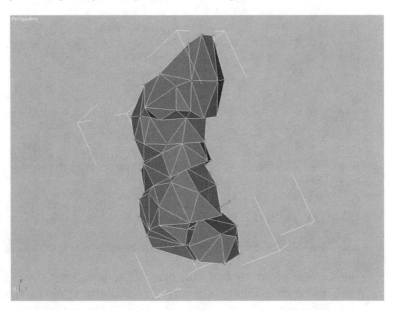

Regardless if it looks *exactly* like mine, your boot should weigh in at about 216 faces. That's over the desired 200 faces so you need to optimize it a little. So, either continue with your mesh or load Callisto26.max.

Step 5: Optimize the Low-Res Boot

In Chapter 11 I cover optimization more in depth, but give yourself a little optimizing primer by knocking about 50 faces off of the boot in this section.

Start at the front toe opening area and Target Weld [Target] these two vertices to the respective vertices above them:

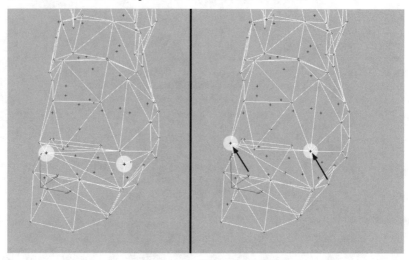

Rotate your view around to the back of the boot, weld these four vertices down to the bottom vertices below them, and then weld the two resultant middle bottom vertices to the outer bottom vertices:

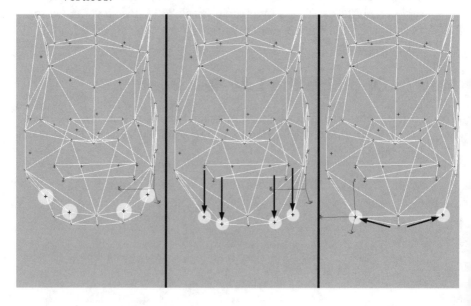

On the right side where the ankle cylinder was, the extra faces created to accommodate this design element are relatively flat with no real contribution to any interesting topography. Weld vertex 1 to 2, 3 to 4, and 4 to 5.

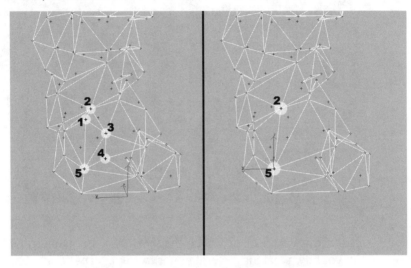

Looking at the cylinder-end area up at the knee, the same sort of flat, wasteful face usage can be optimized as well. Weld vertex 1 to 2, and 3 to 4.

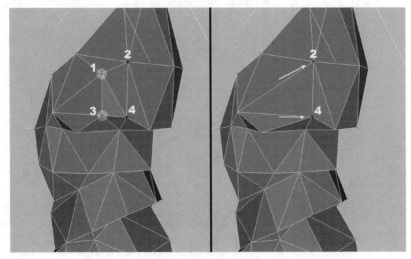

Next, turn edge 2, then edge 1.

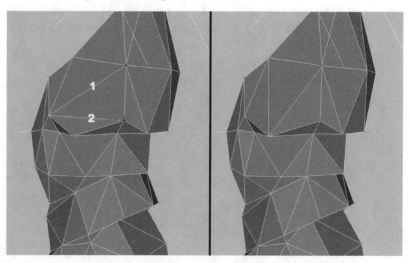

Is there anyplace else? Check the mesh closely. Spend some time on your own making several minor tweaks, turns, welds, and nudges. You should end up with 174 faces and 91 vertices; the almost 2:1 ratio still holds up and you now have a mesh with nearly one-tenth the faces and vertices as the original!

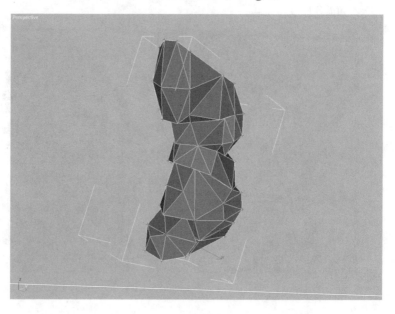

Step 6: Mirror the Boot to the Other Side

Finally, unhide and unfreeze everything, delete Boot and the remaining guide objects, Mirror/Copy low boot, and move it into position.

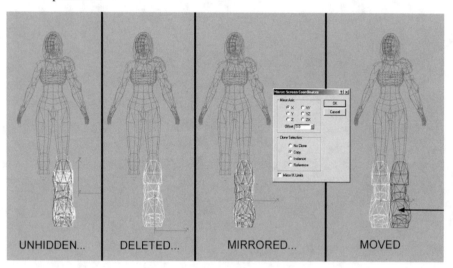

UNHIDDEN...   DELETED...   MIRRORED...   MOVED

Cool! Now Callisto is almost ready to rumble, but at more than 2,100 faces she's *600* over budget. Time to get into some real hack and slash optimization!

CHAPTER 11
Optimizing The Mesh

While building Callisto you went well over the 1,500-polygon budget — that's generally the reality of modeling a character in max or any other tool. Having a higher res version of the character lying around isn't such a bad idea either, because if you need it it's there (easier to go down than up, remember?). I've dedicated this chapter to optimization because in a polygonal, real-time environment like *Quake III: Arena* or *Unreal Tournament*, reducing your poly count on a regular basis is a part of life. This is an important concept and an important skill to have if you want to be an effective modeler.

Optimization Explained

Virtually a modeling technique in its own right, optimization is the mantra for real-time model makers and the programmers with whom they work. Optimizing literally means making the most of what you have, lowering the number of polygons used to convey the design of your mesh at every possible chance. Gaming platforms like Xbox from Microsoft and PlayStation 2 from Sony are very alluring because of the *lack* of optimization you must inflict upon your geometry. They give you nearly *triple* the normal polygon count for creating figures like the one you've just created. In the online PC gaming scene, however, keeping the meshes as low as they can go is still the reality. Fifteen hundred polygons for even a *Quake III: Arena* character is pushing the limit of Carmack's engine's technological might.

The key to successful optimization is to understand the methodology behind deciding what can be optimized. I've boiled it down to four fundamental approaches or ideas when it comes to reducing your mesh. "Consolidation" is the act of streamlining or gently smoothing the topography or surface of the mesh. Find that vertex or edge that doesn't *really* contribute to the shape and merge it into the rest of the mesh. "Hidden geometry" involves deleting any vertices or faces that won't be seen, even when the character is animating. "Sacrifice" involves sometimes severely modifying the geometry of your mesh, prioritizing the various design elements involved and even sacrificing one or two of them to meet your face-count budget. And lastly, "relative face distribution" refers to a comparative look at the size and number of faces in various areas of the mesh and evening them out accordingly. This is the most personal aspect of optimizing since the importance of various design elements of the model tends to lean toward the predilections of the individual.

Consolidation

Start with consolidation. Check out the following:

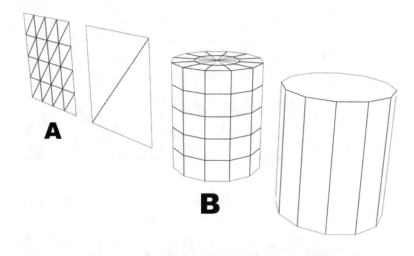

In Plane A and Cylinder B, there's just no purpose for all those extra segments in communicating their respective shapes; the optimized versions beside them are more efficient. All those extra lines and vertices don't contribute any uniqueness or interest to the meshes. During the building process you may need this extra real estate to build up a shape, but, if it's the finished product and you see this needless addition to a surface, then merge the extra vertices to their respective neighbors. Save the vertices and the faces they describe for something more useful.

Looking at Callisto's mesh, her legs can be optimized using this line of thinking. Load Callisto27.max and zoom 🔍 in to the front of the thighs. The curves made by these four vertices at the front of her thighs are close to being straight.

Go ahead and weld [Target] the vertices to their lower neighbors:

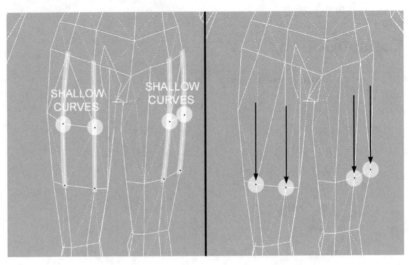

Turn [Turn] the edges made by the welds so there are no divots in the leg surface and the mesh keeps its volume.

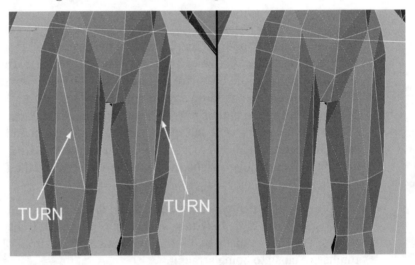

While it would be nice to keep that extra segment in the middle of the leg to describe the fullness of the quadricep better, it's necessary to consolidate the mesh.

FYI: *USING THE OPTIMIZE MODIFIER* You may be wondering why I don't start a chapter dedicated to optimization by extolling the virtues of the Optimize modifier. That's because it's not a very useful tool (in my humblest opinion). The results are often unpredictable and the settings don't seem to correspond to any logic I know! I encourage you to try it and see for yourself, but I think you'll agree that the best way to bring the mesh down is to do so manually.

Hidden Geometry

If you don't see it, what good is it? Getting rid of geometry that is unseen seems straightforward enough but sometimes those caps at the ends of cylinders go ignored when they could be deleted. In the case of the following, it's easy to see where to delete the excess faces and vertices.

Object B has 16 faces less than object A because the hidden faces were deleted. Even if only one face can be gotten rid of this way — do it. However, when deleting hidden parts of the mesh, keep in mind the impact of the deletion if the character animates. Make sure the resultant hole won't be exposed when the character starts moving or bending the area being optimized this way.

An example of hidden geometry is the insertion point of Callisto's legs into her boots. This is a great place to delete intersecting and useless geometry.

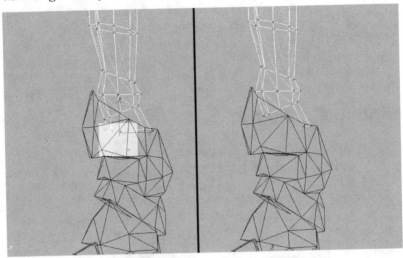

With the way the knee area is designed when the leg bends, the front boot structure will dip down, exposing the front part of the kneecap geometry on her leg. So even though it intersects and is hidden when the leg is straight, it's still necessary. Drag ⊕ these vertices down into the boot so the gap you just created won't be seen.

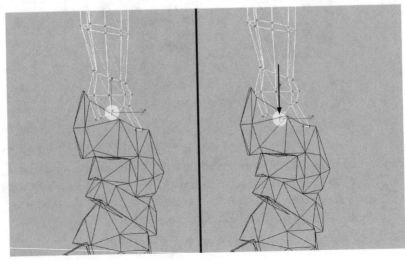

Sacrifice

Sacrifice is entirely different from consolidation because it's purely a balancing act: target face count versus desired shape. An example of a sacrifice you need to make on Callisto would be her left arm pad. I mentioned earlier it might get optimized, and it seems this is the time to do it. Hide ⬚ Hide ⬚ the tubing element and the vertices of the rest of the arm to make it easier to see what you're doing and weld the following vertices of the arm pad:

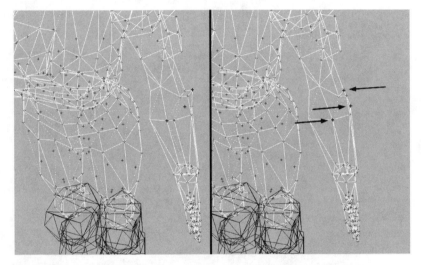

Welding the vertices the way you did — leaving the two near the top untouched — optimizes the geometry but still hints at the pad element.

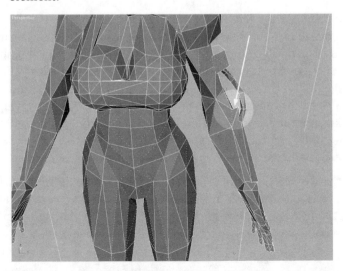

Of course, the arm could be optimized even more, but you'll get to that later.

Relative Face Distribution

Making sure your mesh has an even face distribution is probably the most painful part of the optimization process. It involves all of the other optimizing methodologies and comes down to an almost personal prioritization.

The following best illustrates the difference between unevenly and evenly distributed faces:

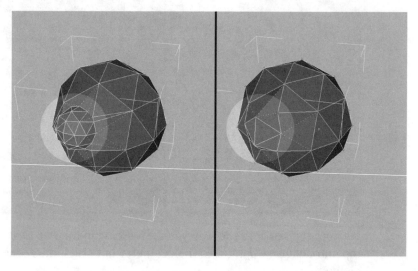

The image on the left shows a small, high-res sphere that has been Booleaned into the side of a low-res sphere. The smaller triangles need to be optimized so they still impart the sense of a "bump" on the surface of the larger sphere, but with larger triangles. The image on the right displays a better relative face distribution. Don't obsess on this optimization approach too much, though. Trying to make sure the face disposition is equitable is almost impossible sometimes, but the closer you can get, the better the mesh will be — especially when you're over your budget of triangles!

So that covers the main principles that should guide your optimization work on any mesh in need of reduction. Now you're going to put them to use while optimizing the rest of the character, going from body part to body part. You'll begin with the head.

The Head

Load Callisto28.max from the CD. The head is definitely more detailed and face-dense than the rest of the character so it will be a challenge to optimize it and retain the features you've built into it.

Step 1: Optimize the Hair

Hide everything but Bangs and study the following to guide you in how to make the optimization.

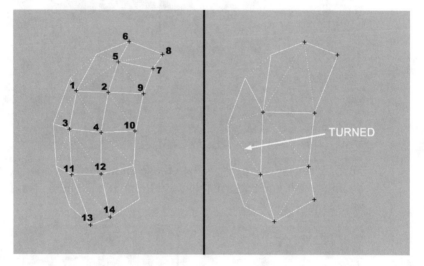

Start with vertices 1, 2, 3, and 4. Increase the Weld Selected value to 100 and hit Selected Selected . Target Weld 5 to 6 and 7 to 8. Select 9 and 10 and hit Selected, select 11 and 12 and hit Selected, and select 13 and 14 and hit Selected. Turn the edge that goes concave. Now the face distribution is a little more even.

Next, unhide Hair and hide Bangs. Start with the top of the head. With the setting still cranked up to 100, alternately Weld Select each pair of the following vertices one at a time and you reduce the faces by 12.

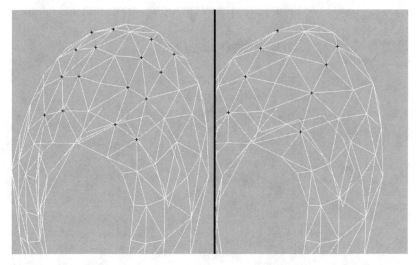

Further working in pairs, isolate these eight vertices (four vertices on either side) and alternately weld them, too: 1 and 2; 3 and 4; 5 and 6; and 7 and 8.

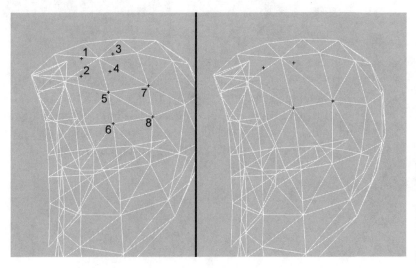

Going to the back of the head, weld the following vertices. Start by
target welding 1 to 2 and then 3 to 4. Select 5 and 6 and hit the
Selected button, 7 and 8 and the Selected button, 9 and 10 and the
Selected button, and then 11 and 12 and the Selected button.
Finally, Target Weld 13 over to 11.

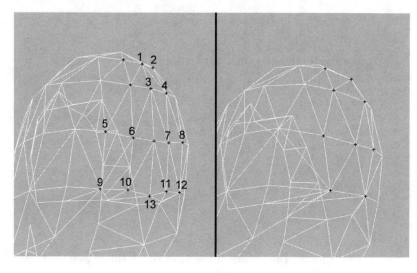

Work on the sides now and Weld Select these pairs one by one,
drawing them into each other:

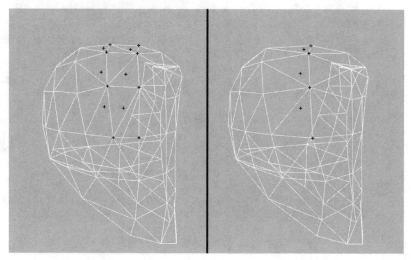

MODELING

Turn any edges ✍ that look like dents and move to the front. Bring the outer row of vertices in and then select the two pairs near the bottom of the front edge and Weld Select them.

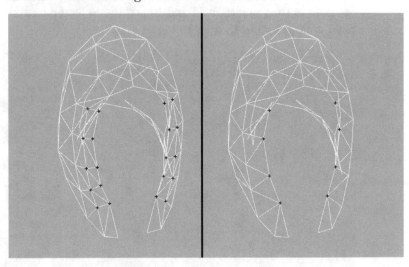

Don't forget the inside of the hair. Bring these two vertices down to the ones below them:

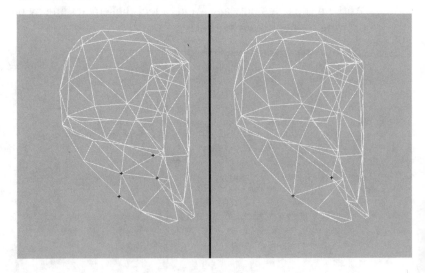

That takes care of nearly 100 faces just on the hair! Hopefully I didn't go too fast and lose you, and you recognized the combination of consolidating the vertices to achieve that *face parity* I keep rambling on about. Speaking of faces, it's time to move on to the face.

Step 2: Optimize the Forehead and Eyes

Load Callisto29.max from the CD.

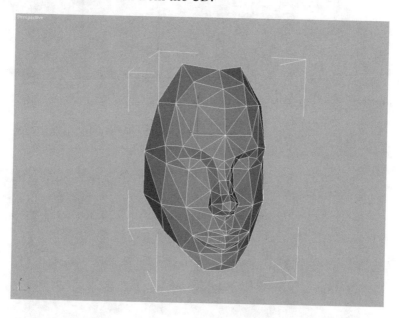

There doesn't seem to be too much that can be done with Callisto's mug, but I bet you can knock, say, 54 triangles off of it. Start with the forehead as shown in the following illustration.

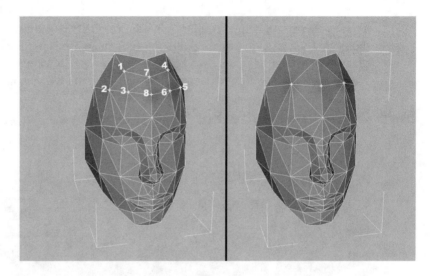

For the eye area Target Weld vertex 1 to 2; Weld Select 2 and 3 as well as 4 and 5. Repeat for the other side.

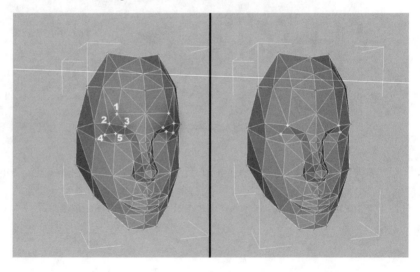

Step 3: Optimize the Mouth and Chin

Tilt up to see the lips and optimize the mouth a little. Target Weld 1 to 2 and 3 to 4. Then Weld Select 5 and 6 together.

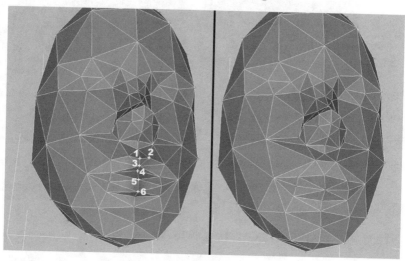

Weld Select 1 and 2; 3 and 4; and 5 and 6.

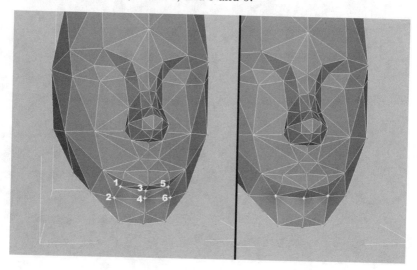

Flip up underneath the chin and Weld Select vertices 1 and 2.

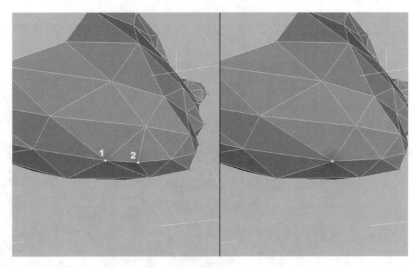

Step 4: Optimize the Nose

Select 1, 2, and 3, Weld Select them, and then turn the bad edges.

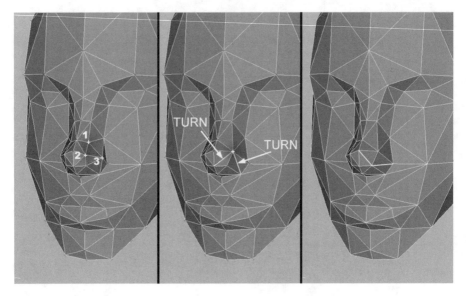

The left nostril looks too far back so move it forward a little.

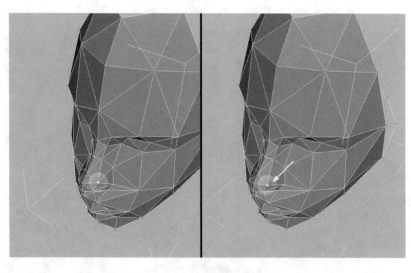

Repeat the weld and move for the right nostril.

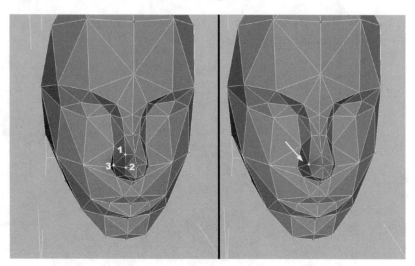

Underneath the nose you can get rid of this small detail. Weld Select 1 and 2, then Target Weld it to 3.

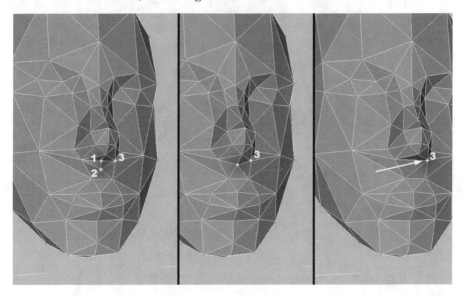

Voilà. What do you know? I guessed *exactly* right! 54 triangles later, the face is now optimized.

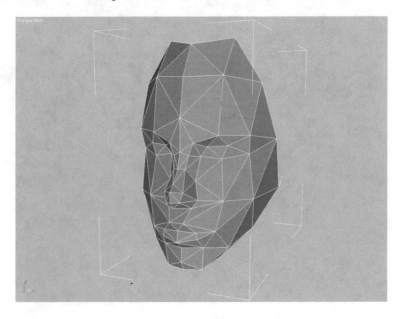

Now, time to move on to the body.

The Body

To effectively optimize the more complex Torso mesh, it's necessary to divide it up again into sections. This will make it easier to see what you're doing. First, load Callisto30.max from the CD.

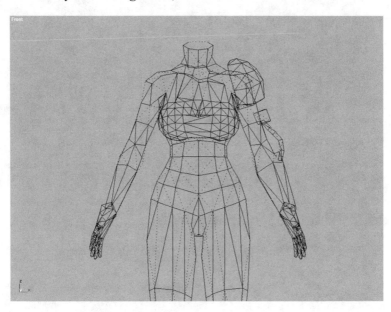

Step 1: Detach the Arms

Since you'll be concentrating on the torso, first detach the arms. In the Front viewport, hide the left shoulder pad element and select the faces of the arms below the shoulders at mid-bicep.

Detach them to an object called Arms, then hide it.

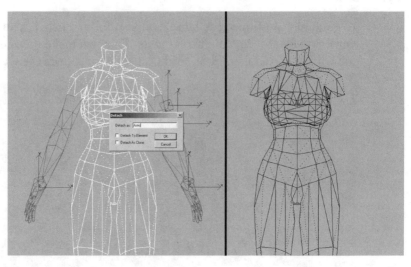

Step 2: Use Polygon Counter

Select File|Summary Info and check your face count.

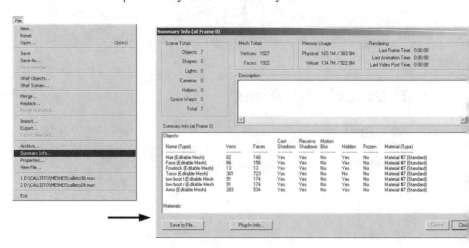

Summary Info is a great way to take a look at your scene and verify how many objects, faces, and vertices are in use, which materials are being used, and more. Now you know the scene has 1,922 faces and since there's nothing else in the scene but Callisto, there's still a total of 422 too many!

Another useful tool similar to Summary Info is Polygon Counter. This is a great way to monitor your optimizing progress on both a scene and object basis. Go to the Utilities panel **T** and hit the More button More... .

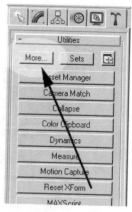

Select Polygon Counter from the list and hit OK.

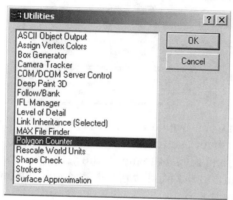

A Polygon Count window now appears in your scene and will stay onscreen until you close it, even if you go to a different panel. The way you use this tool is simple. In the All Objects area, highlight 10000 beside Budget and change it to 1500.

MODELING

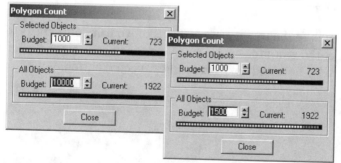

You just gave yourself a 1,500-polygon budget for the scene. Notice how the color bar underneath Budget has changed to include yellow and red. This is just a visual way to tell you you're over your budget; when the lights are all green, you're good to go.

Since there are some faces that can be trimmed from the hidden arms, there's no sense trying to chop all 422 extra faces from Torso. Compromise and tell yourself you only need to knock off 250 from the torso (you can always revisit the mesh after doing what you can to the arms). Currently, the Polygon Counter tells you the

Selected Objects (Torso) is 723 faces with a budget of 1000. 723 minus 250 equals 473, so enter that value in the Budget box beneath Selected Objects. Now you have a hard target to get the mesh down to.

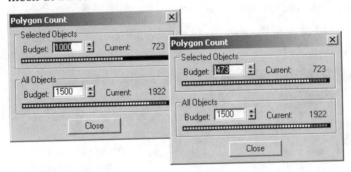

Any time the Polygon Count window gets in your way, simply close it. It will keep all the current settings with the scene file, so even if you quit max, restart, and reload the mesh, the settings for Polygon Count will stick. Return to the Modify panel and begin optimizing the unique parts of the torso.

Step 3: Optimize the Throat and Upper Shoulders

Zoom in to the throat area, select the two pairs of vertices to the left of the gratuitous strap connector geometry, enter a value of 1 in the Weld Selected box, and hit the Selected button.

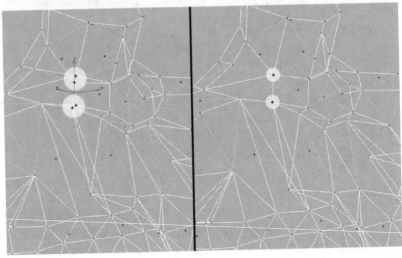

These two angles are shallow enough to be a straight line so Target
Weld vertex 1 and 2 to 3. There's no need for the extra center vertex, so weld 4 to 5.

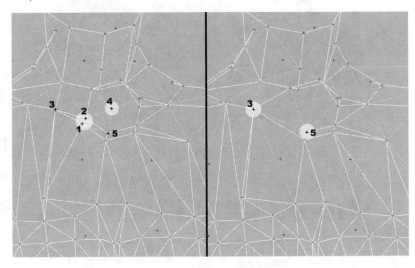

Take a look at the neck in profile. That extra vertex just above the
strap is unnecessary so weld it to the one above it.

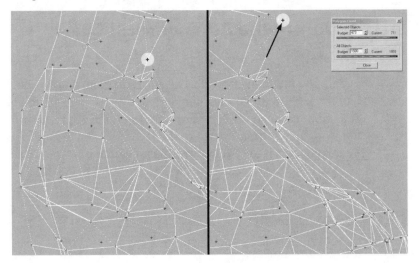

Turn this edge to get rid of the surface divot.

That covers the asymmetrical area at the top front of the torso. If you were to take away those faces, the rest of the body would be decidedly symmetrical. Since you'll be doing a substantial amount of optimization next, and the rest *is* symmetrical, it would behoove you to only work on half and Copy/Mirror/Attach it.

Step 4: Detach the Asymmetrical Chest Geometry

Isolate the uniquely shaped faces and hide them before you delete half the body. Start by checking Ignore Backfacing and dragging a selection marquee ⬚ across the front of the torso as shown in the following illustration. Deselect the faces you don't want to include by holding down the Alt key and clicking on them.

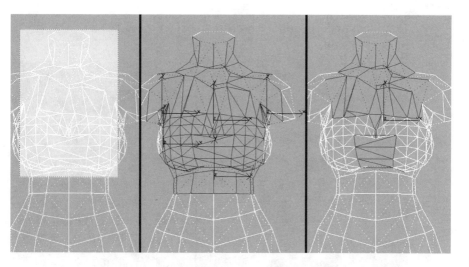

You checked Ignore Backfacing so you could quickly select the front asymmetrical faces without selecting the symmetrical ones at her back. Unfortunately, because Ignore Backfacing is checked, some of the ones you *want* selected at the front were ignored because of the way they're facing.

Rotate your view so you're looking down at Callisto's top, and select these faces at her cleavage and the top of the strap connector that *weren't* selected.

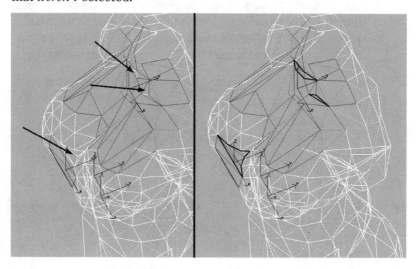

Rotate up underneath her breasts to select these faces that were missed as well:

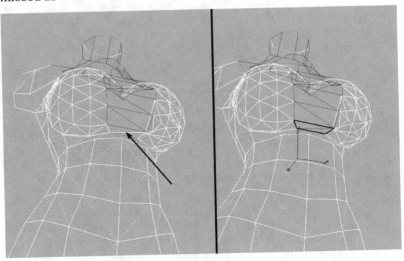

 FYI: *DESELECTING WHEN YOU WANT TO SELECT*

Sometimes you can unknowingly deselect a face when you're trying to select one. When hunting down certain triangles to select, you'll rotate your view trying to get the best angle for seeing them. Make sure as you place your cursor on the face that there isn't a selected face on the *other* side of the face you're about to select. For example: You have a bunch of tri-angles selected and want to add triangle A underneath the selection set.

Holding down the Ctrl key and clicking on triangle A (outline) in any of the shaded area (B) would be fine — it's selected imme-diately. Selecting anywhere else *on top of a selected triangle in the background* (C) would first *deselect* the background triangle clicked, and clicking again would then select triangle A. This accounts for those times you swear you clicked on that triangle and nothing happened!

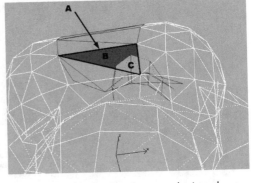

Hide all the faces you've selected. You can see what's left represents nearly equal halves.

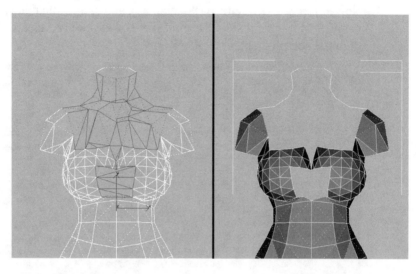

Hit Ctrl+Z to bring the faces back, and then detach them to an object called Frontal.

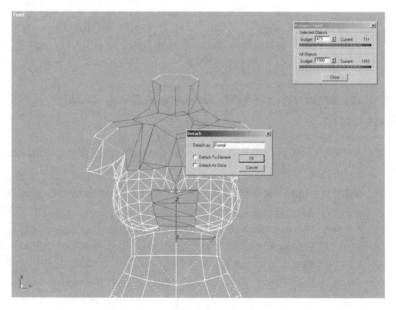

This way those unique, asymmetrical faces are easily identifiable.

MODELING

Step 5: Delete Half the Body

Now, *uncheck* the Ignore Backfacing box and select and delete the vertices of her *right* side. Be careful at the back of the mesh with the intersecting geometry of her buttock.

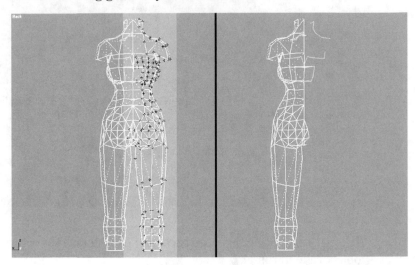

Hide Frontal and close the Polygon Count window for now since its effectiveness is a little skewed with half the geometry gone for "mirroring-later-on" purposes.

Step 6: Optimize the Back, Sides, and Midsection

Load Callisto31.max as shown in the following illustration to make sure you're on the same page.

When optimizing a model, don't just think in terms of *faces*. Many times it's better to look at the mesh in terms of *lines*. For example, it takes two vertices to make a straight line. If the line needs to be curved, it takes at least three vertices. Of course the more vertices you put into a curve, the more round it will be, but using more vertices to describe the curve depends on your polygon budget.

One of the things you can look for when optimizing a mesh is to see if the curved lines can still be achieved with fewer vertices. Can the shape be communicated with *less*? This is what I mean when I say, "Make every vertex count" — fewer, more effective vertices communicating detail in the mesh.

Looking at Callisto's trapezius area, consider the following two lines:

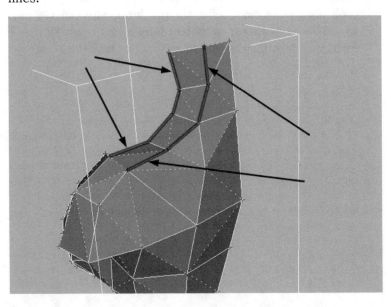

They're important because they make the sweep of the neckline look feminine. However, given the resolution at which the character will be seen most of the time, you can afford to optimize this area and still communicate the intent of the shape. Make sure your Weld Selected value is set at 10. Select vertices 1 and 2 and then 3 and 4, and merge each pair.

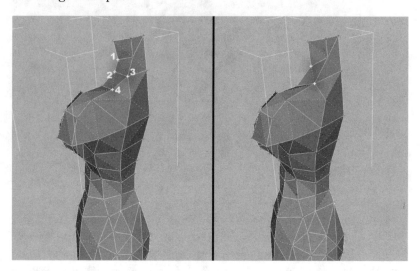

Comparing the lines now, they're definitely less curved, but the density of faces of the neck area now matches the surrounding geometry better. Also, that extra detail in the trapezius area would probably go unnoticed given the resolution at which the model would be seen. As you optimize, don't forget to check your lines and turn any edges that need turning — don't wait until later.

Rotate your view so you're looking down on the area you just optimized and turn this edge to shorten its line length:

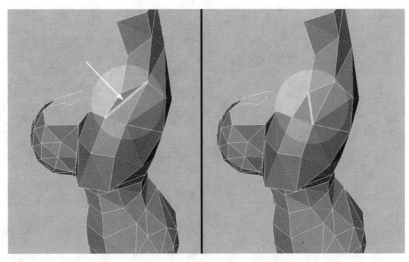

In general, as you've built your mesh you should have been paying close attention to your lines and tried to make them in a somewhat uniform manner when applicable, that is, the spacing of the lines appear even. Most of the time open, flat areas don't need as many triangles or as much complexity as curved areas unless those flat areas are going to deform when the character animates. So, while a geodesic configuration is appropriate for spherical parts of your mesh, areas like the waist and abs don't need to have as much detail or as many faces.

MODELING

Rotate your view so you're looking at the front of the body from a three-quarters angle and look at the following two lines:

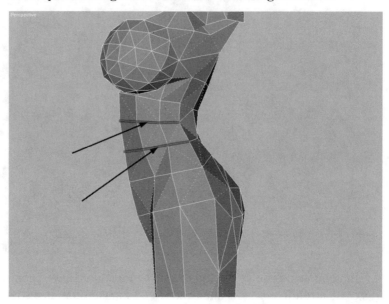

As I look at the model and search for faces to consolidate and vertices to weld, I find the two lines I've highlighted can be merged.

With a Weld Selected value of 10, alternately select and weld the following pairs of vertices: 1 and 2, 3 and 4, 5 and 6, and 7 and 8.

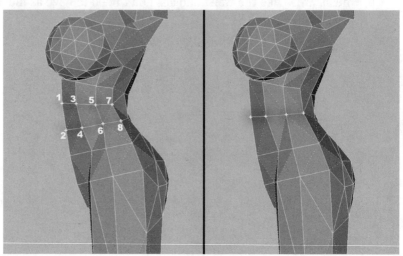

Now the relative distribution of faces is a little more spread out. Of course the breast has much more detail in it and a higher number of polygons, but you'll get to that later. Rotate your view so you can work on the back.

The three lines I've highlighted are nearly straight so the opportunity to merge vertices should be obvious. However, on female characters the small of the back as it ties into the waist is an important detail to keep since it helps define the more narrow, curvy waist — a distinctively feminine feature. Merge these three pairs of vertices to knock another five faces off the mesh:

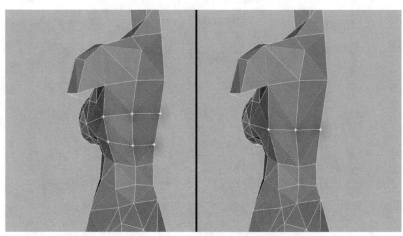

MODELING

Those merges create a nice line that defines the back, but in order to make the lines suggest the "V" of the back muscles, turn these edges:

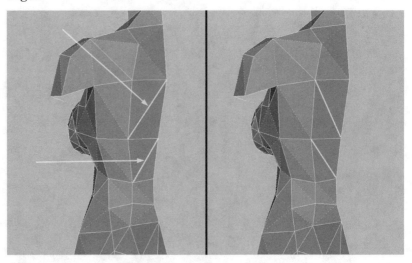

This is a very minor detail to be sure, but thinking like this will make your models *feel* better and adds to your intuitive modeling sense.

Now that you've taken care of some of the latitudinal lines of the torso, it's time to reduce some of the longitudinal lines. Rotate to the side, or abdominal obliques, of the torso, select these vertices, and Weld Select them:

Select the two vertices below the one you just merged and Weld Select them as well.

Turn this edge:

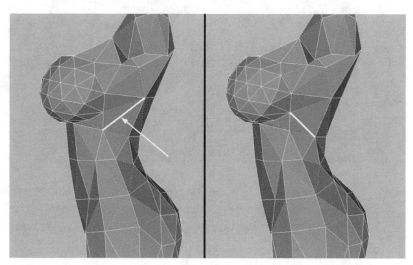

Now it's time to move on to the next area — Callisto's chest.

Step 7: Optimize the Chest

While the design calls for rather buxom proportions, the relative distribution of faces of Callisto's breast shape is just too great compared to the rest of the mesh. She needs some *polygonal* reduction this time. However, because of its spherical aspect, the breast needs slightly more faces than normal. Still, half the number currently used will bring it in line proportionately with the rest of the mesh and easily suggest the roundness of the shape.

To best see what needs to be done, rotate your view until you're at the front of her breast.

The cross marks the spot. Notice the convenient almost grid-like arrangement of the faces. Increasing the size of grid "blocks" by reducing the number of triangles could give you the results you're after.

However, at a lower resolution this approach goes away from the more efficient geodesic sphere shape and becomes a traditional lat-long spherical shape as shown in the following illustration.

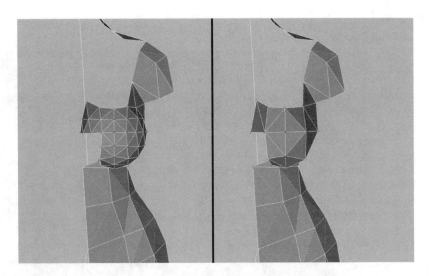

While this is a straightforward approach and appears neat and tidy, it lacks the roundness necessary to communicate the design. You need to try for a more geodesic shape. Think about *triangles* instead of grid lines this time; merge *triplets* of vertices instead of pairs. Aim for a relatively uniform triangle size and disregard the perfect "cross" formed by the lines of the geometry. Start by merging vertices 1, 2, and 3; then 4, 5, and 6; then 7, 8, and 9; then 10, 11, and 12; then 13, 14, and 15; and then 16, 17, and 18.

MODELING

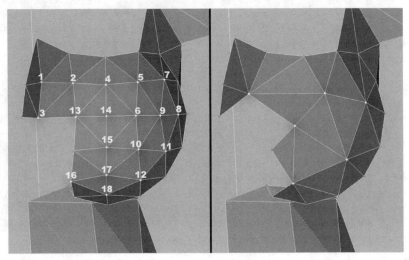

Next, Weld Select 1 and 2, and delete vertices 3 and 4.

Rotate your view so you're looking up underneath the breast and merge vertices 1, 2, and 3, then 4, 5, and 6. Turn [Turn] the awkward edge that the Weld Selects created.

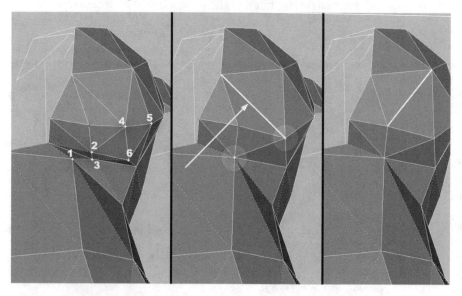

Select vertices 1 and 2 and Target Weld them to vertex 3.

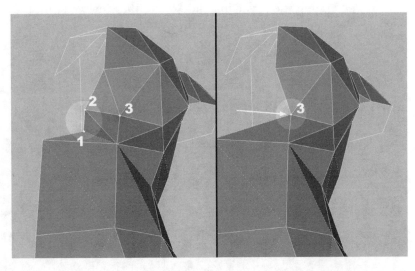

Rotate your view to the side, select these three vertices, Weld Select them, and turn this edge:

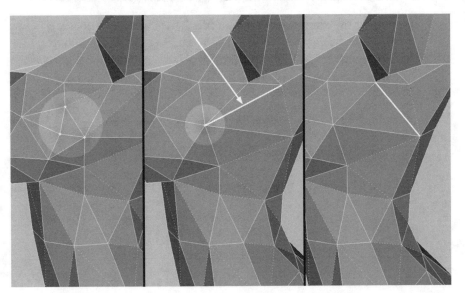

MODELING

Finally, make one last tweak by getting rid of the "dent" formed by the optimizations you just did. Rotate the view, and turn the dent's edge.

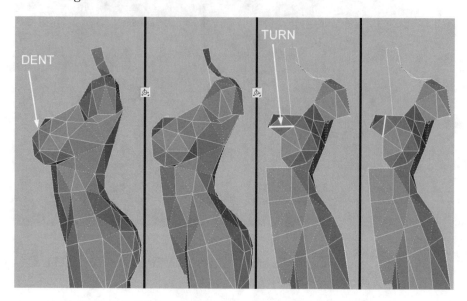

So while the simple reduction of the "cross" to a less detailed version works and cuts the polygon count in half, maintaining a geodesic shape results in a rounder object using *the same number of faces or less*.

Step 8: Optimize the Rear

Load Callisto32.max from the CD. I mentioned earlier the importance of having extra geometry at the small of the back to cue your eye that it's a feminine figure. Looking at Callisto in profile you can see there's potential for a bit more optimization without sacrificing this key detail.

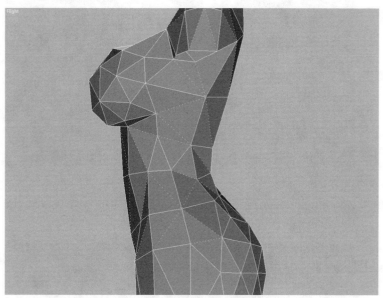

Rotate your view so you're looking at her back. Alternately select and merge vertices 1 and 2; 3 and 4; and 5 and 6.

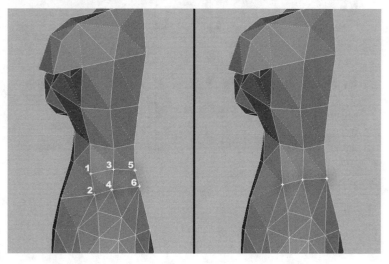

Rotate the view back around to the side, select vertices 1 and 2 and weld them, then select 3 and 4 and weld them.

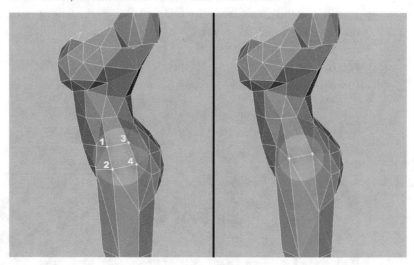

Zooming in and rotating the view back to the rear, merge the next four pairs of vertices:

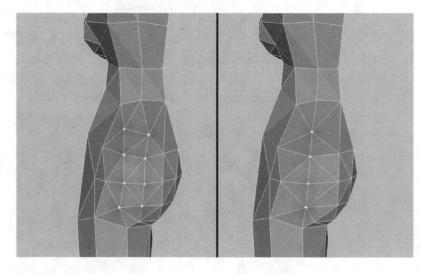

Rotate your view slightly to see these two vertices and Weld Select them as well:

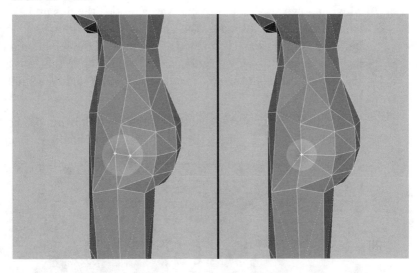

Finally, move vertex 1 up along the Z-axis $\boxed{z}$ about .8 units and vertex 2 in along the Y-axis $\boxed{Y}$ by about .4 units.

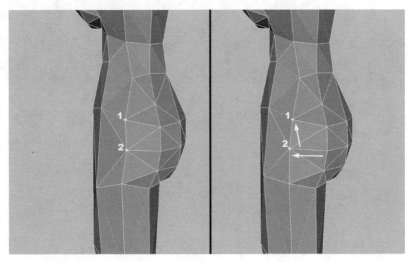

That's all I want you to sacrifice from Callisto's rear for now. You could optimize it further, but I'd rather wait and see how many faces you can shave off elsewhere.

MODELING

Step 9: Optimize the Legs

Moving down the leg to the knee area, notice the design has the back of her leg encircled by the kneepad strap. When a real leg bends, a single crease is formed at the back of the leg behind the knee assembly. In a lower poly character mesh like this, the geometry there can be optimized as well to mimic life and be a single crease.

Rotate to the back of the leg at the knee joint. Starting on the left, merge vertices 1, 2, and 3; then 4, 5, and 6; and finally 7, 8, and 9.

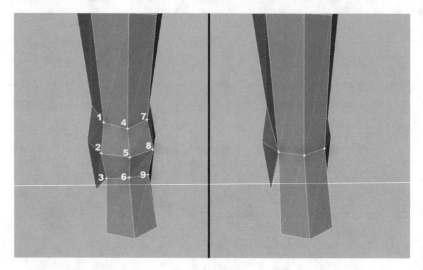

Rotate your view around to the front of the knee and optimize the bottom of the kneepad that will be mostly hidden by the large boot top. Target Weld vertex 1 to 2 and 3 to 4.

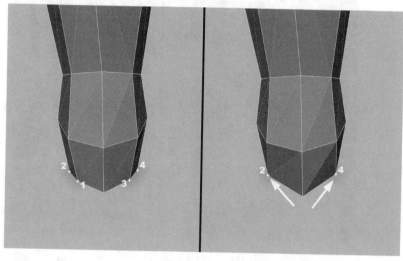

Notice how the edges aren't turned symmetrically on the leg. This is because you started with a cylinder primitive that by default has its edges turned in a uniform direction. Neaten the leg up a little by turning those edges:

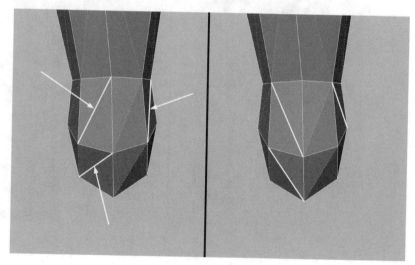

MODELING

Swing your view around to the side of the knee and create the face that's missing there:

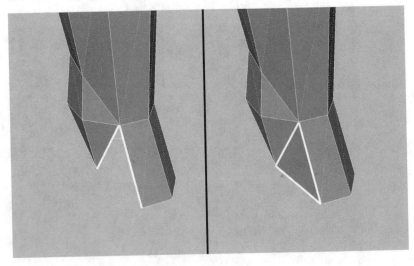

Zoom out and rotate the view a little more so you're at the back of the leg again and turn these two edges:

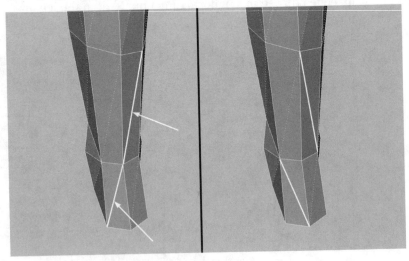

I spoke earlier of making sure every vertex counts — that every vertex has a visible contribution to the shape of the mesh. Looking at Callisto's leg profile in the Right viewport, you can see the back of the leg is nearly a straight line. You might be thinking those vertices in the middle of the thigh could be merged to the ones above or below since the line is so straight. That normally would be the case, but here those vertices are needed to form the subtle curve of the back of the hamstring. What's happened is the vertices you optimized at the crease at the back of the knee have come *out* slightly and *taken the curve away*. The remedy, of course, is to push them back in. Select and move these vertices in a little along the X-axis **[x]** as shown in the following figure.

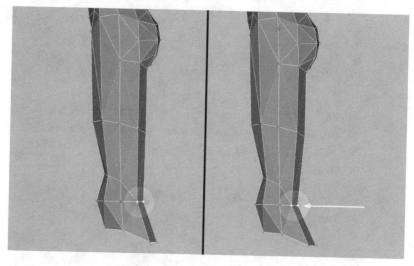

Now, the vertices at the middle of the thigh serve a more tangible purpose, helping to make the leg look more organic by being slightly curved.

Step 10: Give the Body One Last Look

With all the areas covered, it's time to give the body a "once-over" before you copy, flip, and attach that copy to itself. Unhide the hidden shoulder pad and look at the front of the abs and hip area.

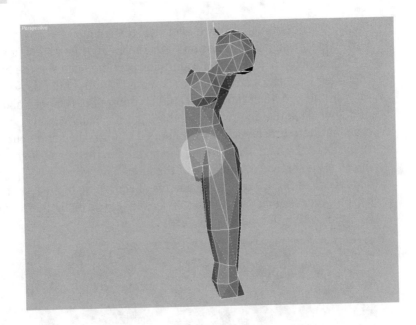

This area where the leg meets the torso is a candidate for further optimization. There is an extra line around the stomach, and vertex A seems unnecessary given the distribution of faces in the now-optimized mesh.

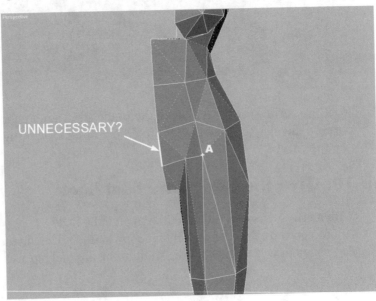

Select and weld vertices 1 and 2. Then select and weld vertices 3, 4, and 5.

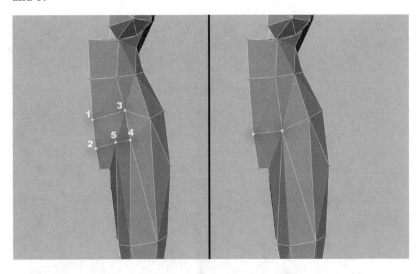

Now it matches the surrounding level of detail. Rotate your view a little, check Ignore Backfacing, and turn these edges that have become a little concave:

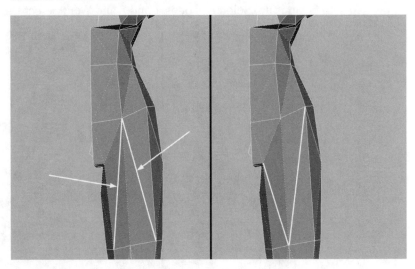

MODELING

Much better. Now, rotate around to the back and give it another look as well. Like the area in front, this area bothers me:

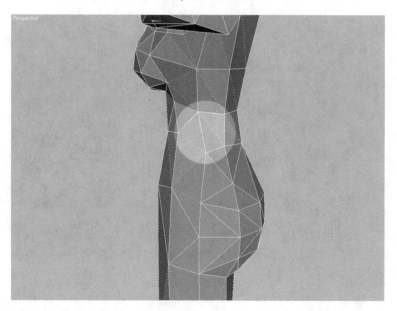

The lines are a little jumbled and it seems like there's an opportunity to clean it up. Select vertices 1 and 2 and Weld Select them.

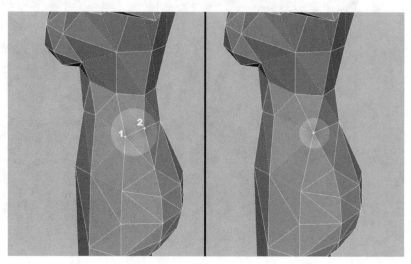

Now you need to adjust the line that runs around the waist so it isn't so jagged. First, select the following two vertices and Uniformly Scale 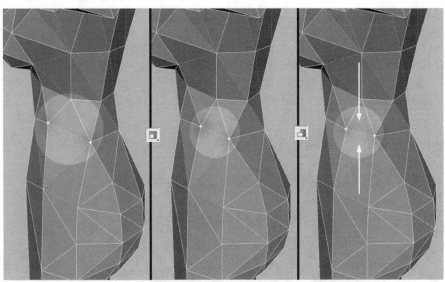 them 65%. Then switch to Non-Uniform Scale and scale the vertices 45% along the Z-axis — all in the Perspective viewport, of course.

Turn the following edge; and that should do it for the waist and hip area. Note that although turning it results in a *longer* line than before, it makes the surface of the mesh more smooth.

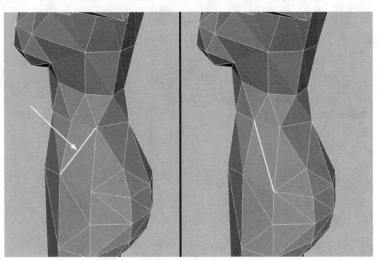

MODELING

You've made all the optimizations you need to make for now on the body, so it's time to Copy and Mirror the optimized/tweaked geometry.

Step 11: Copy, Mirror, and Join the Optimized Body Half

Load Callisto33.max. Select Torso, go to the Element sub-object menu, select just the body (not the shoulder pad), and Shift-drag the faces, cloning them to an object (just keep the name, Mesh01, since you'll be attaching it shortly).

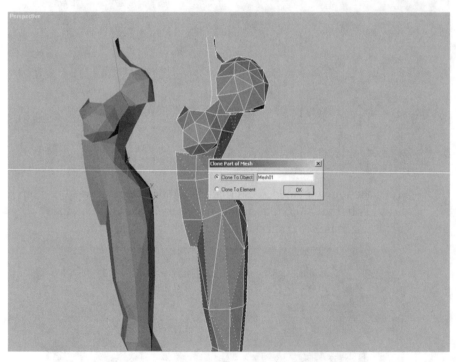

Make sure Use Selection Center is the active coordinate system and Mirror the object. Move it over along the X-axis until the middles of the two torso halves meet.

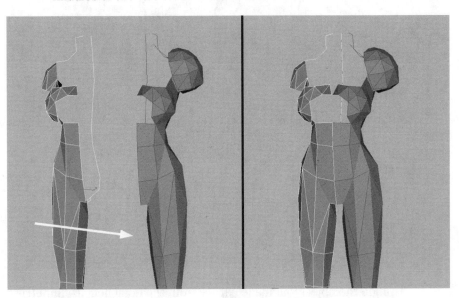

Switch to a Front viewport and attach the copy to Torso. While the line of vertices running down the dividing line between the meshes should be perfectly straight, some of them seem a little off. Select just those centerline vertices where the two elements meet, make sure that Use Selection Center is active, and NU Scale them down as far as they will go along the X-axis four or five times. (Just select and drag the mouse a few times until you notice no change in the position of the vertices.)

MODELING

Once you get them all lined up, set your Weld Selected value to .1 and hit Selected.

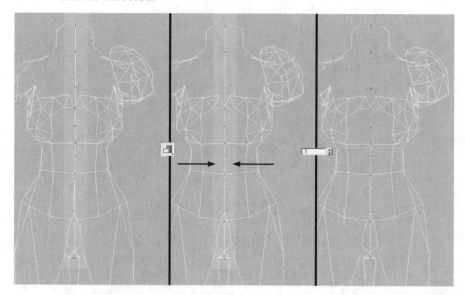

Unhide the object you made earlier from the detached, asymmetrical faces of the chest area and move on to the next step, tweaking it to fit the newly optimized Torso.

Step 12: Tweak and Attach "Frontal"

Continue with your mesh or load Callisto34.max from the CD. Unhide Frontal from the list of hidden objects.

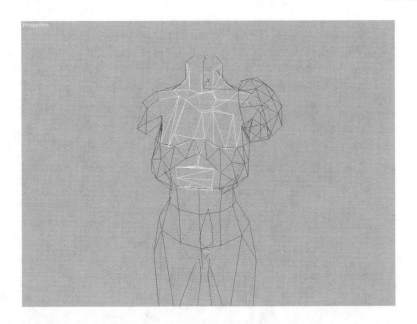

With all the optimizing you've done to the Torso mesh, now you need to play catch-up with the faces of the front chest you detached earlier: Frontal. When the Attach Options window comes up, just hit OK to confirm the Match Material IDs to Material option.

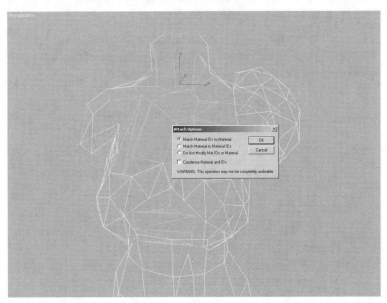

First, isolate just the vertices where the two elements meet, go to Edit|Select Invert, invert the selection, and hide all the vertices you don't need for the moment. Select all the vertices that are left, enter a value of 1 in the Weld Selected box, and hit Selected.

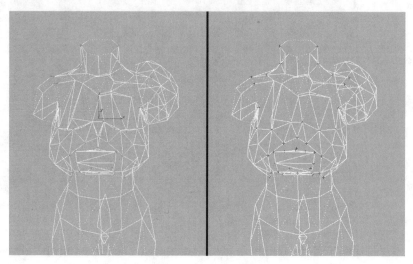

That is the quickest way to take care of all the flush vertices and the ones relatively close. Now you need to do a little work to close the mesh and complete the attachment of Frontal.

Rotate your view so you're looking up at her bosom. Using Target Weld, close the gaps by welding the vertices of the former Frontal object *to* the optimized Torso.

Start by selecting and welding vertices 1 *and* 2 to 3. Then select and weld 4 to 5 and then 6 and 7 to 8. Weld 9 and 10 to 11, 12 to 13, and 14 and 15 to 16.

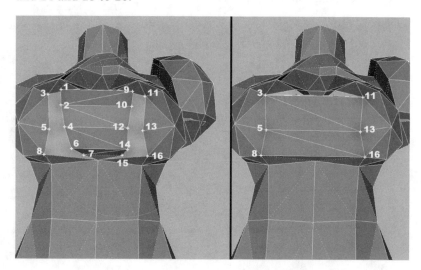

Now rotate your view again so you're staring down at Callisto's chest and close the gap there by merging the following sets of vertices using Weld Selected: 1 and 2; 3, 4, and 5; and 6 and 7.

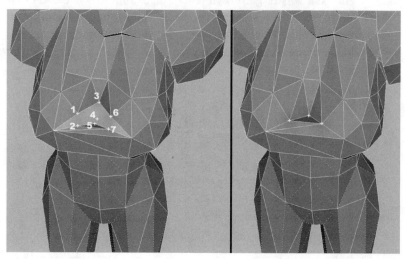

Unhide the rest of the vertices, select the vertex used to give dimension to the strap on her right, and slide it over a little along the X-axis so it's not so far to the left:

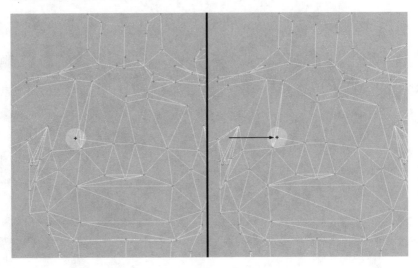

Now unhide everything. Bring up the Polygon Counter and see where you sit on face count.

The goal was to get down to 473 faces, but 485 is close enough for the torso. The scene total is still at 1,684 so that means you still have another 184 faces to trim. Hmmm. The boots are pretty much dialed down to as low as they're gonna go, so all that's left are the arms.

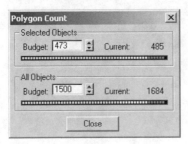

Step 13: Optimize the Arms

Load Callisto35.max from the CD.

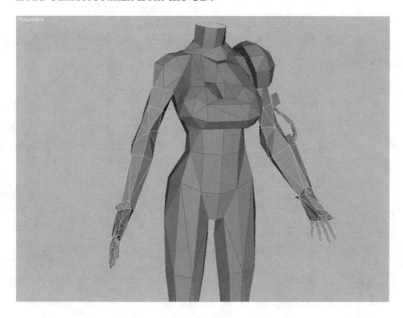

I've made some minor tweaks to the arms because I didn't like how the elbow joint and the elbow pad were looking; it seemed a little too low. Hide Torso Hide Selected , and select and hide the right arm, upper arm shroud element, and tubing elements as well.

MODELING

Rotate your view so you're looking at the outside elbow area a little from the rear. Push vertex 1 away from the body along the X-axis about .3 units, Target Weld vertex 2 just below it to vertex 1, and then merge vertices 3 and 4 using Weld Selected.

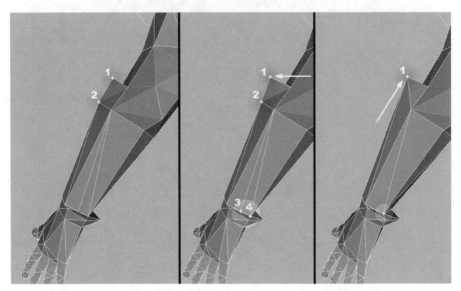

Rotate around a little more to the front of the mesh and Target Weld vertex 1 to 2, and 3 to 4.

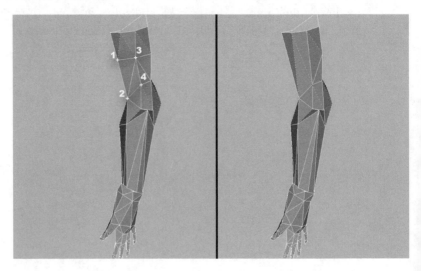

Geometry like the upper arm and thigh don't deform, so those extra segments that help define the shape can be sacrificed and consolidated when looking for areas to optimize. It's unfortunate, but a necessity. Rotate your view to the inside of the arm and weld vertex 1 to 3 and 2 to 4:

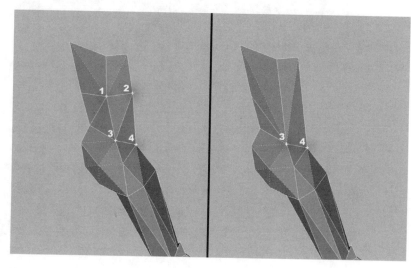

Rotate again to the outside of the arm, looking slightly down on it. Turn the following edge and pull this vertex out along the Y-axis about .3 units, making it more useful as it adds shape to the front of the bicep:

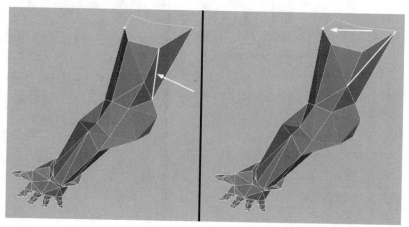

Rotate your view back around to the inside of the arm, looking slightly down on it. Line A is too short compared to line B, so move this vertex over along the XY axes ⟨XY⟩ to distribute the faces more judiciously in the forearm.

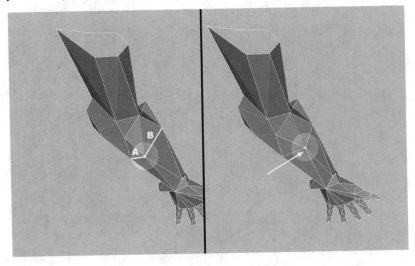

Moving down to the wrist area, merge vertices 1 and 2, and turn this edge to complete the optimization of the forearm:

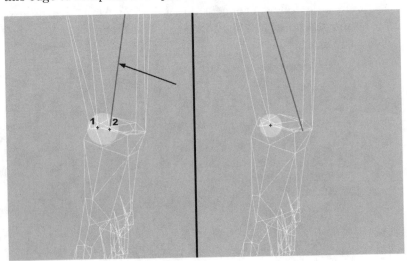

Unhide the other elements of the arm, and zoom in to the front of
the arm where the tubing is attached. Merge vertices 1 and 2, then
3 and 4 using Weld Selected.

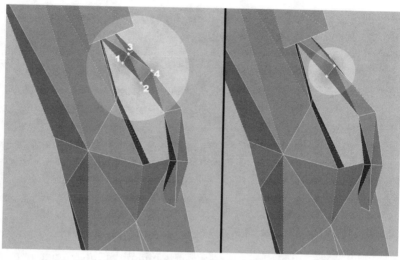

Rotate the view a little and notice that even with the optimization,
you still get the sense that the tubing is more complex than it actually is by *not* merging the vertices that make up the outer part of
the curve and keeping this line.

Go over to the right arm and get rid of that middle line at the bicep, making the same welds and edge turns you made on the bicep of the left arm.

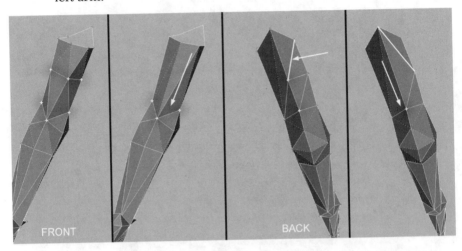

FRONT   BACK

I had you keep this vertex at the middle of the outside of each arm instead of merging it because it helps add shape to the upper arm:

Unfortunately, when you check the face count in Summary Info, it's 1,658 — still 158 faces more than you are allowed. So you're going to have to sacrifice the shape detail by welding that vertex to the one below it on both arms.

Turn the long edge on the outside of the arm because doing so shortens its length without making a "dent" in the surface.

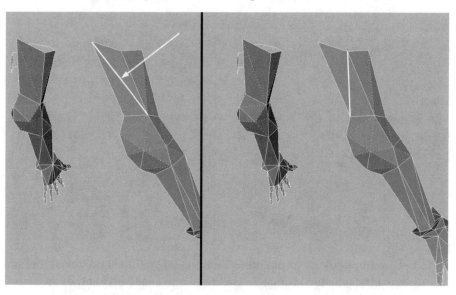

Unhide [Unhide by Name...] the torso mesh. Hide the shoulder pad element so it doesn't obscure your view, and reattach the arms to Torso.

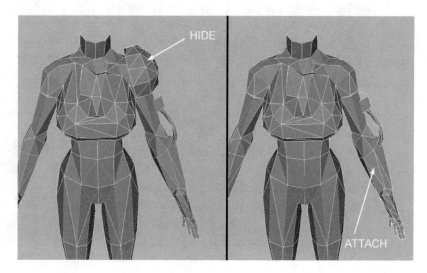

Rotate your view so you can Target Weld [Target] vertices 1 and 3 of the torso to vertices 2 and 4, respectively, of the arm.

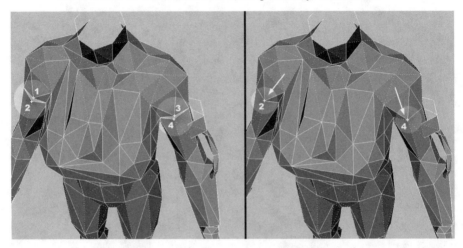

Hmmm. Looking at the torso from this angle, it seems this detail of the strap can be optimized. Go ahead and shave off another two triangles by merging these two vertices at the top of this shoulder strap piece. While it's nice to flesh out this kind of detail, chances are it would never be noticed anyway.

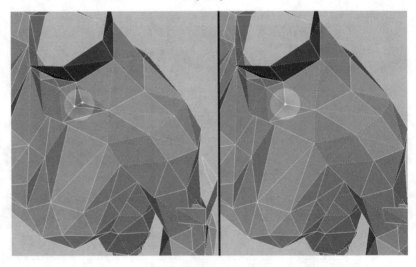

Select all the intersecting vertices from when you attached the arms a few minutes ago, set your Weld Selected threshold to 1, and merge them. Be careful *not* to select the vertices of the torso that lay close to those penetrating vertices of the arm geometry.

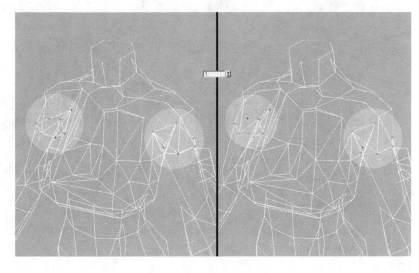

Seems like you're running out of things to optimize. Give the mesh another once-over to see if you can squeeze out another triangle or two. Rotating your view so you're looking at the back, see if there's some consolidating you can do there. It seems you're going to have to bite the bullet and sacrifice all that detail of the trapezius and neck area.

MODELING

Starting at the top of the neck, set the Weld Selected value to 10 and merge vertices 1, 2, and 3. Then merge vertices 4, 5, and 6; then 7 and 8; and lastly 9 and 10.

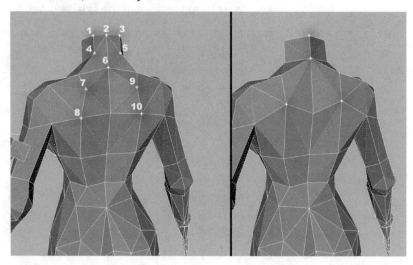

Turn these edges to clean up the lines of the neck and back:

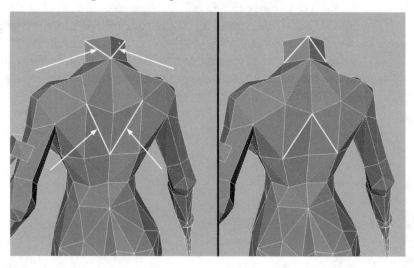

It's unfortunate you have to delete all the detail of the back you added earlier, but hey, sacrificing for the "cause" is what optimization is all about. Doing a quick check, the face count is still up at 1,640. It's time to try something more extreme in order to get down to your target face count of 1,500.

Step 14: Optimize the Hand by Turning It into a Fist

Fingers are key to adding life to a character because animated digits imbue expression and attitude. Fingers are also *very expensive* in a low-poly model because they're so small relative to the rest of the mesh and need extra faces to be animated properly. Load Callisto36.max from the CD. Looking at Callisto's hands, there's definitely some disparity when it comes to the faces of the fingers and the rest of the body!

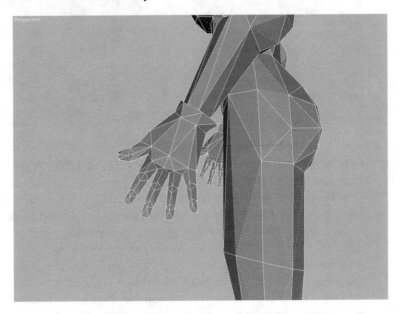

As much as I'd like to see Cal have complete articulation and expression with her hands, being almost 150 faces over budget leaves you little choice but to target her polygon-rich fingers. Most of the time real-time game characters like this one will tend to carry weapons, so the hand holding that weapon is closed into a fist. This presents the perfect opportunity to trim down at least one of her hands. First, select the faces of the right hand and make a copy of them. When performing major surgery like this it's best to work on a copy instead of the original. This always gives you a backup. Hide everything but the hand copy. Build a skeleton for the hand using Bones or Biped and attach the mesh to it using Skin or Physique.

However you decide to do it, once the mesh is attached, pose the skeleton hand into a fist.

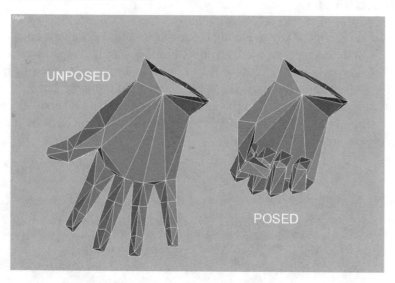

FYI: *POSE, DON'T MODEL... ALWAYS USE A SKELETON*

The benefit of posing a mesh by attaching it to an underlying skeleton and posing those bones or biped objects is simple. By using a Skin or Physique modifier you can always default back to the original state of the mesh by turning the modifier off or deleting it from the stack. If you simply add an Edit Mesh modifier to the stack, you lose the benefit and utility of having a bone system and are limited to the shape you end up with. Adding a bone to your mesh gives you the freedom to pose it in *any* shape and much more quickly and accurately than pushing your vertices around. Think of it as *posing* instead of *modeling*.

Once you've posed the hand, snapshot it by going to Tools | Snapshot and taking a "picture" of the mesh in its posed state, creating another copy of the hand.

The reason you snapshot the geometry is because you may need the original boned and weighted hand for another pose or the other hand. Like the reasoning behind using copied faces of the original mesh, it saves you time if you use *copies* in this way so you don't have to re-bone and re-weight the hand. In fact, once you take the time to bone and weight a hand mesh, it doesn't hurt to keep a copy of it "on hand" as a reference to bring in pose and snapshot for cases like this in the future.

Once you have the hand posed and snapshotted, optimize it using the techniques I've shown you, but make sure you retain the most distinguishing aspects of the fist so that it *looks* like a fist.

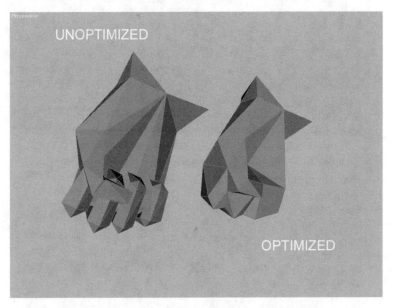

MODELING

If you want to see the differences between the unposed, posed, and optimized fist, load Fist.max from the CD and see what I did to knock the faces down. Optimizing the hand into a fist nets 110 faces!

With the pose and optimization of the right hand, the face count is now 1,530.

It's easy to see where a bunch of polygons can get eaten up pretty quickly. Looking at the other hand, how can you optimize it to shave off those other 30 faces? It takes two hands to hold a rifle — one hand on the pistol grip, one hand holding it up to aim. If the hand holding the weapon can be a fist, the hand holding it up can be a

"mitt." Like the fist, merging the fingers into a unified mesh means the *texture* will have to imply the fingers the geometry represents.

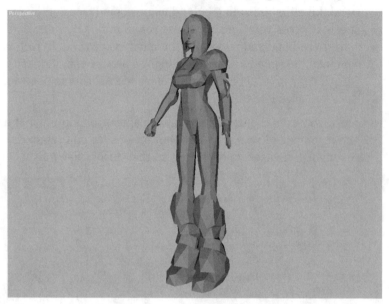

So take the boned and skinned hand from earlier and pose it into a mitt that could hold a weapon steady.

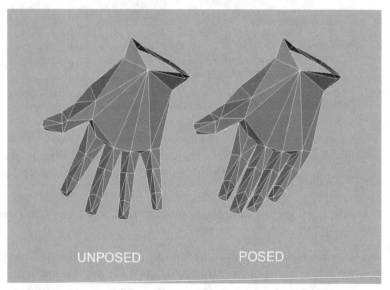

Next, optimize it like you did the fist, keying on the features of the hand so it looks like it should and hits your target face count. Keep in mind the mitt hand still needs to animate to some degree — gripping the rifle, curling into a fist, whatever — and the outside of it is more visible than the inside.

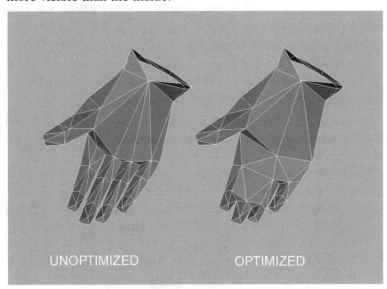

UNOPTIMIZED   OPTIMIZED

If you're interested in comparing the three states — unposed, posed, and optimized — load Mitt.max and see how I did it. Delete the current left-hand faces, mirror and attach the mitt, and voilà! Callisto is now proudly wearing 1,500 triangles and the model is built!

MODELING

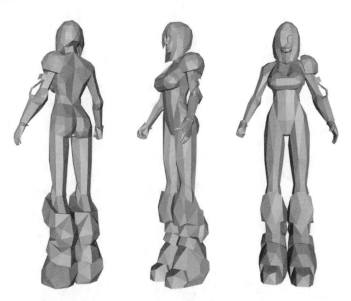

Load Callisto37.max if you want to check over the final mesh, but that does it for the optimization process. Hopefully I've not left you scratching your head in a daze! I've spent a lot of pages on optimization because in the end, it really is the heart of low-poly modeling for characters. Why? Because as you model, you should constantly be asking yourself where you could save a few faces. Unless there is a definite need or use for a high-poly version, do your best to optimize as you go and crunch the mesh down even further at the end to meet your target face count.

Too often I see a mesh or a game that has models in it that could have been optimized and reduced. After a while the sum of all those extra faces could easily be a little more detail in the world or even another character! Try your best to achieve the design of the character with the polygons you have been allotted or even fewer. At the very least, be sure to make the detail of the mesh match its environment. Even if you have a 5,000-face limit for your character, be smart in the distribution of polygons! Cramming faces into a mesh for the sake of saying it has that many polygons (not because it needs them) is just plain *bad*. Those faces can always be used elsewhere and result in a better scene or even a better game.

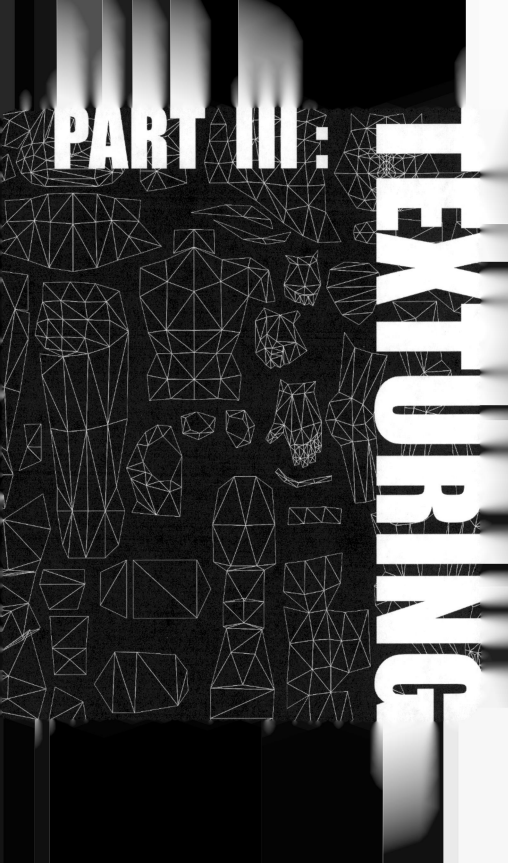

PART IIII: TEXTURING

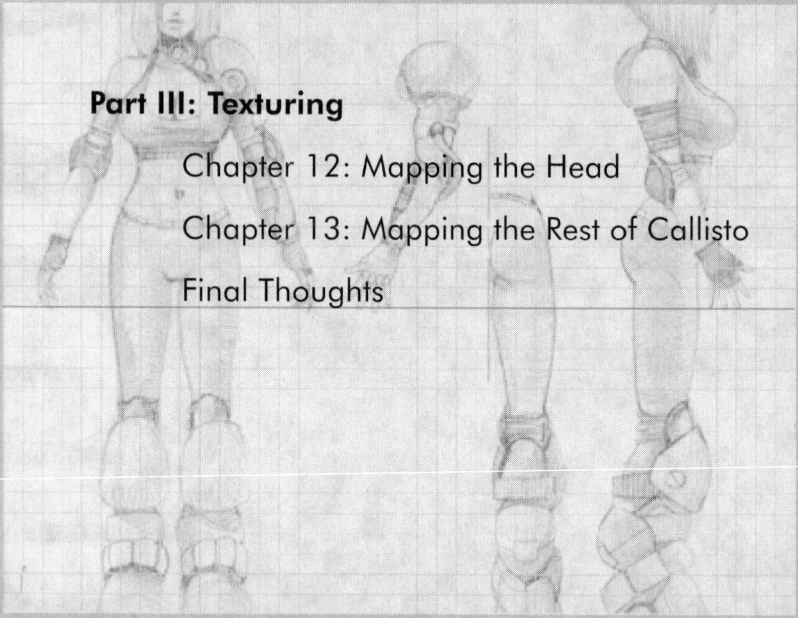

Part III: Texturing

CHAPTER 12
Mapping The Head

The best way to illustrate mapping theory and technique is to just do it. In this chapter, I'm going to show you step by step how to do Callisto's head. The following chapter then briefly covers how each of the rest of her body parts were mapped.

Texturing Explained

First, though, let me discuss the basics of texturing. As I mentioned at the beginning of the book, my intent is to show you how to build a character in max, not how to exclusively use the program. You should know what a "bitmap" is and what "texture coordinates" mean. Being a self-taught artist, it would be presumptuous of me (not to mention embarrassing) to teach you the fundamentals of painting or color theory. In fact, when it comes to texture mapping, an entire *book* could maybe begin to cover how to create some of the beautiful masterpieces of artwork that grace characters in many games today. I'd be one of the first to buy a book like that, too! What I will do in this part of the book is review some max texturing basics and concentrate more on the "*skinning*" of a character — the laying in of the UVW mapping coordinates — than to feebly attempt to show you how to create that lush texture you've been dying to paint!

UVW and XYZ

"Texturing" and "texture maps" refer to the application of an image or the "coloring" of your mesh usually done via a 2D paint program such as Adobe Photoshop or CorelPHOTO-PAINT. This is sort of like using those warm-water removable decals you put on that model car you built as a kid. However, before you can see the image on your mesh you need to embed, or "lay in," the "mapping coordinates," or UVWs. In other words, any object in max that's been assigned a material that contains a "bitmap" or image file such as a .jpg or .tga has to have UV mapping coordinates assigned to it.

I say "UV" because although referred to as "UVW," the "W" only really applies to procedural texture maps. It represents a third mapping dimension much like "Z" represents the third dimension in the Cartesian coordinate system. Even the letters themselves are derived from XYZ; UVW are just the three letters preceding XYZ. Procedural maps (i.e., noise, dent, marble, etc.) don't require mapping coordinates because they aren't based on an actual image.

They approximate and/or simulate an image *type* by generating it programmatically via adjustable parameters in the Material Editor.

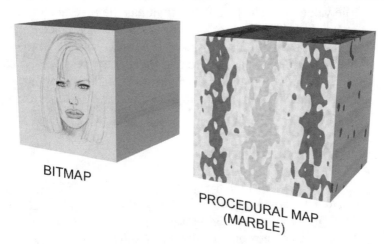

BITMAP

PROCEDURAL MAP
(MARBLE)

Thus, while universally you'll hear everyone refer to mapping coordinates as "UVW," they most often truncate the non-acronym and just say "UVs." Typically, when you "adjust your UVs" you're dealing with tiling. Like the tiles you lay on your guest bathroom floor after having ripped up all the old linoleum, "tiling" refers to the repetition of a pattern via the texture coordinates. Basically, you're telling max to take the image applied and repeat it across the surface of your mesh.

When tiling a texture and making the association of which tiles to lay in what direction, I've found a good rule of thumb when it comes to UVs is to think of "V" as "vertical" (doesn't matter what you think of "U"). In other words, increasing the Vs means the image will repeat up and down, increasing the Us mean the image will repeat horizontally.

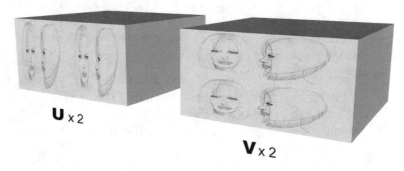

U x 2

V x 2

TEXTURING

Both of the boxes in the previous image have been assigned mapping coordinates. The box on the left has a U Tile value of 2 and a V Tile value of 1. The box on the right has the reverse: a U Tile value of 1 and a V Tile value of 2. Tiling is a great way to add detail to a character's texture map by increasing the resolution at the price of making sure the edges of the texture all meet seamlessly. The main thing I want you to understand, however, is the directional correlation of U and V as it applies to the bitmap and to the texture coordinates of the mesh.

Applying Coordinates

There are two ways to assign mapping coordinates in max: Apply a UVW Map modifier UVW Map or check the Generate Mapping Coords. check box on the parametric rollout menu of most primitives.

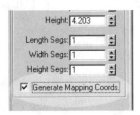

Compare these two boxes:

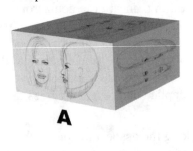

A

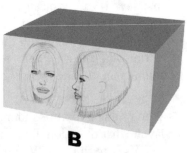

B

Box A has been created with the Generate Mapping Coords. box checked; regardless of the dimensions of the box, the image applied to it is mapped onto each side automatically. Box B has been assigned a UVW Map modifier with Planar mapping selected; the image assigned to it only appears on the surface where the modifier gizmo has been oriented (if you could see the back of Box B, the image would be in reverse).

Since max doesn't have a Character primitive for which to check the Generate Mapping box, you need to get used to using the UVW Map modifier to texture your character. While there are seven types of mapping to choose from in max, I tend to only use Planar, Cylindrical, and/or Spherical.

Planar is the most common type of mapping because it projects a texture onto a mesh much like a square "light" being shined on it. It's the most useful, but it does have its limitations. It will streak across faces of your mesh that are perpendicular to the orientation of the mapping "gizmo," or adjustable indicator of how your map is being applied.

Here are two basic shapes that have planar mapping assigned to them:

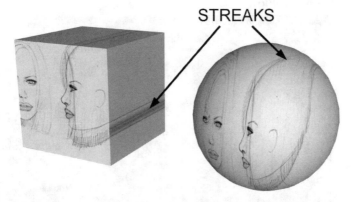

If you make that "Flat Man" superhero you've always wanted and three dimensions aren't being considered, then planar works fine "as is" for your character. If you want to apply a nicely detailed texture map to your character, wrapped around the three-dimensional aspect of your beefy or buxom hero/heroine, then you need to use a *combination* of mapping modifiers and techniques.

"Skinning" Your Character

There are a variety of methods to apply a texture, or "skin," to your model using the tools that come with max. Sometimes you're only limited by your imagination to come up with creative ways to lay in your UV coordinates. I've read about some pretty wild and sometimes pretty convoluted processes both online and in various magazines. Here are two of the more mundane ways to apply mapping coordinates and a texture to your mesh.

TEXTURING

Method One

1. Apply an appropriate UVW Map modifier to a group of selected faces.

2. Assign an Unwrap UVW modifier to adjust the UVs as necessary.

3. Repeat steps 1 and 2 until all the faces of the mesh have UVs assigned and arranged to fit on one square texture page.

4. Collapse the stack.

5. Apply one last Unwrap UVW modifier and bring up the Edit UVWs window.

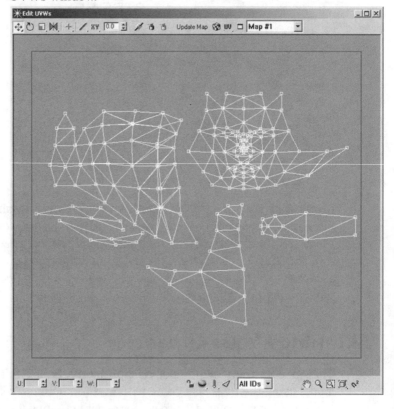

6. Hit the Print Screen button on your keyboard to take a snapshot of the UVs.

7. Load the captured image into Photoshop.

8. Crop the Edit UVWs portion of the image.

9. Save it as a square image and use it as a texture map template.

10. Create and apply the bitmap material to the mesh.

11. Look at the mesh with the template texture applied, and tweak and adjust the UVWs to fix any problem areas with the coverage.

12. Repeat steps 6 through 10 until everything looks cool and then use the final template image as a guide to paint a real texture in Photoshop.

This method is great if you have an image already done that has to be used as a texture "sheet." However, doing it this way can result in a pretty large stack as you alternately select the appropriate faces and apply the mapping to them. For me, large stacks are cumbersome and, as I've mentioned before, sometimes unstable. You also have to remember where each selection set of faces is on the texture "background," stitching them together as you go or in the end when you collapse the stack. This makes the process pretty lengthy, and the low fidelity of the screen grab from the Edit UVWs window in Unwrap UVW also makes for a pretty crude texturing template.

Method Two

Here is the second method.

1. Strategically detach faces on your mesh as elements.

2. Make a copy of the mesh.

3. Hide it.

4. Rearrange the detached faces of the remaining mesh, tweaking the vertices as necessary so that the mesh is laid out neatly for a planar mapping projection to be applied.

5. Apply a UVW Map modifier to the arranged mesh.

6. Render the arranged mesh in wireframe to use as a base or template to paint a real texture in Photoshop.

7. Create and apply the bitmap material to the arranged mesh.

8. Unhide the copy you made earlier.

9. Apply a Morpher modifier to the arranged mesh, and pick the unhidden copy to morph to transform the shape back to its original state.

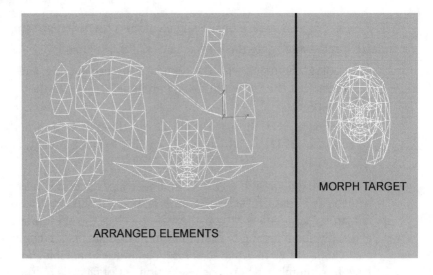

10. Collapse the stack and weld the vertices of the mesh that were previously detached.

11. Delete the copy used as a morph target.

This method isn't bad because what you've done is apply the same philosophy of manipulating the UVWs like you would in Unwrap UVW, but you have the full power of max's transforms in 3D instead of just the 2D of the Edit UVWs window. It's also quicker and you can render the wireframe "template" image to whatever color or resolution you want. The problem with this method is that if you arrange all the pieces like you want and discover you didn't detach the elements correctly, you have to start all over again. Morpher works on the assumption and the limitation that the morph target mesh consists of *exactly* the same number of vertices and faces. Detaching a face after you've made a copy to morph to later will make that copy useless.

Steed Method

The method I prefer for laying in the UVs on a character mesh is a combination of the techniques above. I've also added a little twist (with the help of WildTangent modeler David Johnson) and the use of a third-party plug-in for max written by Cuneyt Ozdas and Sinan Vural called Texporter (available at www.cuneytozdas.com/software).

The twist is a take on the Morpher approach — without the Morpher modifier. The plug-in is a tool for extracting the UVWs of your mesh and exporting them to a bitmap of your choosing and resolution. After downloading Texporter from www.cuneyt-ozdas.com/software, simply install it by closing max if you're in it and copying the Texporter.dlu to your max/plugins directory. Relaunch max and you'll be able to access it through the Utilities panel T.

For my method, the process goes something like this:

1. Attach all geometry using the same texture map page into a single mesh.
2. Apply an Edit Mesh modifier to the object.
3. Arrange the faces of the mesh to accommodate a planar mapping assignment.
4. Apply a UVW Map modifier and make it a square aspect.
5. Apply an Unwrap UVW modifier to lock in the UV coordinates.
6. Use Texporter to create a wireframe texture map template.
7. Create and apply a material using the template bitmap.
8. Delete the Edit Mesh modifier.
9. Improve the texture in Photoshop and reload it into the material.

This method works because it's simple and it's quicker than the other two. It incorporates the utility of the Morpher technique without actually using it or worrying about having detached the elements correctly. However, like the limitation of a morph object, *never detach* any elements of the mesh after applying an Edit Mesh modifier as you arrange them. This will cause a very big frown on your face when you delete the Edit Mesh modifier at the end of the process and the UVs don't conform to all that work you did (trust me, I know the feeling of that kind of pain). Using Unwrap UVW to "lock" in the UVs is one of those happy accidents you can discover if you spend just a little time in max poking around and trying different things. Texporter can, of course, be used with any technique you want to use for applying the UV coordinates. It just takes *whatever* UVs you've assigned to the mesh and turns them into a wireframe image. Rather than drone on about it, let me show you how to effectively create the right mapping coordinates for Callisto using the Steed Method.

TEXTURING

Load Callisto38.max from the CD.

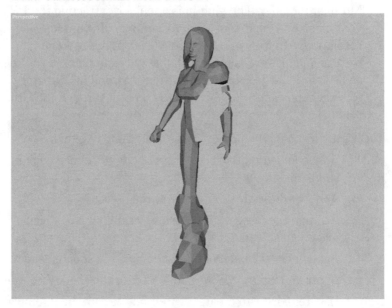

The first thing you'll notice is all the symmetrical parts of the mesh have been deleted and the mesh has been merged into three objects: Head, Bangs, and Body. The Bangs are separate because they will use a different texture than the rest of the body. The Head will use the same texture as the body, but I've not attached it for instructional purposes. It will, however, be attached later.

There are two reasons for merging the rest of the body parts into one object: technical and mapping technique requirements. Technically, it's always a good idea for real-time game characters to consist of as few objects as possible. Individual character parts are usually only separated when they're using different textures, or the parts are separated so they're easier to get to in the animation process.

FYI: MULTI/SUB-OBJECT MATERIALS   Some game engines support an alternative to detaching parts on a mesh to support unique bitmaps: a Multi/Sub-Object material. This is a typical M/SO setup with two slots dedicated for textures:

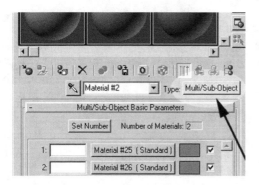

This material type allows you to assign different bitmap materials to different sub-object elements of a mesh *without* detaching them. You can apply as many different textures or material types as you want. Most of the time, regardless of the game engine, the biggest reason you'll see parts of a mesh separate instead of all attached is for ease of weighting and animation.

The best approach is to associate each texture "page" or bitmap image with a single mesh object of the character. A more consolidated mesh allows the game engine to "digest" the object in the best possible way and contributes to making the game run faster. Another reason to attach all the objects into a single mesh per bitmap is that the technique I'm about to show you only works if you've collapsed the various parts into a single object. For example, assigning an Unwrap UVW modifier to multiple objects *will not* allow you to see all the UVWs in the Edit UVWs window at once; you have to select each object separately. This basic limitation applies to Texporter as well (i.e., you can only generate a texture template per object, not for multiple objects).

I've deleted all the symmetrical faces of the mesh for the same reason I would if I were going to make some major tweaks in the model. Why double the work? Once the UVs are set for the mesh, any copied portion of it will have those coordinates as well. However, if the portion is mirrored, the UV coordinates *will not* be mirrored. This way, the mirrored geometry will use the same reference and same texture as the original geometry. Mirroring geometry that uses half a body part image is also a tried-and-true method for saving texture space, keeping the texture page size within reason. Again, if for some reason you don't want a

TEXTURING

symmetrical texture on a mirrored piece of geometry you can easily flip the UVs of the copied and flipped faces using the mirror function in Unwrap UVW. Just rearrange them so they won't overlap the other UVs *before* you reattach the geometry to the main mesh.

The Head

Now let's apply the theory to Callisto's head.

Step 1: Apply an Edit Mesh Modifier

The first step after dividing the mesh into the appropriate objects and deleting symmetrical faces is to apply an Edit Mesh modifier.

> **FYI: *IT'S EASY TO FORGET THE UVW MODIFIER*** Since the Modify panel ⟋ looks the same for an editable mesh and an Edit Mesh modifier, it's *very* easy to forget the first step of this mapping technique. When writing this book, I would first just do what I was trying to show you a couple times, working out the kinks and deciding how I was going to present the information. Believe it or not, I forgot to apply the Edit Mesh modifier about *four* times. Be careful and don't forget! You'll be in for a jaw-dropping disappointment when you spend several hours arranging the mesh and go to delete the Edit Mesh modifier only to realize *it isn't there*.

Go to the Front viewport; hide everything but Head and add an Edit Mesh modifier Edit Mesh to its stack.

Step 2: Arrange the Elements

Next, you need to select and arrange the elements of the head so they can receive the mapping properly. To make it easier, I've preassigned specific smoothing groups to areas of the mesh for a quick way to select and isolate groups of faces (smoothing groups can always and easily be changed later on). Scroll down to the Surface Properties sub-menu for the Face

sub-object 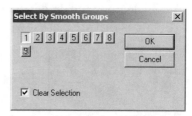, open it up, and hit the Select By SG button in the Smoothing Groups sub-menu.

When the Select By Smooth Groups window comes up, hit the 1 button so it's "lit." Make sure no other number is depressed so only faces with smoothing group 1 assigned to them will be selected and hit OK.

Note that even though there are 32 smoothing groups, only nine numbers appear. This is because the faces of the mesh only have smoothing groups 1 through 9 assigned to them.

Selecting all the faces with smoothing group 1 causes all the triangles of the face to become selected. Hit the Detach button under the Edit Geometry sub-menu to detach the faces to an Element. Zoom out a little and slide the face over to the right of the rest of the head so it's out of the way.

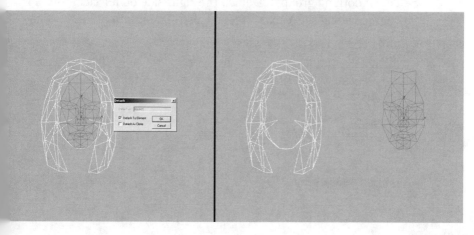

Zoom out a little and turn on Snap ![snap icon]. Select smoothing group 2 next and detach the left side of the face. Rotate ![rotate icon] the element –90 degrees and drag it over to the right. Snap it into place at the vertices that are closest without the two elements overlapping.

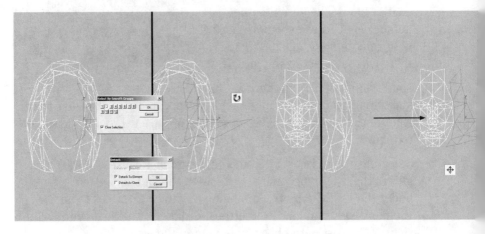

Select smoothing group 3. Detach the right side of her face, rotate it 90 degrees along the Y-axis ![Y icon], and also slide it into place.

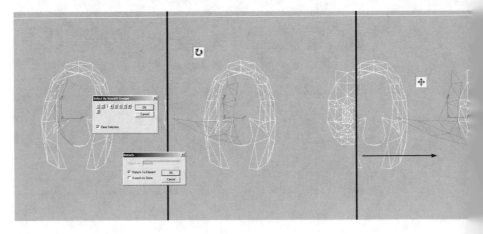

Now, before you create any more elements, select the remaining
geometry of the head and rotate the faces 90 degrees along the
Y-axis and slide them over to the left.

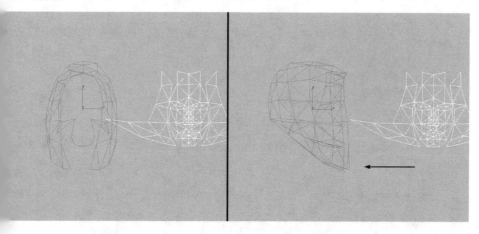

Select the underside of the head by choosing smoothing group 4.
Detach and rotate the element 20 degrees along the Z-axis $\boxed{z}$, –90
degrees along the X-axis $\boxed{x}$, and then another 180 degrees along
the Z-axis. Move it so it rests just below the face.

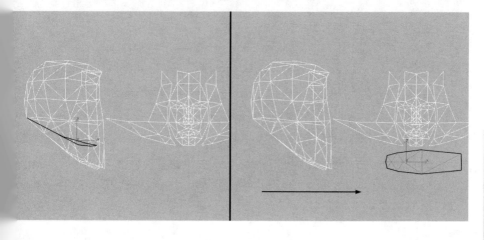

Pan your view to the left a little and select the outer hair elements, highlighting smoothing groups 5, 6, and 7. Detach and move them to the left.

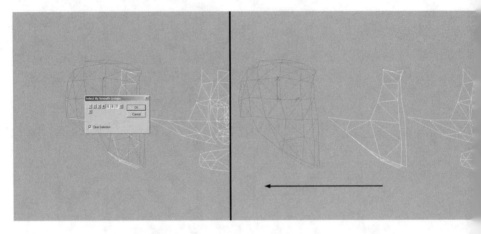

Pan over a bit more, select only smoothing group 7 (the back of the head), detach, rotate 90 degrees along the Y-axis, and position it like so:

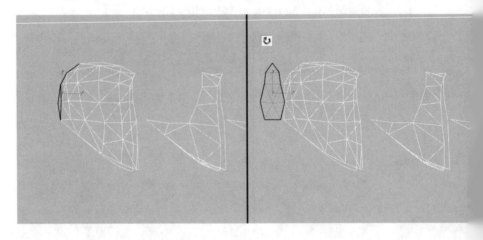

Finally, zoom out a little and select smoothing group 8. This is a group of faces that make up the *bottom* of the hair, and would be easy to miss if you didn't look closely (or build the model). Detach the faces, make sure you're using the Use Selection Center 🔲 coordinate system, rotate the elements 30 degrees along the Z-axis, and rotate them 90 degrees along the X-axis. Position these "slivers" just underneath the remaining element of the head — the *inside* hair geometry.

Now the elements should be nicely detached, laid out, and ready for the next step.

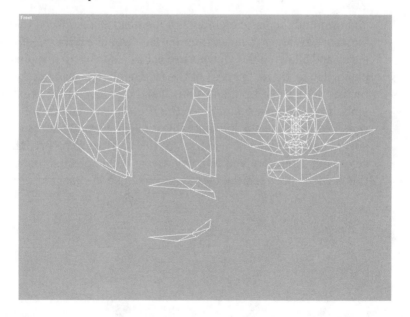

TEXTURING

Step 3: Adjust the Vertices for a Planar Projection

With the elements separated, it's now time to refine the vertices
similar to how you would in Unwrap UVW. Select and hide Hide
all the elements of the head except for the front and two sides.

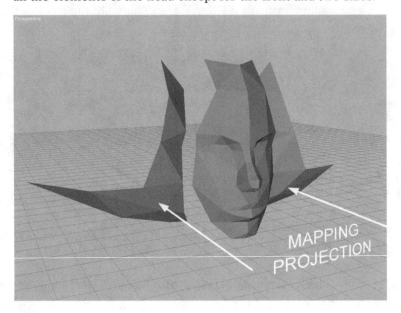

You oriented the basic elements of the head so they faced the Front
viewport, rotating them so their surface would get the most "exposure" and allowing the viewport to act as a surrogate mapping
plane. These three "pieces" of the face need to be arranged even
further so that the front and sides blend together and are textured
smoothly without a seam. Since the Edit Mesh modifier will be
removed from the stack eventually, it doesn't really matter what
sort of deformation you use to align the vertices to receive the most
coverage. Therefore you're going to use Weld Selected to merge
the vertices between the elements and close the gaps.

Go to the Front view. Click on the Vertex sub-object ⊡, set your
Weld Selected value to 10, and alternately select and merge the following pairs of vertices:

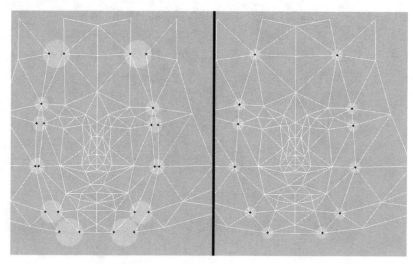

Because the face is curved, it needs to be widened slightly to
accommodate the planar mapping projection, especially around the
nose area. Make sure Use Selection Center is active, select all the
vertices of the face except for the two end ones on either side, and
scale ⊿ them along the X-axis by 110%.

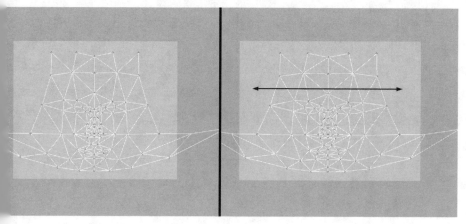

Then select all the vertices that make up the middle of the face and scale them by another 110%.

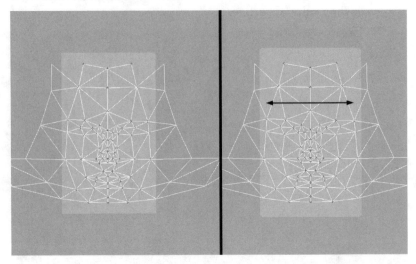

Next, select all the vertices below the bottom of the nose, including those vertices that make up the *bottom* of the nose, and lower them by .5 units along the Y-axis.

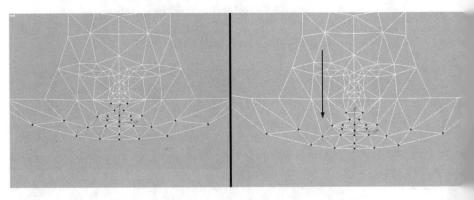

Then scale those selected vertices by 135% also along the Y-axis.

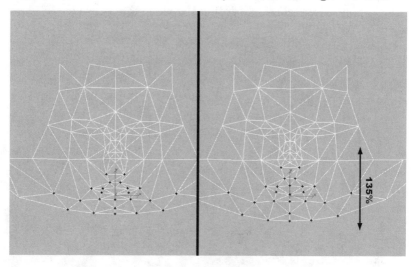

Now compare the following front and profile render of the nose area.

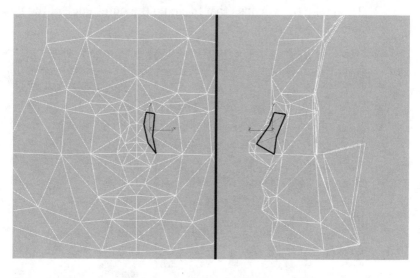

From the front, the faces are narrower than from the side. This means the texture will stretch as it runs across the surface. When adjusting the shape of the mesh, make sure this kind of difference between front and profile doesn't happen.

Since the tip of the nose doesn't really have to be as wide as it currently is, scale those vertices in along the X-axis by 70%.

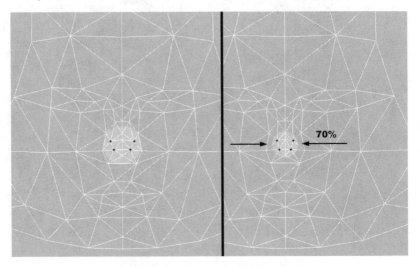

Then take the vertices that make up the outer edge of the nostrils and widen them by 120%.

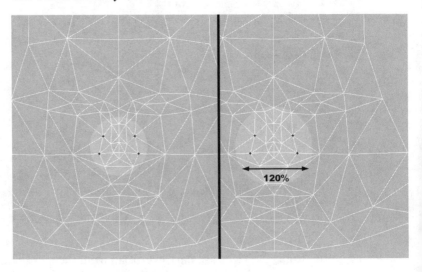

Now compare the front and side again; notice they seem a little closer in relative scale:

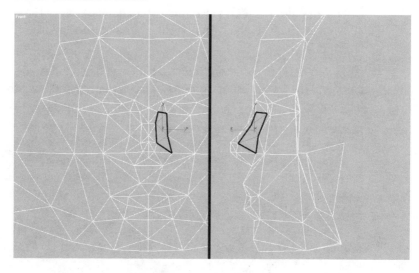

The next thing you need to do is to detach and rotate these four faces 180 degrees along the Y-axis, then move them over to the other side, matching them vertex for vertex since they're basically symmetrical. This saves space on the texture page since they can share the same lower side cheek texture. Just make sure there's no seam from not matching one side to the other.

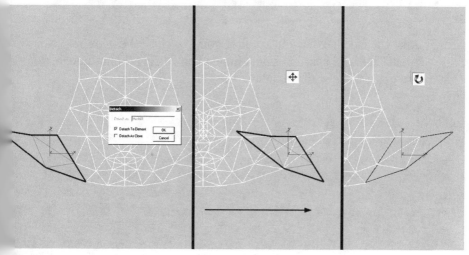

Unhide the rest of the head so you can shape up the other elements as well. The underside of the chin and head element is fine as is. This element isn't seen very much and keeping it near the chin allows you to more easily match the colors of it to the face texture later on.

Now, you need to focus on the hair. Hide the face, underside of the chin, and the two crescent groups of faces that go underneath the hair mass.

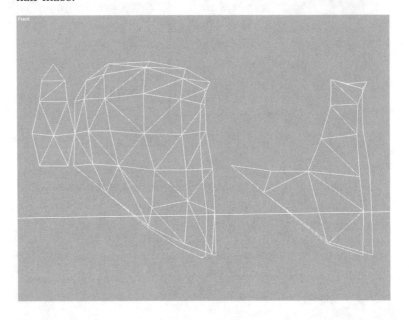

Like the face halves, you are first going to close the gaps between the back of the hair and sides. Instead of welding them, though, you are going to use Snap to adjust the vertex positions.

Pan your view over a little, zoom in to the back hair element, and turn on Snap. Select all the vertices at point 1 and move them to point 2. Then select all the vertices at point 3 and move them to point 4.

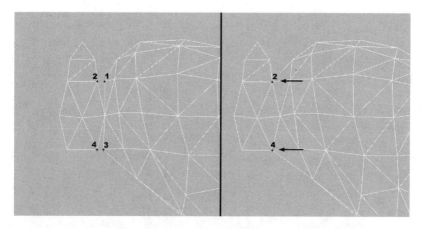

Moving the vertices is better than welding in this case since the back of the hair is a symmetrical group of faces. Using Weld Selected to close the gap would make the right side different from the left. This in turn would affect how the mass of hair facing the back would fit to the back of the hair element.

Now, pan over to the *inside* hair element. You'll notice a line that runs in front of the faces in view. This is basically the edge of the triangles facing the opposite direction (or the other side of the hair). To save texture space, you're going to map the same texture on both sides of the hair. Although the front edge of the hair mass is asymmetrical, for mapping purposes it's better to make the UVs symmetrical. This applies only in a case like this since the difference between the edges isn't that great. The important thing to remember is to use the vertices of the outermost edge as a target to snap to.

TEXTURING

A texture compressed will almost always look better than a texture *expanded*. However, before you move the vertices so they line up on both halves, rotate your view and look at the faces at the *top* of the inside hair element.

The triangles are facing *downward*, so take the top two sets of vertices and move them up along the Y-axis about .8 units and the vertices just below them up .2 units:

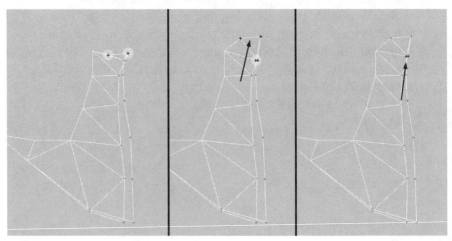

This will prevent streaking. Going back to the leading edge of the inside hair element, line the vertices up, moving the inside vertices to their outermost counterparts:

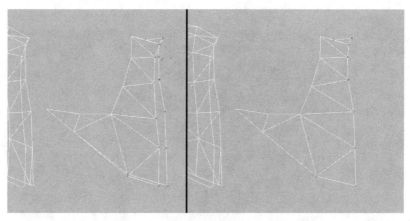

Now, before you do the same for the outer hair element, zoom in to the bottom of the front edge of the hair:

TEXTURING

Hide the inside hair element and rotate your view a little. Now you should see that those vertices at the bottom actually make up the bottom of a triangle on either side of the front of the hair that's facing almost directly to the right.

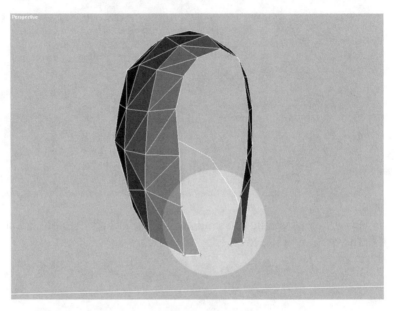

If a planar map were applied from the Front viewport the texture would streak across these faces. An easy fix is to grab the leading vertices and drag them to the right about 1 unit.

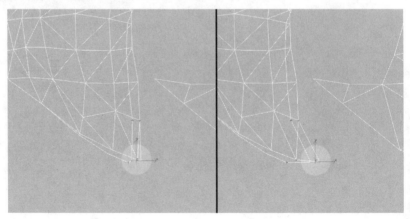

Now, match up the inner vertices of the front edge to the outer vertices of the front edge like you did for the inner hair element.

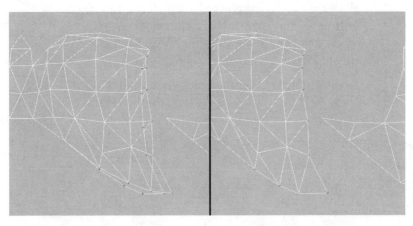

Cool. Now unhide the rest of the elements and arrange them so they look like so:

When arranging the elements, think of them as puzzle pieces. The better you can make them "fit" together, the less amount of texture space will be wasted. Rotate and adjust them however you see fit, but avoid warping the geometry too much or making the pieces unrecognizable when you apply the real texture later.

Step 4: Apply a UVW Map Modifier

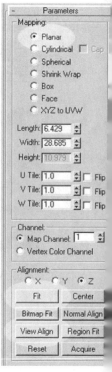

With the head still selected, turn off the sub-object button 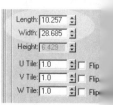 and apply a UVW Map modifier to the stack. Over to the right in the UVW Parameters menu, Planar should already be selected.

Go down to the Alignment sub-menu and hit the View Align button View Align , then the Fit button Fit .

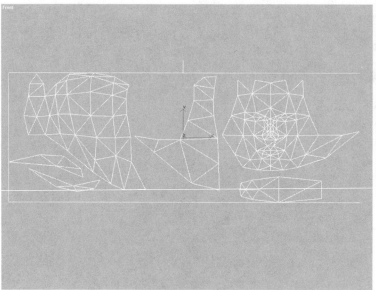

This aligns the mapping gizmo so it's oriented with the current view and snaps to the outermost vertices of the mesh. Over to the right you'll notice the Length and Width values for the mapping gizmo.

Think of the mapping gizmo as your texture page. It can be whatever resolution or value you want, but the aspect ratio is important. In Callisto's case (as with all real-time characters), the texture page is going to be a power of two. Going with a resolution of 1024 x 1024 is ambitious and may seem needlessly detailed. Keep in mind that when she goes into a game engine that image will get knocked down to at least 512 x 512, or even more likely 256 x 256. Having a higher resolution image to knock down in size is *always* advisable when creating characters.

Like a higher poly mesh, a higher resolution comes in handy for those gratuitous screenshots if nothing else! The important thing here is that the aspect of the gizmo be *square*. Therefore, the actual *value* for width and length don't matter at this point, just the fact that they're the same.

Enter a value of 40 for both Length and Width. That should leave you plenty of room for both the head and rest of the body you're going to map.

Step 5: Use Texporter to Create a Bitmap Template

Now you're going to use the Texporter plug-in to generate a bitmap. Again, to install the plug-in after you've downloaded it from www.cuneytozdas.com/software, save your work, quit max, and copy the Texporter.dlu to your max/plugins directory. Restart max and go to the Utilities panel . Click on the More button and select Texporter from the bottom of the list.

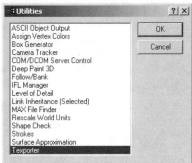

If you don't see it, follow the instructions that come with the plug-in and make sure it's installed properly. Once you have Texporter installed and active in the Utilities panel, go to the Texporter menu and make a few changes to the default settings.

Enter 1024 for Width and 1024 for Height, setting the bitmap size. Set the rest of the Display properties as shown in the adjacent figure.

Leave the Map Channel set to 1 since that's the default map channel assignment in max. Unchecking Polygon Fill and checking Edges with All Lines rendered makes the image easier to see and works better as a template. Leave the rest of the settings as is except for the Colorize by sub-menu. Select Constant and click on the color swatch beside it. Change the color to white.

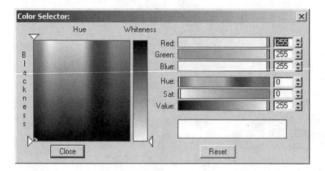

 FYI: *TEXTURE RESOLUTION*   Whenever I texture I do so at double the target resolution. For example, if the texture page is 512 x 512, then I'll create the texture 1024 x 1024. This is in the event you need a high-res render of the character for something special. It's also just a good idea to create a larger than required bitmap since it can be reduced very easily with minimal touchup required to make it fit to the mesh.

Click the Pick Object button 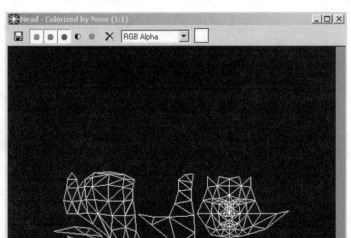 and then click on the head.

An image window should now pop up similar to the one seen when rendering an image in max. You should see a wireframe of the head elements on a black background. Click on the Save icon 🖫 at the upper left-hand corner and save the image as Template01.jpg in the Callisto\Images directory. Keep the quality of the JPEG file high.

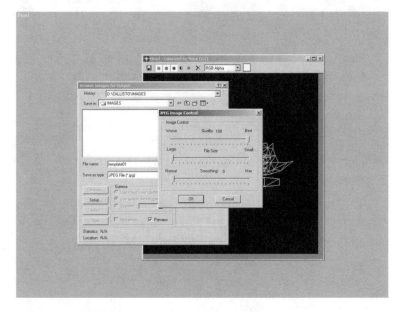

Step 6: Create and Apply the Material

With the image saved, you can now make it into a material, apply it to your mesh, and see if there are any problem areas you need to tweak with the UVs. But first you need to create the material in the Material Editor.

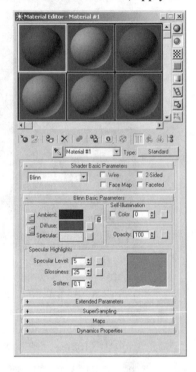

Click on the Material Editor icon ⠿ in the upper right-hand portion of the screen. The menu shown at right pops up.

The first material in the slot will be active and can be renamed to whatever you want. Normally I name the texture after the bitmap it uses, so click where it says Material #1 and rename it to Template01.

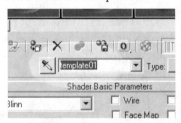

Next, you need to make the material a bitmap material. Go down to the small box beside the Diffuse color swatch and click on it.

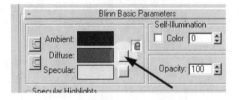

This is a shortcut to opening up the entire Mapping sub-menu, and with real-time characters is all you need most of the time. When you click on the map button, another menu appears.

New should already be marked indicating this is a new material, so
select Bitmap from the top of the screen and hit OK.

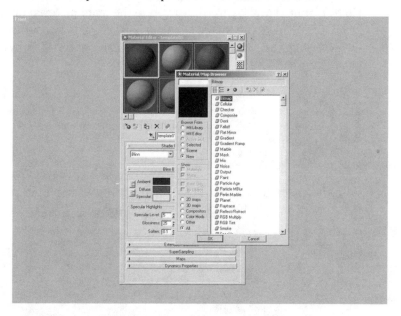

Now max prompts you to find the bitmap (image file) you want to
slot into the map channel. Choose the image you just saved in
Callisto\Images — Template01.jpg — and load it. The menu kicks
back to the Material Editor with the image now mapped onto the
sphere in the material window.

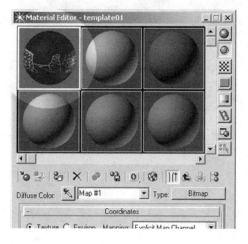

TEXTURING

To make sure you'll see the image when you apply it to your mesh, click on the Show Map in Viewport button ⚙, and then click on the Go to Parent arrow ⬆ to return you to the main material menu. Once there, make the image show up better as you tweak the UVs by increasing the self-illumination of the material to 100% by entering 100 in that field:

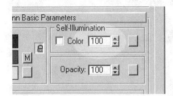

With the character mesh still selected, hit the Assign Material to Selection icon ⬆; the material is now assigned to your mesh.

Pretty cool. I'm taking for granted this is *not* your first texture, but if it is — congratulations!

Step 7: Apply Unwrap UVW and Turn Off Edit Mesh

Now comes the beautiful part about this technique. You're going to add an Unwrap UVW modifier Unwrap UVW to the stack to lock in the UVs and then turn off the Edit Mesh modifier to see what the mapping looks like on your mesh.

First, apply the Unwrap UVW modifier and hit the Edit button Edit... .

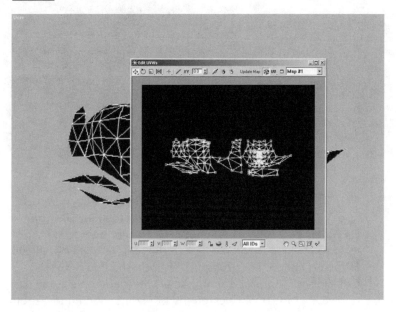

With the Show Map icon active, you'll see that the UVs line up perfectly with the bitmap image.

Now, go down the modifier stack and turn Edit Mesh *off* by (1) clicking on the small arrow beside the current modifier name (in this case, Unwrap UVW). (See the figure on the following page.) Then (2) go down the stack list and select Edit Mesh (the mapping now goes nuts on the objects). (3) Click on the Active/Inactive modifier toggle to turn the modifier off. (4) Click on the small arrow beside Edit Mesh, and go *up* the stack back to Unwrap UVW.

TEXTURING

Your mesh should assume its previous shape and also retain its UVs thanks to the "pinning" of the Unwrap UVW modifier.

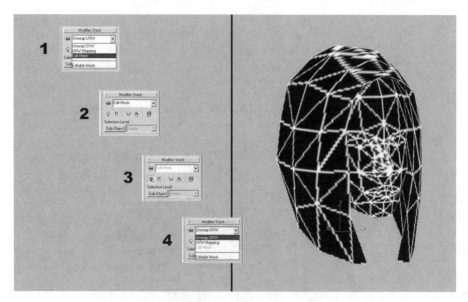

 FYI: *USING THE NEW UNWRAP UVW TOOL*   In max 6 and 7 you have a very powerful tool with the new Unwrap UVW. It is very robust and chock full of neat ways to quickly map your objects. The most powerful feature of it is the Flatten Mapping button. For example, if I had used it to map Callisto's head I would simply select the Head object and apply Unwrap UVW. Click on the big Edit button under Parameters, zoom out so you can see the UVWs in the Edit UVWs window, arrange your viewport view so you can see your mesh, and it should look something like this:

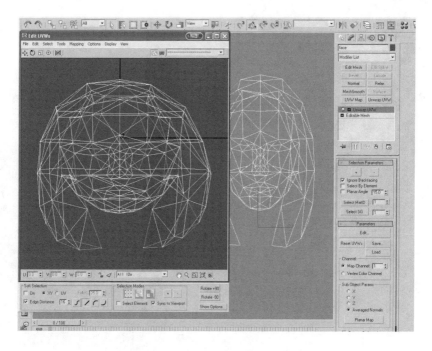

The scale is such with Callisto's Head object that it's way bigger than the outlined mapping space, but that's no biggie. Notice how I did *not* apply a UVW Map modifier first. This is because with the Flatten Mapping feature you don't have to. Go up to the Mapping pulldown at the top of the Edit UVWs window and select Flatten Mapping (1), go with the default settings (2), and hit OK. (See the figure on the following page.) The screen suddenly shrinks down to the normal mapping dimensions that now fit in the outlined mapping area, so hit the Zoom Extents button and the mapping is now "flattened" out in your Edit window (3).

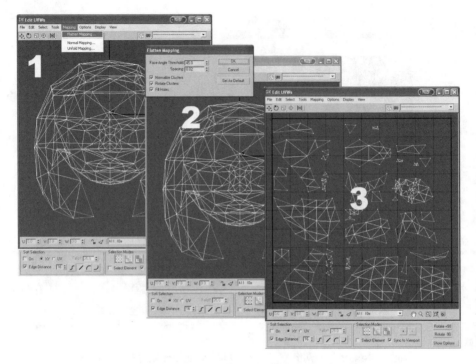

Next you'd rotate, move, and connect the "broken" pieces using a variety of tools in Unwrap UVW like Sketch and Stitch and others until you have a mapping scheme that makes sense and works for you. You can also reflatten the mapping any time you want by going up to the Mapping pulldown and typing in a different value. The higher the number the less the mesh becomes fractured because the value represents an angle threshold between contiguous faces before being broken apart. Compare values of 60 and 90 with the default 45:

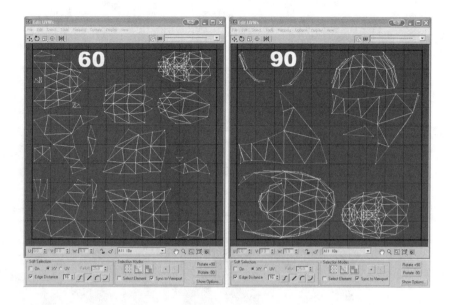

While I like what Discreet and the developers at max have done with this tool, I still like doing it my way by manually breaking the mesh apart. I'm sure once I tried it on a few characters or objects and got used to the workflow it'd be fine, but there's nothing that really compels me to use it extensively. However, I do encourage you to try it and see if you like it.

Step 8: Tweak UV Problem Areas

Turning the modifier off instead of deleting it gives you the opportunity to check your mesh over, fix problem areas (like streaking), and reapply the UVs. The first step, though, is to examine your mesh in a Perspective view, rotating and panning around it and looking for any streaking or warping.

TEXTURING

The most obvious areas that need adjusting are at the top of the head.

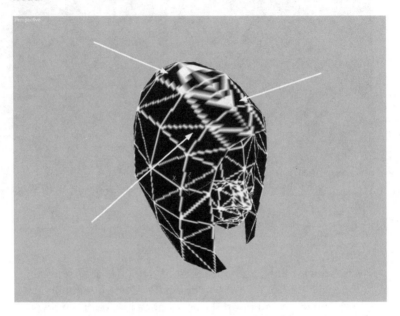

In addition to obvious streaking, look for areas that have *thicker* lines from the render of the wireframe than the lines nearby. This means the pixels are being stretched, which in turn means the UV coverage isn't enough. In the case of the top of the head, you need to compensate for the curve of that part of the noggin and adjust the UVs accordingly.

Delete the Unwrap UVW modifier so the changes you're about to make stick. If you don't delete the modifier, then no matter how you go back down the stack and adjust the mesh, the changes won't appear in the UVs. Go back down the stack to Edit Mesh and turn it back on.

Going into wireframe mode, zoom in to the outer hair element in the Front viewport.

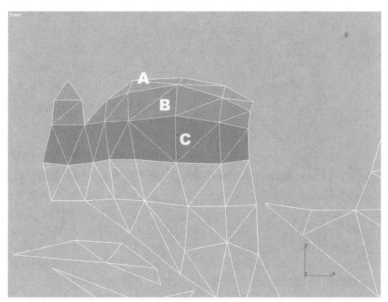

Compare the width of the faces in strips A, B, and C, and you'll see another sign the UVs need adjusting. Since the head is an oval shape, strips A and B need to be closer to the same thickness as C for the UV coverage to be equal. That should be your guiding thought when readjusting the vertices of the mesh.

Move the vertices of the top and back of the outer hair element so they look like so:

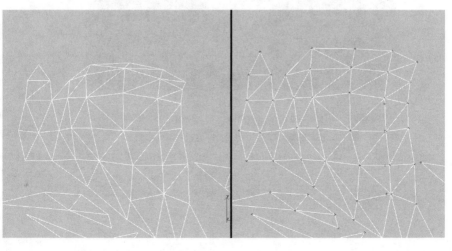

FYI: *USING UNWRAP UVW INSTEAD*   Keep in mind you could've just made the adjustments to the top of the head by moving the UVs in the Unwrap UVW editing window. I just think it's always a good idea to be consistent if you can.

When applying mapping coordinates to your mesh, these back-and-forth adjustments are expected. It takes a while to get the coverage just right, but in the long run it's time well spent. Without proper mapping, it doesn't matter how good a texture artist you are — the character's skin will be lacking.

Step 9: Use Texporter, Make a New Bitmap, and Reload It

Now you need to create a new bitmap to use as your texturing "template." Go back to the Utilities panel; Texporter should still be the active plug-in. The settings should still be the same as before so hit the Pick button active/green and click on the head.

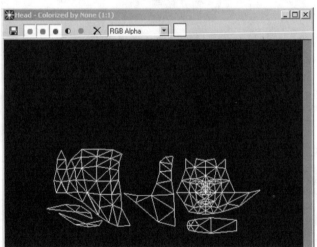

Overwrite Template01.jpg and go back to the Material Editor. You'll now notice a letter "M" in the small box beside the Diffuse color swatch because there's been a mapping type (bitmap) assigned to the diffuse channel.

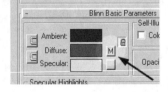

Click on it and it takes you
to the map channel you
applied the bitmap to earlier. Hit the Reload button
and you'll refresh
the bitmap you just
overwrote.

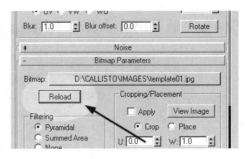

Apply another Unwrap
UVW modifier to the stack
and turn off Edit Mesh again. The top of the head should look
better.

So that covers applying the UVs to your mesh as well as creating
and applying a material that uses an image that serves as a "template" to give you a guide to create a real texture. The next step is
the creation of that more refined image.

TEXTURING

Step 10: Refine the Bitmap in Photoshop

Once the UVs are applied and the template created, you need to go into Photoshop and create the real texture for the character. I'm assuming you use Photoshop 4.0 or higher, but if not, any 2D texture tool that supports layers will work. Load Template01.jpg into Photoshop and copy and paste the entire main image *twice*, creating two additional layers.

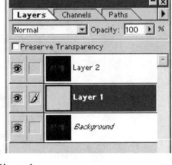

Now go to the middle layer, select everything, and hit Delete. Using your Paint Bucket tool ⬛, fill the empty middle layer with an arbitrary color. (I use a flesh tone since it's for the head, but you can use whatever you like.)

Go to the top layer, deselect everything, and activate your Magic Wand tool ⬛. Under Options, *uncheck* Anti-aliased.

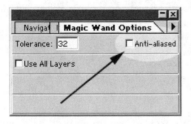

The template for the UVs of the head is white lines on a black background with *no* anti-aliasing. Start with the face part of the template and select each chunk of black texture *inside* the face element by using your Magic Wand tool.

Zoom in to the face element by holding down the Ctrl key and Spacebar at the same time and left-clicking in view (an icon that looks like a little "+" sign inside a magnifying glass will appear; Alt and the Spacebar will zoom *out* when clicking in view). To select multiple areas of black, simply hold down the Shift key when using the Magic Wand tool to click and select.

When you have a few sections selected, just hit the Delete key and the underlying color of the middle layer will show through the white wireframe as shown in the following illustration.

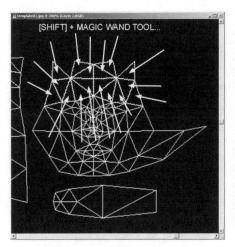
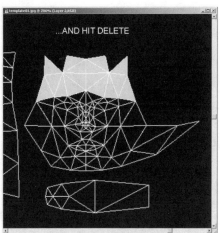

Leave the background black. This will give you a clear contrast for placing the other elements of the body later. Also, by keeping the main layer (Background layer in Photoshop) a copy of the template, you always have it to fall back on in case the top layer is lost or corrupted. Eventually when you're done, you will have a 2D wireframe that serves as an even better template to create a realistic texture.

Here's what the texture for Callisto looks like with the white template overlay. The top template is 50% opaque so the white lines aren't as stark.

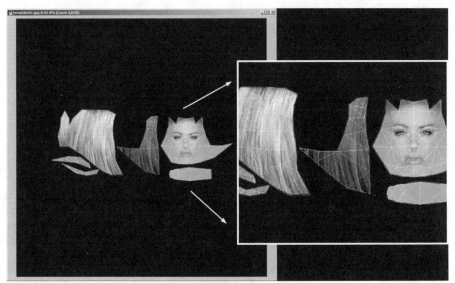

TEXTURING

If you're asking yourself, "Huh? Isn't he going to show me how he actually made the texture?" Unfortunately, no. I'm not going to chronicle how I ended up with the texture for Callisto. That book would be titled *Texturing a Character in max Using Photoshop* and there are too many people out there more qualified than yours truly to write it! Also look for any sites or books that will help you more quickly master Photoshop or your 2D texturing tool of choice.

So even though I won't attempt to teach you how to paint in Photoshop, I *have* hopefully succeeded in showing you a *process* by which you can assign the UV coordinates, give yourself a texture map template, and make that template a functional helper to paint a texture in a 2D paint program like Photoshop. The way I make textures may or may not be the way you do it, but I encourage you to train yourself or receive training on traditional painting techniques. The skills and knowledge you can gain by being around an instructor who understands color theory and how to apply it to a canvas can only make you a better character modeler and computer artist.

I will share this with you, though: Typically when I texture a character, I begin with a scan or combination of scanned *features* like eyes, lips, and hair. Then I blur ⬦. and/or smooth the areas of plain color so they don't retain those "scan artifacts" of random colors that often accompany scans. Finally, I retouch and alter it to fit the template using Smudge ⬦., Airbrush ⬦, Rubber Stamp ⬦., and other tools or filters in Photoshop.

Using scans or not using scans is up to you. I know many artists who do use scans, many who say they don't but are too proud to admit it, and a few purists who adamantly refuse to do anything but unique works of art for every texture they create (of course they have the skills to eschew such scanned images so they're allowed their peccadilloes).

 AUTHORIZED DIGRESSION: *ADRIAN CARMACK'S RUBBER DUCKY* While at id Software I was continually amazed by the pencil and pixel-pushing prowess of co-owner/co-founder/artist Adrian Carmack. He *never* uses a scan and rarely uses reference for anything. Trained as a traditional artist, he spent internships working for morgues where he honed his anatomical mastery made famous in the work he did on *Doom* and other id titles. His raw talent for taking a blank page and filling it up with a bunch of tiny, colored squares

▼

that soon resembled an image rivaling a render from a 3D model has been the source of inspiration for many digital artists. One of the *coolest* pieces of art I watched him create was a DPaint rendering of a rubber duck that sat on top of his monitor. Dubbed his "only true friend" at the time, the duck was painted for a secret area in *Quake II*. The thing that impressed me the most was the speed with which he created it and his unerring eye for a consistent *light source*. Of all the masterpieces this "Frazetta" of the computer game industry has done — wall textures, Barons of Hell, *Quake* bad guys, and even Commander Keen — perfectly reproducing that rubber duck using 12 colors from a fixed, 256-color palette with DPaint in 1997 stands out the most. Adrian, you rock. Thanks for everything — especially for the time and the impetus to write this book!

Step 11: Load the New Bitmap and Tweak the UVs

Load Callisto39.max from the CD.

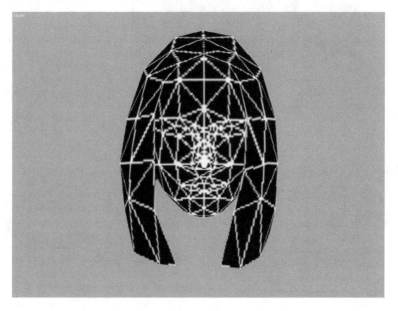

Now you're going to load the refined bitmap for Callisto's head into the material. Open up the Material Editor, click on the M beside Diffuse for the template01 material, and click on the Bitmap path button under Bitmap Parameters.

Instead of Callisto\Images, go to the Callisto\Maps directory on the CD. Click on Callisto1.jpg and the painted image appears in the material sample window.

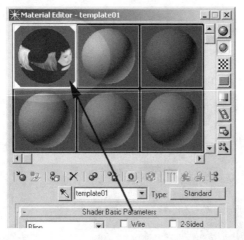

FYI: *IMAGES VS. MAPS DIRECTORIES* I like to think of my Images directory as a temp location for images to be tested or turned into a final bitmap and my Maps directory as the final home for textures that are applied to the character. This makes it easy to identify those important image files versus the throwaway or unimportant image files.

Close the Material Editor and go to a smooth shaded view. Hit F4 to turn Edged Faces on and see how the new image is now mapped onto the head.

Somehow the image is slightly off-center and the face doesn't seem to line up exactly as it should. That's no problem because you have Unwrap UVW. With the head selected, go over to the Modify panel and hit the Edit button under the Unwrap UVW Parameters menu. This will bring up the Edit UVWs window; you should see the UVs with the image assigned to the mesh viewable from underneath. If you don't see an image, click the Show Map icon .

TEXTURING

Use your middle mouse button to pan over to the face just like you would to pan in a regular viewport.

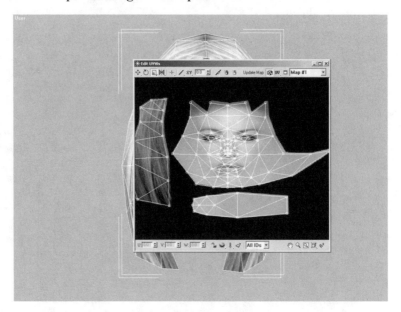

The great thing about the Edit UVWs window is that it can be resized. Move the window to the upper left-hand corner of the view and, grabbing the bottom right-hand corner of the window, resize it so it's slightly larger than the view with as square an aspect as you can make it.

Make sure all the UVs of the "face" are in view.

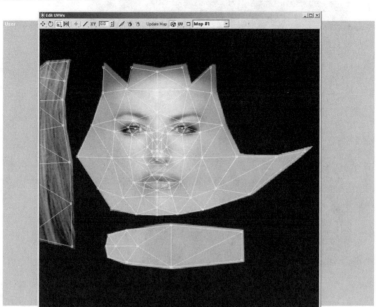

Even with the best planning and the most dead-on templates, the UVs will sometimes need to be tweaked after the fact in order to fit the bitmap. Think of the UVs in the Unwrap UVW modifier as the same as the vertices in the mesh. For example, if the vertices in the mesh aren't attached, the UVs in the window won't be attached. Therefore when you select and move UVs, drag the selection marquee across them instead of moving them individually.

Select and move ⊕ all the UVs of the face (right-clicking on the UVs is the same as in the regular viewport, giving you the three transform choices) so it lines up better with the image. Key on the eyes, making sure the UVs are centered on the face and the UVs are completely covering the texture made for them.

TEXTURING

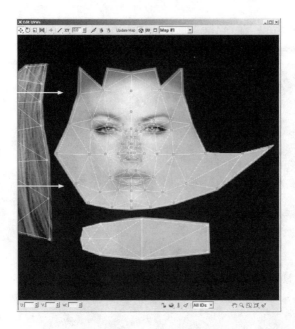

Minimize the Edit UVWs window and now look at the mesh. Turn the view a little in a Perspective viewport and you'll see there's still a little weirdness with the nose.

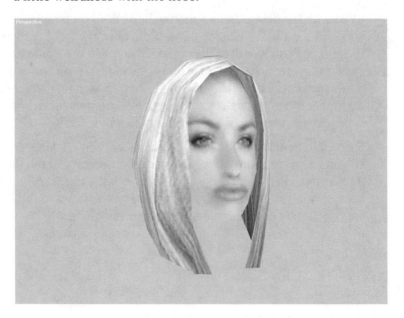

Go back into the Edit UVWs window, and use the Zoom tool to home in on the nose. Drag the following UVs *down* to raise the texture on the nose. Make sure the center eight UVs are just a tad lower than the rest so the soft highlight at the tip of the nose is in position.

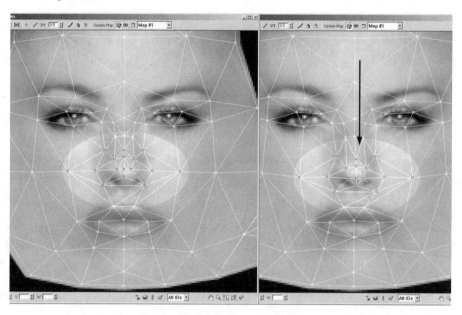

Now when you see the head with the texture on it, it looks better.

Hmmm. Callisto doesn't really look too mean for a butt-kicking her-oine. Let's make her a little less wide-eyed and friendly and give her a nice Eastwood-like *squint*. Resize your UVW window so it's smaller and you can see the mesh at the same time. Select the two UVs just underneath her eyes.

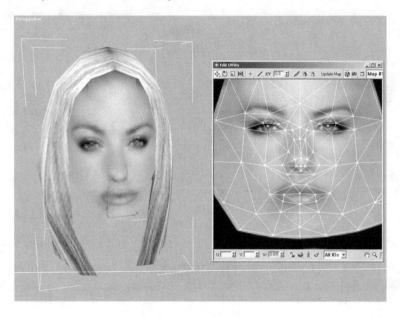

Right-click and hold down the Move icon in the Edit UVWs window, then slide down to the Move Vertical icon ⬍ and click on it. Now when you move the UVs, they will be restricted to going up and down. Drag the UVs down slightly and give Callisto that squint:

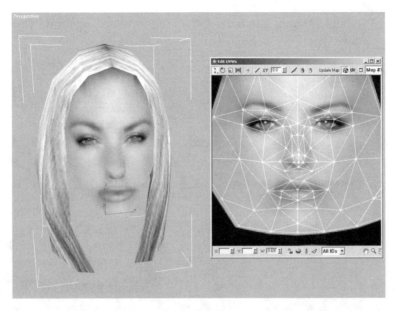

By moving the vertices *down* you squish the texture covered by the UVs, hence giving her a squint. Complete the look by giving her a little bit of a scowl by selecting these three UVs above her eyes…

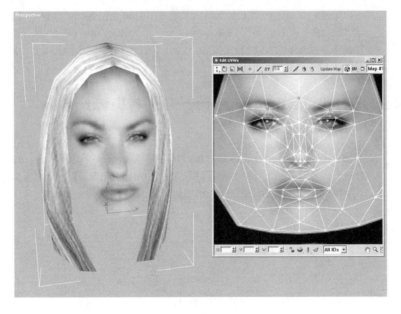

... and dragging them *upward* a little until her eyebrows wrinkle just enough.

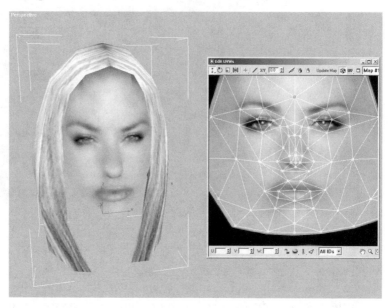

Now, zoom out in the Edit UVWs window and make sure all the UVs of the rest of the head elements are nicely centered on their respective textures. That should do it for the head — but wait a minute. What about the bangs?

Step 12: Assign Mapping Coordinates to the Bangs

Hide the Head and unhide the Bangs. Apply a UVW Map modifier to the Bangs object. Hit the View Align button and the Fit button to center the mapping gizmo on the bangs.

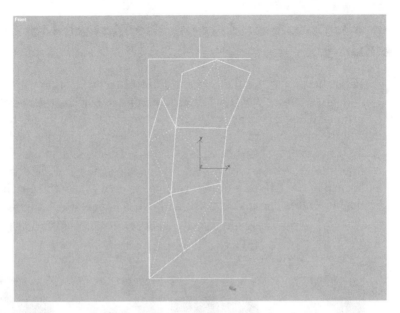

Now, rotate your view to look down on the object and rotate the mapping gizmo –10 degrees along the Z-axis so the planar map is more perpendicular to the surface, resulting in less streakage. Also, change the Length and Width each to 10 to give the mapping coordinates a square aspect (all textures need to be by power of two — mostly a *square* power of two, remember?).

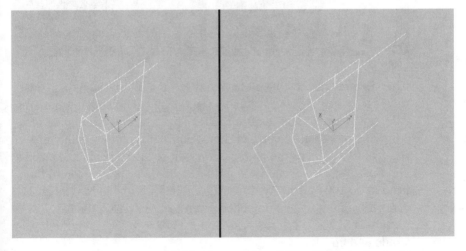

Go to Texporter and this time make a 256 x 256 wireframe image to serve as a template for your final bangs bitmap. Call it Template02.jpg and save it in your Callisto\Images directory.

Step 13: Create and Apply the Material to the Bangs

Paint the texture for the bangs in Photoshop by starting with a black and white cutout where white is the hair and black is the background. This serves as both another template for the bangs texture and the opacity map. An *opacity map* is a way for part of a texture to be transparent; in this case, it's to create the illusion of hair falling in front of the face. With an opacity map assigned to a material, the bitmap in the diffuse channel will appear only where the opacity map is white. The less white it is the less opaque the bitmap becomes until it's completely invisible wherever there's black. Once the opacity map is done for the texture you can create the hair texture knowing where to make it conform to the cutout.

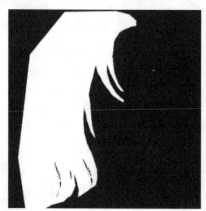

Keep in mind, there doesn't have to be any black in the bitmap, just the opacity map. I just put it in to see the shape better. As a general rule, try to extend the texture past the borders of the template just a little so there's no chance of the background color creeping into the real texture. For the high-res version of the bangs I used a 256 x 256 texture page because it's closest in relative comparison to the head in its 1024 x 1024 texture page. When it's applied to the character in-game it will get knocked down to 128 x 128 if the base texture is 512 x 512. If the base texture is 256 x 256, then the bangs would end up 64 x 64.

Go back to max and load Callisto40.max from the CD.

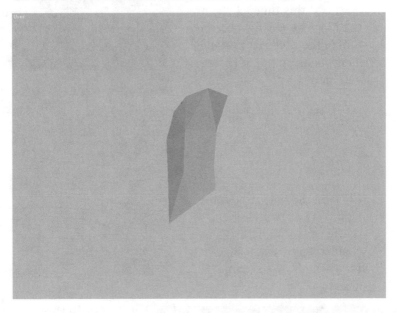

Go to the Material Editor and create the new texture for the Bangs mesh. Typically I start additional materials for a character by just dragging the first material window to the material slot beside it and renaming it. In this case, rename it to "bangs" for the bitmap you're about to load called Bangs.jpg.

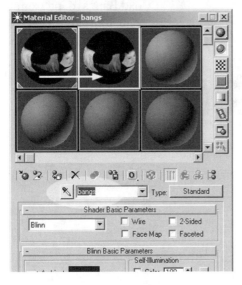

However, instead of clicking on the M this time, click on the Maps button near the bottom of the Material Editor. This opens up the full Maps sub-menu.

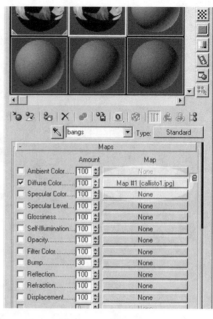

Click on the button next to Diffuse Color where it currently says, "Map#1 (Callisto.jpg)" and load Bangs.jpg from the same directory:

Hit the Go To Parent button to return to the main material menu and click on the None button beside the Opacity channel. Double-click on Bitmap and load Bangs_o.jpg from the Callisto\Maps directory on the companion CD. Now the material window shows hair with transparency wherever the opacity map is black.

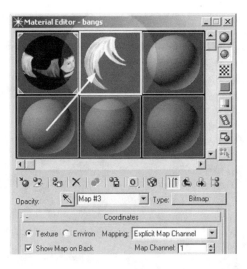

Assign the material to Bangs, unhide Head, and apply an Unwrap UVW modifier to the stack. Hit the Edit button, and arrange your view so you can see both the head and the Edit UVWs window.

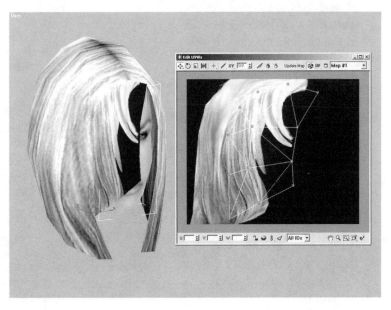

The UVs need a little bit of tweaking to match the bitmap. Move the UVs over so they encompass the texture better.

TEXTURING

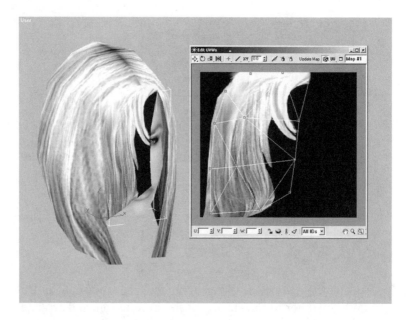

Now, even though you can't tell from the way the model looks in the viewport, render it and you'll see the effect of the opacity channel on the UV-tweaked bangs.

With the head done, that wraps up the blow-by-blow, in-depth coverage of laying in UVWs, making a texture, creating a material, and applying it. If you want, load up Callisto41.max to see the finished result.

All the steps and approaches to taking care of the head will work for the rest of the body as well. In the next (and last) chapter I will briefly cover the mapping and texturing of the rest of the character, explaining how and why I came up with the particular layout for each body part. However, I won't be going into the same detail as I have in covering the head.

CHAPTER 13
Mapping The Rest Of Callisto

The head was a great place to start texturing because it was an isolated piece of geometry that was relatively easy to explain. Now comes the trickier part of setting up your UVs for the rest of the body. Since there are so many different ways to skin the proverbial cat — er, *model* — I want to reiterate that this and any skinning technique is subject to scrutiny and/or improvement. Use what I show you but I encourage you to explore any method you come across.

Minor Adjustments...

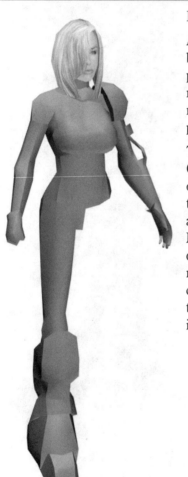

Load Callisto42.max from the CD.

Another reason for texturing the head before the rest of the body is that it compels you (at least it does me) to get the rest of the model textured. It should make you want to see how the complete package is going to look!

The first step in texturing the rest of Callisto is to detach her body into a series of elements. This paves the way for using the technique I just showed you, but can also be done when you apply the Edit Mesh modifier. However, before I break down the body into its appropriately organized pieces, I want to go over some changes I've made to the model in order to help with mapping the UVs and to improve her shapely shape.

First, hide Head and Bangs and notice the way I've deleted the left half of the legs and boots. These areas will be copied and mirrored later on using the same texture page real estate. Also notice the substantial structural change of moving the vertices at the waist so they form the top line of her pants. Compare the tweaks to the original design.

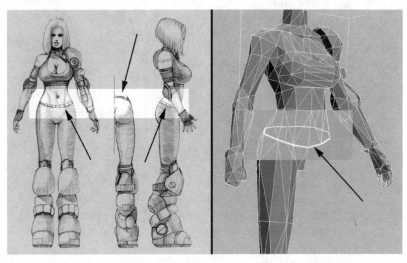

This is for texturing convenience and the fact that where possible I try hard to let the geometry make the dividing line that could be done solely with a texture. Using both geometry and texture just makes the effect that much more *effective*, resulting in cleaner separation between body parts. Delineating geometry like this also makes it easier to apply a different *shader* effect when called for.

FYI: SHADERS   The term "shaders" is just another name for materials. Often when applied to a character or other in-game object, bitmaps can have additional attributes like procedural reflection, glows, and electrical "crackling energy" effects. These attributes have to be applied usually after exporting the character from max. Most complex shader effects rely on hardware acceleration and the particular game engine being used.

TEXTURING

Another area I adjusted to fit the design that could have been accomplished with just a texture is the top she's wearing. Hide the arm elements and you can see the new line that separates her shirt line from her exposed midriff.

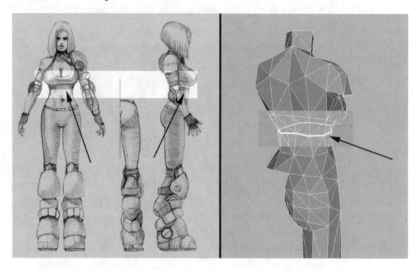

While those tweaks were made for texturing convenience, the next tweaks were made after thinking about how to subdivide the mesh before texturing it. Unhide all the hidden elements and hide just the shoulder pad. I've made a couple more optimizations to the left shoulder and neck strap region:

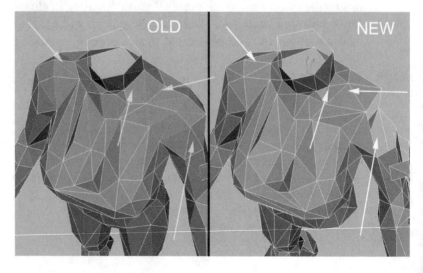

I chopped about eight triangles because there were a couple being effectively hidden by the shoulder pad that I didn't catch while optimizing the model. The texturing logistics of getting to the little top edge of the neck strap wasn't worth the hassle either so I merged it to the neck. I also rounded the neck with the addition of a vertex at the left juncture point. With all those optimizations I gained a few faces to apply elsewhere (hey, if they're there, use 'em!).

Thusly, since I wasn't really happy with the way we took so much off her (ahem) frontal chest region, I put them where they'd do the most good — her *rack*:

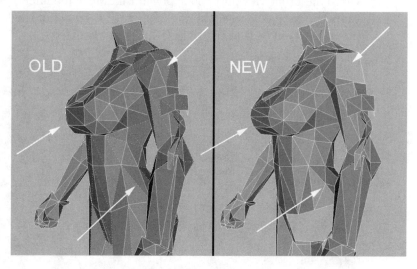

Can't have a rack without a decent back so I added another segment to the hips as well, making them more rounded and feminine. This is to take away from the boxiness it had before. These changes are minor but worthwhile since the mesh is still right at 1,500 triangles.

TEXTURING

Creating a Quick and Easy Leg Texture

Now that I've explained the structural changes I made in preparation for the initial texturing process, I'm going to introduce you to a little trick for making a quick-and-dirty leg texture. It's also a way to generate a starting point or base texture for most body parts (in addition to your Texporter template).

Step 1: Apply an Edit Mesh Modifier

Go to the Front viewport and apply an Edit Mesh modifier [Edit Mesh] to the Body object. Select all the elements [⬚] *except* for the leg and move [⊕] them over to the right (you'll see why later).

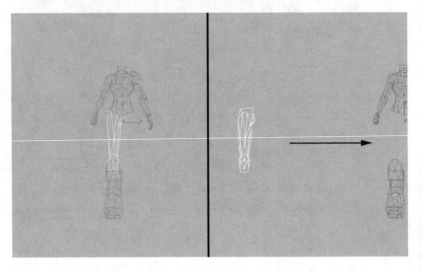

Hit the Hide button [Hide] on the sub-object menu and zoom in [🔍] to the leg geometry. For the sake of expediency I've already detached the faces of the leg (and rest of the body) into the appropriate elements. Take a moment to study the various sub-sections of the body if you like.

The following exploded view illustrates how I broke the leg apart:

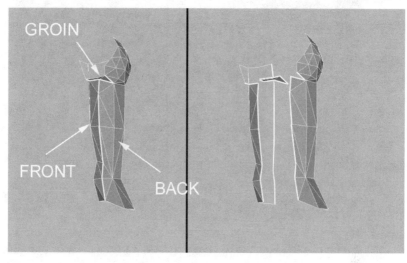

The front and back pieces are easy enough to understand but the groin patch of triangles represents those few faces that are at 90 degrees to the other two elements. Detaching them is the best way to gain texturing access to these polygons. An easy way to determine how to split a piece of geometry like this is to look for the dividing line or seam that makes the most sense where an object could be broken apart. However, even if you forget to factor them in when you build the model, don't be afraid to adjust the geometry after you thought you were all through. Tweaking the character *during* the texturing process is sometimes a necessity if you want to give yourself the best UV coverage.

Step 2: Position and Adjust the Elements

Now you need to position the pieces. You should still be in the Front viewport. Select and move the rear element over to the right and rotate 🔄 it 175 degrees along the Y-axis 🅈 . Drag the groin faces over to the left and rotate them –90 degrees along the X-axis 🅇 as shown in the following illustration:

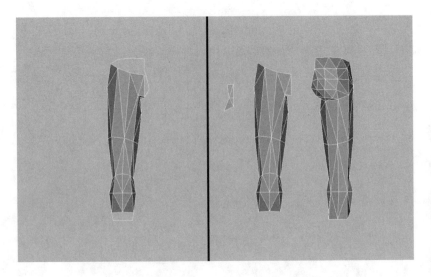

Since the leg is curved, give yourself more access to the outer side faces as seen from the front by simply scaling [icon] the two major leg pieces each 150% along the X-axis.

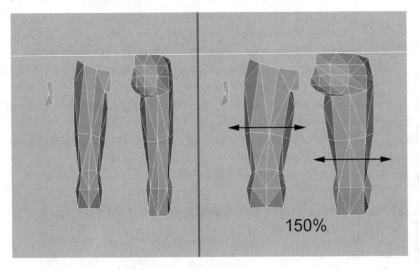

This step isn't really necessary, but it does compensate for the fact that faces on the side of the leg are thinner as seen from the Front view and widening the structure is the quickest and easiest way to provide more texturing access.

Step 3: Apply a UVW Map Modifier

With all the leg elements selected again, apply a UVW Map modifier UVW Map . Hit the View Align View Align and Fit Fit buttons and enter a value of 48 for Length and 64 for Width.

Step 4: Make the Bitmap Template with Texporter

Create a bitmap template for the leg geometry by going to the Utilities panel T and clicking on Texporter (hit the More button and fish it out if you haven't added it to your button set yet). Make the Image Size 640 x 480 (hence the 48 x 64 mapping gizmo dimensions) and select the options shown in the Texporter menu to the right.

It's *crucial* you make sure Only Selected is checked when dealing with a mesh like this when other faces are hidden. The rest is up to you and your personal preferences. I like white lines on a black background, but you may want to experiment with black lines on a white background, etc.

 FYI: *CHUGGING DOWN TEXPORTER* I've found that *not* checking the Only Selected box with a mesh that only has mapping coordinates assigned to *part* of it makes max chew on the image-making process in Texporter a verrryy long time. In fact, the program seems to hang forever and may even crash on you. It may be a wise idea to save before using Texporter for only *part* of a mesh.

When you have the settings how you want, click the Pick Object button ▢ Pick Object ▢ and click on the leg elements/Body mesh.

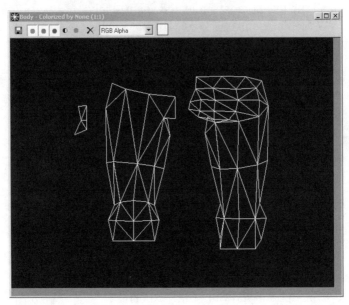

Save the image as Legtest.jpg in your Callisto\Images directory.

Step 5: Align the Mapping Gizmo to the View

Next, still in the Front viewport and with the leg elements selected, go over to the Modify panel 🖉 and click the Sub-Object button yellow and active.

The mapping gizmo will light up and become selected, allowing you to do any of the typical transforms you would to a regular object.

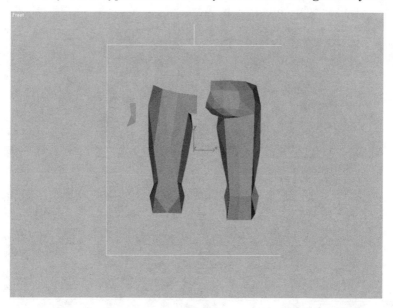

You want it selected so it's easier to see. Now, go up to the left-hand corner of the viewport and right-click on the word "Front." Slide down and click on Show Safe Frame.

Now you'll notice three concentric line boxes in the viewport. On the outside it's ochre, indicating the dimensions of the current rendering settings. The next two boxes are for rendering images to video. The green one is the "safe" frame used for a typical video image and the pale blue box (smallest) is for video *title* images.

 FYI: _SAFE FRAME EXPLAINED_   The reason for the overlap is that many broadcasters intentionally "overscan" video images when playing them back. This results in some of your rendered image being "cut off" around the edges. I mainly use Safe Frame to see what the rendered real estate will be.

TEXTURING

Slowly zoom in and pan 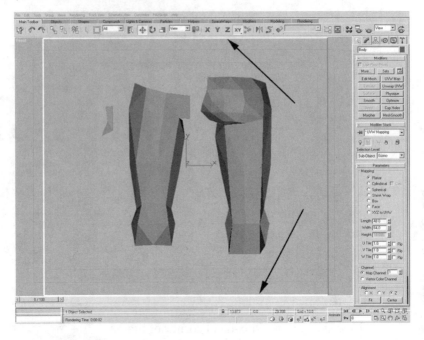 the view until the top and bottom edges of the mapping gizmo touch the top and bottom of the viewport (outer ochre line of Safe Frame).

Aligning the gizmo to the view allows you to get a rendered image as close as possible to the same aspect and same relative size as the bitmap template made in Texporter.

Step 6: Merge Lights into the Scene

While the default lights in max are great for seeing your mesh as you create it, sometimes it's best to set up your own custom lights to get the desired effect. Go up to File|Merge and load Lights.max from the CD's Meshes directory. Bring in the two spotlights from the file by highlighting Spot01 and Spot02 and clicking OK.

Your scene is now lit. I've basically created a *key* light that shines from overhead and slightly to the left and to the front. The *fill* light is down and to the right to simulate radiosity and provide an interesting highlight. I won't go over lighting any more than that since the manuals have very thorough sections on the usage of lights, cameras, and materials. Now the scene seems much more brightly lit.

Step 7: Apply a Material

Now that you have lights, it's time to assign a material to the leg. Click on the Material Editor icon ⬚.

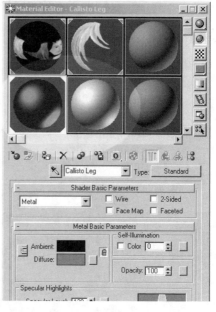

You'll see two new materials already made for you in the material window: Callisto Leg and Callisto Skin. Make sure Callisto Leg is active and assign ⬚ it to the selected Body mesh. Close the editor and you're just about ready to render the scene, but first you need to...

TEXTURING

Step 8: Set the Background Color to Gray

Before rendering the image, go to Rendering|Environment and change the background color to a value of 200 or light gray.

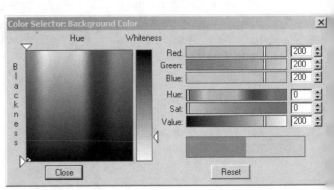

This ensures the UVs will be visible in the Unwrap UVW editing window later on.

Step 9: Render the Scene

Click on the Render Scene icon ⚘ at the top of the menu beside the Material Editor icon. This brings up the Render Scene menu.

Click on the 640 x 480 button 640x480 (if it isn't already clicked) to make the current render those dimensions. Hit the Files button Files... under the Render Output sub-menu.

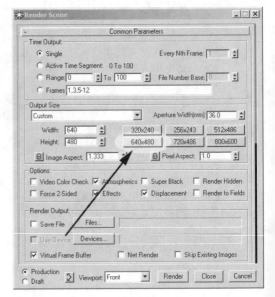

When the dialog box pops up, tell max to save the image under your Callisto\Images directory as Legtest2.jpg.

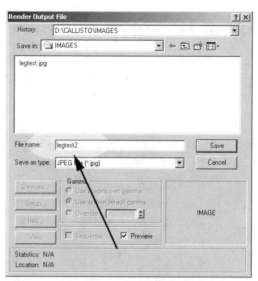

Hit the Render button Render on the Render Scene menu or hit the lone blue teapot Quick Render (Production) icon to watch max render the scene.

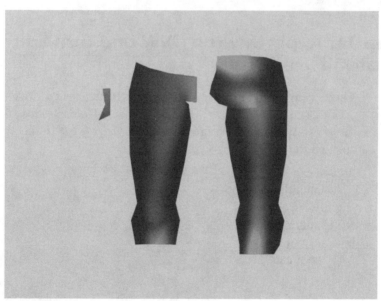

The leg is now rendered in a metallic red, shiny material.

 FYI: *RENDERING OBJECTS WITH HIDDEN ELEMENTS*
Rendering an object in max results in *all* the elements being rendered — even if they're hidden. You moved the other elements of the body out of view earlier to prevent them from being rendered in this step.

TEXTURING

Step 10: Create and Apply a New Material

Go back to the Material Editor and create a new bitmap material using the image you just rendered. First drag the Template01 material in the upper left-hand corner of the Material Editor over to the bottom right-hand corner and rename it Legtest3.

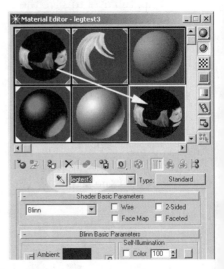

Load Legtest2.jpg into the material channel and apply the new material to Body.

Step 11: Apply Unwrap UVW and Turn Edit Mesh Off

The texture doesn't line up exactly, but that's all right. In addition to pinning the UVs to a mesh, Unwrap UVW can also be used to adjust the UVs. Apply an Unwrap UVW modifier Unwrap UVW to the mesh and click on the Edit button Edit .

As you can see, the UVs and bitmap are slightly off. Select, scale, and move the UVs so they line up with the image.

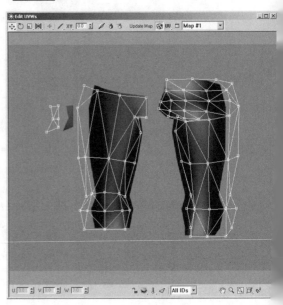

Make sure there's a little bit of image overlap so none of the gray background shows up in the texture.

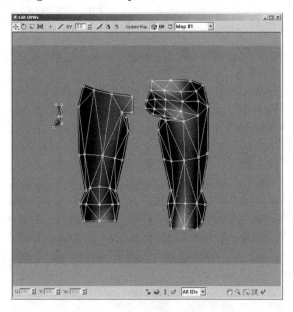

Now, go down the stack and turn the Edit Mesh modifier off. Delete your lights, turn Safe Frame off by clicking on it again, and you'll see that the texture is snugly wrapped onto the leg part of the mesh, looking to all the world as if it's still being lit by the spotlights you merged earlier.

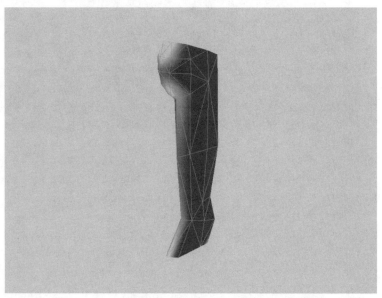

TEXTURING

Again, this a quick and easy way to get a texture started. Of course it needs work, but at least it's a beginning! Now it's time to break down the rest of the body and show you the final textures.

Arranging the Body Pieces

When you applied the UVs to the head, you used one Edit Mesh modifier. For the body, this is still the case, but since there are so many elements, it's better to arrange them into body *parts* first. Save the mesh you've been working on if you want to refer to the "quick texture" technique later on.

Reload Callisto42.max so you can have a fresh start. Go to a Front viewport again, select Body, and apply an Edit Mesh modifier. This time, however, move the elements around so the various body parts are easy to get to before arranging their respective elements.

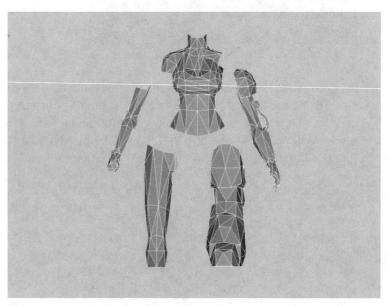

Step 1: Arrange the Torso Elements

If you deform the geometry too much trying to get the best UV coverage it becomes difficult to "see" the shape of the body part as you texture it. Still, even before you think about altering the shape too much you need to arrange all the pieces into a logical order. Hide all the elements except for the torso and arrange *its* elements like so:

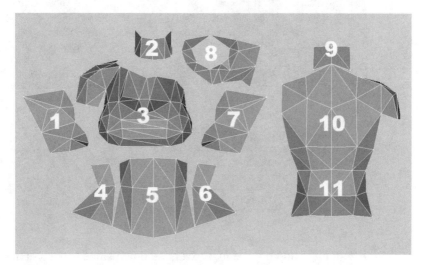

Element 1 is the right side. It could have been with element 7 but since the back and abs aren't symmetrically mirrored halves, it's best to keep the sides separate as well. However, if the texture page starts getting crowded, these two pieces can be merged into one to save space. The chest element (3) is facing forward to make it easy to recognize. The sides of the torso (4 and 6) can also be merged like 1 and 7 if necessary. Element 5 is the abs and like I mentioned, it's best to avoid symmetry if possible (in my opinion at least); that's why this element wasn't split down the middle. Detaching the neck strap and top of the torso and rotating it to face forward (8) allows for access otherwise denied. The back elements (9, 10, and 11) are best kept together since the back is so flat. However, keeping the lower back (11) detached allows for adjusting the UVs later on to provide a nice dividing line between clothed and bare skin. Same goes for the abs (5).

Once all the pieces are arranged in a basic pattern, the surfaces that are facing to the sides need to be tweaked to give them more coverage.

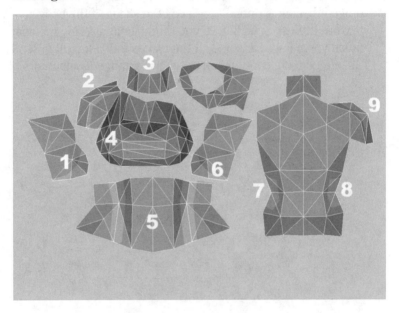

Elements 1 and 6 were just extended down since those vertices at the bottom of the sides were so far back along the Y-axis (as seen from the front). Element 2 is the shoulder area and it needed more coverage because it was basically the top of it. The sides of the neck (3) were scaled outward to receive more texture coverage. Scaling the outer edges of the chest (4) gives more square surface for texturing as well. The sides were welded to the abs (5) and the sides as seen from the back (7 and 8) were scaled outward to fit better into the front sides. Finally, the shoulder (9) was extended to get more surface coverage.

Step 2: Arrange the Leg Elements

I've already covered how the leg should be arranged and why, but here are further refinements to the leg.

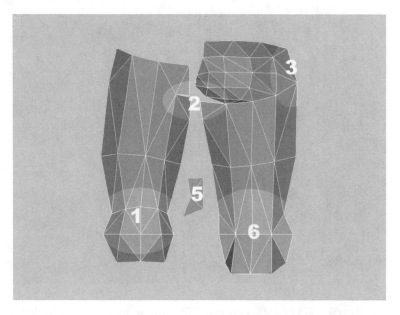

In addition to arranging them so each half faces forward and the groin strip is rotated to face front, some additional vertex tweaking around the sides of the leg halves gives more access to those areas. The knees (1 and 6) were expanded to expose some hidden faces tucked away along the side. The area around the groin and top of the leg under the cheek (2) was pulled out and down to expose those hidden triangles. The top of the outer hip was tweaked (3) as well as generally widening the groin (5).

Step 3: Arrange the Right Arm Elements

The right arm was pretty easy. Here's how it needs to be laid out:

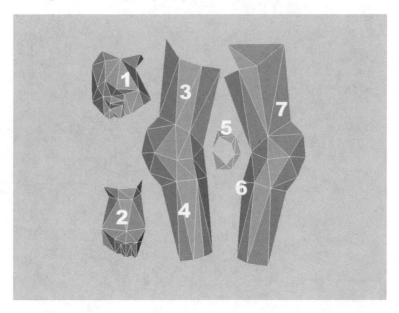

The fist (1) is detached and split into an inner and outer hand. The vertices of the knuckles for both elements 1 and 2 were extended to compensate for being tucked under and those faces turned so that they're perpendicular to the viewport. The upper arm (3) was widened and the inner arm (7) had to have a couple of vertices brought away and down as well as generally be widened. The elbow pads were enlarged slightly to compensate for the curvature and the forearms (4 and 6) were given more texture coverage by widening them.

Step 4: Arrange the Left Arm Elements

The left arm is definitely more complex geometry, but its layout is fairly straightforward:

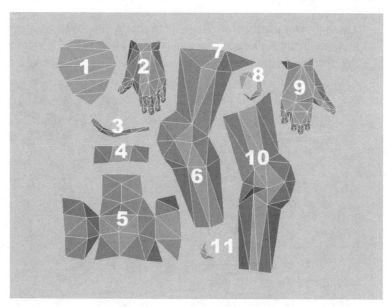

Element 1 is the back and underneath flat surfaces of the shoulder pad. They were scaled down because they don't really need that much resolution (they're hidden most of the time by other geometry). Element 2 is the outside of the hand. The fingers needed to be lengthened just a little to compensate for them curving away from the view. The small tubing element (3) doesn't need any attention except to be as flat as it can, facing the view. The ends of the armband (4) were stretched out to give more access to the curved faces. Element 5 is the rest of the shoulder pad with the center being that element as seen from the side with the front (left), top (top), and back (right) elements welded to it. The inner arm had to be widened at the elbow and wrist (6) like the other arm, but a vertex at the top (7) had to really be stretched outward to expose that lone triangle. Element 8 is just the top of the hand and will rarely be seen. Facing the view as flat as it can, the palm (9) still needed the outer edges pulled away so those surfaces could get texturing coverage. The outer arm (10) was tweaked like the other arm halves with the elbow joint and its forearm plate top exposed for better coverage. Finally, the end of the forearm had these four faces (11) that are mostly obscured by the top of the hand.

Step 5: Arrange the Boot Elements

The boot is a pretty complex design that's supposed to appear faceted and heavy. The approach here is to keep the gross shapes together so that when textured, the pieces are easily seen.

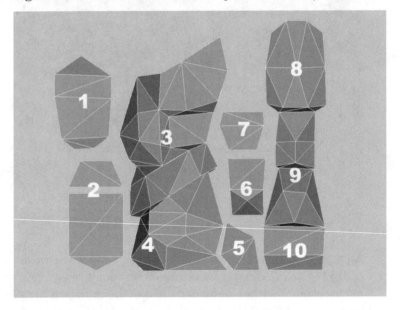

Element 1 is the very top of the boot where the leg inserts into it. The sole (2) is an important element since Callisto will more than likely put it in some interesting place, leaving a nice imprint of her feelings at the time. The sides (3) are practically identical in shape and geometry. Since they're going to be mirrored, it may be better to give each side a different texture, but since the shapes are so close, what the heck. The sides of the toe (5) are also similar in shape so they can stay intact, sharing the same texture. Rotating the top of the toe slightly in the X-axis as seen from the front (6) gives more surface exposure. Element 7 is the inside part of the toe that faces the boot and can be shrunk if necessary since it will hardly ever be seen. The big huge knee cover (8) is going to turn out cool with all that texture surface, and the rest of the boot front (9) is well exposed as well. Finally, the hidden surface behind the toe (10) won't require much in the way of texturing, but still — it's there.

Step 6: Arrange the Elements and Assign the UVW Map

With the elements all arranged per body part, now they all have to be situated to fit together in a big square texture page. With the head already done, it will be a little tricky for the character to have only one bitmap applied to it. The best thing to do in that case is to roughly arrange the pieces so a UVW Map modifier can be applied to them. Then, position the head's UVs roughly to match the space left in the body's UVs and attach the head to the body.

Unhide all the elements of the body and roughly place them so they fit within a square border leaving a strip at the top for the head.

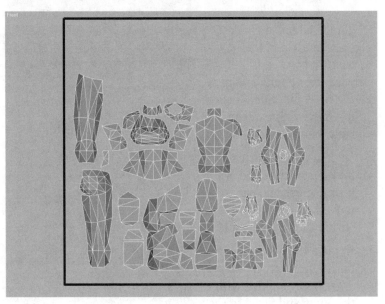

Unhide the head and double-check the layout of its UVs using an Unwrap UVW modifier.

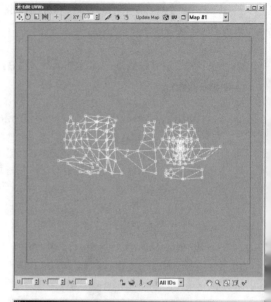

The head takes up a rectangular strip of the texture page so it'll fit in with the general layout of the body just fine — once it's moved up into the right-hand corner, that is.

Of course this means the texture for the head is now useless and has to be moved up there as well within the bitmap itself.

Apply a UVW Map modifier to the Body now. After being aligned with the View and fitted to the dimensions of the mesh, it needs to be squared with a value of 105 for both Length and Width.

Select the mapping gizmo and move it along the X- and Y-axes
so the elements rest near the bottom left corner.

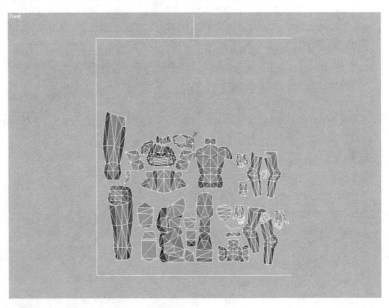

Step 7: Attach Head to Body and Reorganize the UVs

Apply an Unwrap UVW modifier to Body and turn Edit Mesh
off. The body snaps back to its original state with mapping coordinates intact. Apply another Edit Mesh modifier to Body, unhide the Head, and attach it to Body. Apply another Unwrap UVW to Body's stack and click on the edit button.

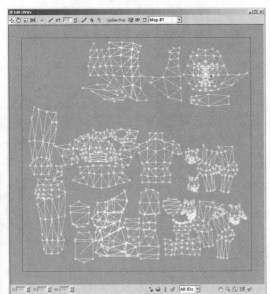

Turn the background bitmap image off by hitting the Show Map button and look at the new distribution of UVs for the composite mesh.

TEXTURING

When arranging the UVs on a character like this it's best to think of them as "puzzle pieces." They need to fit nicely together with the least amount of background or "dead" space between them. In their current state, Callisto's UVs fit a little too easily within the UVW background "square."

The most effective way to reduce all that empty space is by *increasing* the size of the body UVs by scaling them up a bit.

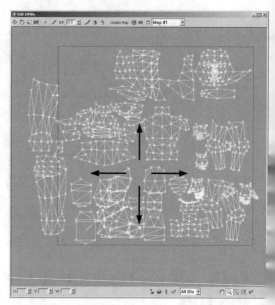

This way they take up more space and cover more of the texture page. Don't worry if the UVs spill off the borders of the square. Once the pieces are moved around they will be back on the page.

Speaking of rearranging, the head elements that were mapped previously can be moved so they fit more tightly by moving them up and over to the right-hand corner.

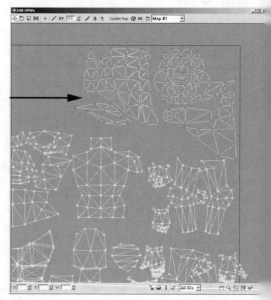

Of course, this means the corresponding texture has to be adjusted even more than it would have before. Next, move the torso and leg pieces up into the upper left-hand corner.

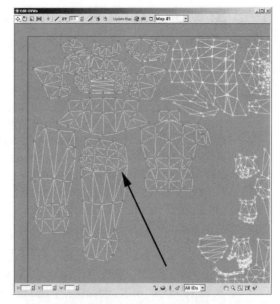

This frees up a substantial chunk of texturing real estate so that the rest of the body can easily be situated within the texture square. Finally, after giving it some thought and experimenting with various combinations of moving, turning, and scaling the UV elements, the figure to the right shows how they ended up.

Note I actually did end up mirroring ⋈ the sides of the chest area and combining them into one texture. There will always be some texture waste, but with some thought and planning the pieces can fit nice and snug.

TEXTURING

Step 8: Make a New Bitmap Template with Texporter

With the UVs all taken care of and the mapping in place, it's time to make the bitmap template so the *real* texturing fun can begin. Start by loading Callisto43.max. Right-click on the Body mesh and convert it to an editable mesh by highlighting and clicking on Convert to Editable Mesh (no need to have any extra modifiers around and it's a clean start for the next phase of creating the character).

Go to the Utilities panel next and bring up Texporter again (it should still be active from the last time it was used).

This time set the image size to 1024 x 1024 and *uncheck* the Only Selected box (otherwise, only the faces that are selected on the mesh will be used to generate a bitmap template).

Save the image as Callisto_base in your Maps directory.

Step 9: Create and Apply the Template Material

Click on your Material Editor icon, change the Template01 material to Callisto_base, replace Template01.jpg with Callisto_base.jpg, and assign it to Body.

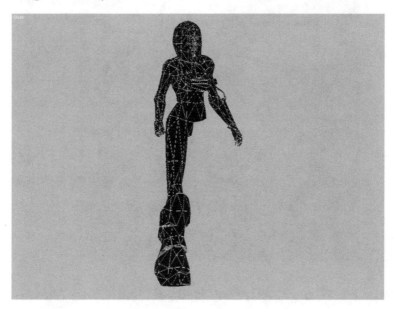

Voilà. Now she's ready to have her face adjusted and the rest of her texture created in Photoshop.

Step 10: Create the Final Texture/Material

For me, making the texture for a character means having both max and Photoshop open, and going back and forth between the two programs. I work on the texture in Photoshop, creating layers as I go — adding colors, highlights, and other details — and building the texture up. I use Photoshop's powerful History feature to alternately flatten all the layers, save the image as a successive number of versions of the bitmap, undo the flatten to restore the layers, then pop over to max, reload the bitmap, and see how it's shaping up. I easily do this 50, 80, or even 100 times before I'm finally through!

TEXTURING

Swapping this image for the bitmap template image automatically applies it to the mesh. Be sure to rename the material to whatever name the final texture ends up being.

Step 11: Copy, Mirror, and Attach the Missing Geometry

Now that the texture is finished it's time to copy, mirror, and attach the geometry that's missing from the model and weld it back to the body.

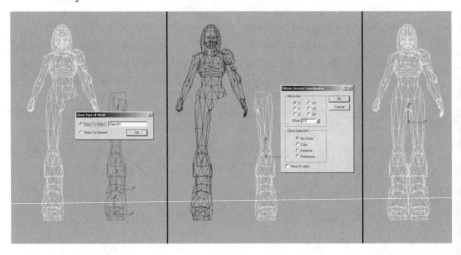

Now that she's whole once more, Callisto is looking pretty niiicce.

Now our femme fatale is fully "clothed" and ready to go forth and kick some digital butt, frag some bad guys, and generally not be embarrassed because she's only in *wireframe*.

So, with the texture applied to the character using 100% illuminated ("full-bright") material, notice I've added some manual highlights, painting them into the texture itself. In real life we don't walk around with highlights painted on us, but for dramatic effect and emphasis on shape, it's necessary to apply some degree of shading and highlights. However, don't go *too* crazy with highlights and shadows on a character's texture. If, for example, you put a shadow underneath a character's arm, then as a 3D model it will look like a dark stain or smear when the arm is raised. The same goes for the inner thighs and underneath the neck. While some shading is necessary, be smart when applying the amount of shading and remember it's designed to be lit and rendered *real time* in a game engine.

TEXTURING

That concludes the part of the book devoted to texturing and consequently finishes the creation of a single character from start to finish. I hope you've gleaned some useful information and helpful techniques in this paltry tome dedicated to character modeling. Now on to my Final Thoughts...

FINAL
Thoughts

In this second edition of *Modeling a Character in 3ds max* I've tried to give you an updated tweaking of a book that hopefully will work with any version of max from now until 10. I also hope it makes you think and expands your thoughts on making real-time characters.

My order of preference when it comes to making real-time game characters is: animating, modeling, designing, and texturing. The reason for this is simple: teamwork. I have no problem with others texturing my models or building a model based on someone else's design. It's not that I can't texture or design, I just know I can find many more people more talented than I am to do those two things. It's just really hard to find someone who is tops in every aspect of character creation. They're out there but they're few and far between. But imagine if instead of competing with the artist next to you to conceive, model, texture, and animate each of your own characters you instead combine your abilities and come up with an even *better* character.

I wrote this book because I simply couldn't find one like it. In the end it is more of a glimpse into the mind and methodology of how a professional game artist makes a character. If you're reading this and you're working for a game company, consider writing a book yourself. Your contribution to the rest of your peers and aspiring hobbyists cannot be overstated.

When designing a character I draw on a wide range of sources and inspirations, but mainly I make something when I think it's just plain *cool*. When showing you modeling techniques, I've concentrated on the polygonal, low-level tools available in max. The techniques and tips I've presented are the ones I have used to create hundreds of models over the past nine years. This book has been primarily about sharing the way I do what I do with you — the artist, designer, or hobbyist who wants to get over the hump and learn a few things about making characters. I want you to wear this book out — dog-ear some pages as you refer to a section more than once. In other words, I want you to *use* it.

As you go forward in your modeling career, never stop learning and never stop asking others questions. Always be there for someone else in need of a little help and don't ever be covetous of your "secrets." I learn things all the time simply because I *ask*. Writing this book taught me a great deal about a program I use every day but have barely begun to explore (seems that way, anyway).

Finally, here's some food for thought and a sort of summary of what I've covered. Keep them in mind when you use the material I've presented to create your *own* Callistos and other models that will one day perhaps inspire you to write a book about their creation. Good luck and good modeling!

Design

- One of the most influential factors on a real-time game character's design is *limitations*. Polygon count, animation system, and design document specifications are just some of the limiting factors for capping the ambition of your designs.

- Another overriding consideration when it comes to character designs is to make it *cool*. Cool is usually defined by your personal taste combined with how well the character fits into its game world or environment.

- The importance of anatomy and proportions can never be stressed enough, and there are plenty of ways to hone your figure drawing skills like life drawing and copying photographs.

- It's important to practice drawing frequently and develop your skills in order to communicate your designs to others and have a clear idea of what you want to turn into a 3D model.

- Reference material and other artists can provide that initial spark or continued inspiration for creating awesome characters for real-time games.

Modeling

- Never be intimidated by a tool like max or any other piece of software. The learning curve is sometimes steep, but it is a *curve*. Time and perseverance will get you over the hump and you will eventually chuckle at the frustration you felt at the beginning of the learning process.

- Always use reference, whether it's a quickly doodled sketch tacked on the wall or carefully prepared orthographic drawings scanned into your computer. Working out the shapes and function of the parts of your model beforehand in your head will only make the modeling process faster and more effective.

TEXTURING

■ Tracing your reference images into a 3D line drawing for use in any angle can assist you in building the mesh better than just a dropped-in background image.

■ Start your character by building the head. This allows you to think about the character, instilling a little empathy for it. As crazy as that sounds, making a memorable character starts with putting effort into giving it life, giving it a consistent look and feel. When it's animated, the feeling of life and attitude is more apparent, but the process starts with the model.

■ When possible, make use of the primitives max has to offer. There are 10 standard and 12 or 13 (depending on your version) extended primitives to choose from with highly customizable parameters.

■ A geodesic sphere is much more effective than a normal latitude-longitude sphere. In silhouette, it describes a much rounder shape usually with fewer polygons.

■ If your mesh is symmetrical, build half at a time, copy, mirror, and attach it, merging the resultant cotangent vertices. Sometimes it's necessary to copy, mirror, and position a *reference* copy of the mesh that allows you to work on one half and see the results on both halves as you build it out.

■ As a low-level polygonal modeling tool *nothing* is more powerful than edge manipulation. Turn Turn edges to shorten line length and to get rid of any concavity at the surface.

■ Working in one window gives you more visible real estate to look at, while working in a Perspective viewport will give you a more intuitive approach to modeling your character.

■ A faceted shaded mode will point out surface problems like unseemly creases and edges that need turning. Faceted with Edged Faces turned on can allow you to see edges and vertices better when working in a sub-object mode.

■ It's important to think of your character in terms of gross geometry, breaking it down in your mind to as basic a shape as you can get it and then adding the detail where appropriate.

■ Extruding a shape or face is another way to quickly build a model. It works great for a variety of body parts including hair.

■ When building a head, try to add a little asymmetry to the face to avoid an unnatural quality that results from a perfectly mirrored half.

- Using Surface Tools (Surface and Cross Section) is a great way to build any type of mesh but is more suited for high-res organic shapes. The great thing about it, however, is the ability to use a spline cage that gives you the power of describing any level of curve and translating it instantly into a mesh.

- Boolean operations are quick and effective ways to combine objects into a unified mesh, but come at the cost of much cleanup and optimization. You can increase the effectiveness of a Boolean by making sure the two shapes involved are optimized for the operation.

- Use Soft Selection to adjust parts of the mesh in a pliable fashion, scaling or moving vertices in one area to influence the vertices surrounding it with diminishing influence based on distance.

- Make it a habit to collapse the stack of modifiers applied to a mesh if you don't need to reference them later on. It's been my experience that large stacks can make max unstable and you run the risk of crashing the program and losing work.

- One of the key tenets I ascribe to when I model is to establish the rough mass of the shape I'm after and then tweak it into the desired shape.

- Knowing anatomy is crucial to good character modeling. Take the time to study the anatomy book of your choice, but at least be familiar with why various body parts look the way they do.

- Right-clicking on any active transform icon will bring up the Type-In Transform window that allows you to enter values for move ⊹ , rotate ↻ , or scale ◧ .

- Use Snap to align parts of a mesh to be attached or to align vertices correctly based on a template object.

- Keep in mind the character will have to be animated and factor that into the mesh as you build it by adding enough vertices and faces at joints like the elbows and knees to accommodate deformation during movement.

- Hips and shoulder areas are some of the most difficult areas on a character to animate so pay special attention when building them.

- You can change the object color of any mesh by simply clicking on the color swatch to the right of its name on most of the command panels in max.

TEXTURING

■ When geometry overlaps and you need to delete faces underneath others, it's sometimes easier to select and delete edges instead.

■ Cannibalizing other max files to quickly add parts to your current model is a widely used and accepted modeling technique. Sometimes it's even beneficial to have a standard character mesh that serves as a source for a hand here or a leg there. Simply merge the object you need and fit it to your current design.

■ Lofting a shape along a path is a great way to create tubing and wires. Make the object even more natural looking by adjusting additional attributes like Scale and Twist.

■ Another form of cannibalization is to use a high-res object as the template to build a lower-res version. Simply identify the vertices that are absolutely crucial to building the lower polygon representation, copy them, make the vertices visible, and build the faces like a 3D version of "connect-the-dots."

■ Optimizing a mesh entails much thought and understanding several key reduction concepts. The overriding principle behind optimization is to identify and keep important features of the mesh that, when reduced, still impart the intent of design.

■ In the Utilities panel T, the Polygon Counter is a great way to watch the face count of your mesh and set targets during the building and optimization process.

■ Optimize your character body part by body part, doing your best to keep an overall even face distribution throughout.

■ Sometimes it's necessary to pose your character, snapshot that pose, and optimize it (like turning a hand into a fist) in order to reach your target polygon budget.

Texturing

■ "Texturing" and "texture maps" refer to applying an image or bitmap to your mesh using a program like Photoshop.

■ UVW represents the mapping coordinates of a mesh and is named after the three letters preceding the Cartesian coordinate designators XYZ.

- Most of the time, mapping coordinates for an object are referred to as "UVs" because the "W" doesn't really get used unless you're dealing with an automatic or procedural mapping scheme.

- When it comes to tiling UVs, think of the V as being vertical and you'll remember the effects of applying a larger or smaller number to U or V.

- The two ways to apply mapping coordinates are via the Generate Mapping Coords. check box or the UVW Map modifier.

- When using the UVW Map modifier, the most common types of mapping to use are Planar and Cylindrical.

- Unwrap UVW is a powerful way to adjust and refine your mapping coverage.

- "Skinning" your character simply refers to the application of mapping coordinates and subsequent painting of a bitmap texture or "skin" that makes the character look more realistic.

- There are many different ways to skin your character, but the method I prefer involves adding an Edit Mesh modifier to the mesh, detaching and placing the triangles in logical groupings so they face forward, and then adjusting their placement even further so the geometry receives the most "exposure" it can get using the Front viewport as a mapping plane simulator.

- Smoothing groups are an additional way to group faces together as selection sets.

- Texporter is a great plug-in for max that quickly generates a bitmap "template" for you to paint the full texture in a program like Photoshop.

- When texturing the character, apply a material that is 100% self-illuminated to give you the best view on how the mapping coordinates and the final textures are being applied.

- Using scans or not using scans is up to the individual artist. If you do use scans, make sure you integrate the image into the map so that it doesn't look like a cheap cut and paste job.

- Finally, never be afraid to go in and tweak the UVs after you have made and applied even the final texture. It's your model to do with as you see fit. Tweak, tear, push, and pull that thing into shape any way you can to ensure the best results!

TEXTURING

APPENDIX
Building Cover Callisto

I hope you've found the preceding chapters and the creation of the real-time Callisto useful. Hopefully, you've gotten over any humps you felt you were stuck upon in your bid to become the greatest character modeler of all time.

I had a lot of fun making the higher resolution cover version of Callisto for this second edition of *Modeling a Character in 3ds max*. As I did, I found myself using tools and techniques that I didn't cover earlier, so I felt this would be an excellent opportunity to share some more techniques with you. I can't go over how I made the cover version of Callisto from start to finish, but the following are the more useful and interesting tools to consider next time you make that perfect character.

Using the Push Modifier

One of the modifiers in max you don't see used too often is Push. It's perfect for making tight-fitting clothing, so I used it to create cover Callisto's top. First I selected my base model and hid all the faces except for the top torso geometry. Then I created a line to roughly represent the sport-bra top.

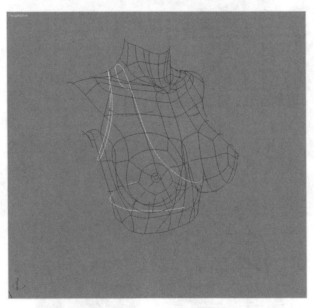

While I could use the spline to make the top via Surface Tools, it's easier and faster to use the existing geometry and MeshSmooth. So I deleted the MeshSmooth modifier and copied just enough torso geometry to approximate the top delineated by the line. Then I shaped the copied geometry by cutting, dividing, turning edges, and welding vertices.

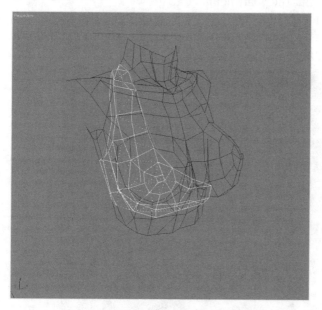

Because I didn't want to delete the underlying geometry and follow a "clothed" analogy all the way, the top as is won't work because many of its vertices and faces are identical to the underlying geometry. This would cause problems when you went to render it because they would "Z fight," i.e., the renderer wouldn't know which triangle to draw first in the geometry that overlapped. Here's where the Push modifier comes in — it basically "pushes" geometry *outward* (or inward with a negative value). So I selected the modifier from the pull-down menu list...

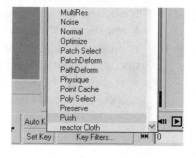

...and applied it to the sport-bra half. To get it to work I typed in a Push Value of .01, but this setting always depends on your scale.

Trial and error will determine the best number, but the goal should be to grow the geometry just enough so it won't Z fight with the underlying geometry. With the setting entered, the geometry grows outward accordingly:

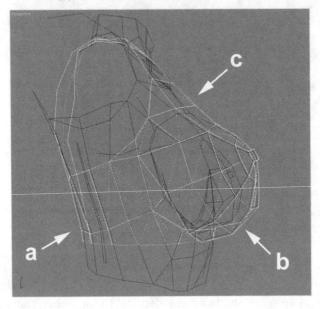

Notice the small gap that's created between the top and the geometry beneath (a and b). I manually adjusted the top part so it looks like it resembles taut cloth (c). Next it's just a matter of mirroring a copy, attaching it to the first half, welding vertices, and making any necessary adjustments to the geometry so the underlying geometry isn't pushing through. Assign another MeshSmooth modifier to both objects and a two-sided material to the top and voilà...

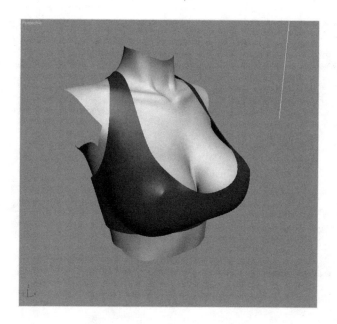

...cover Callisto is no longer topless! It took about half an hour to make it and it works because of the Push modifier. Naturally if this were for in-game use, the Push modifier wouldn't be necessary and the two objects would be merged and optimized like we did earlier in Part II for the real-time Callisto.

Using Slice Plane

Another useful tool that's always been in max is Slice Plane. It's a quick and easy way to create a line in your geometry based on a plane in XYZ space. I used this tool to create cover Callisto's pants line. First I selected the object, then made the edge sub-object active, and hit the Slice Plane button (a). (See the figure on the following page.)

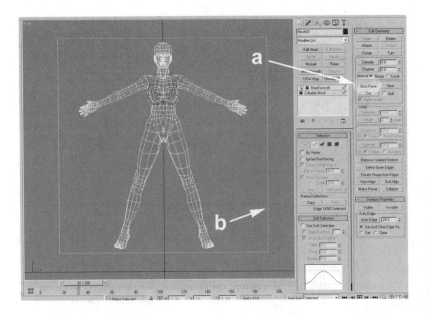

Notice the yellow square gizmo-like...gizmo that appears (b). This is your slice plane. Now it needs to be moved and rotated according to where you want your new line to appear. I went to the Side view and positioned it to approximate the top of her pants.

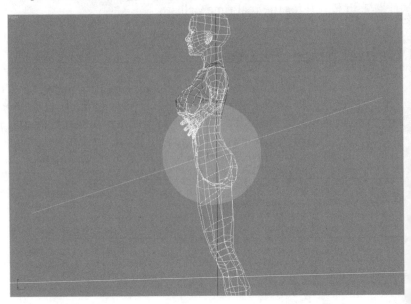

Then I simply hit the Slice button (next to the Slice Plane button), and a new line of edges appeared where the plane bisected the mesh.

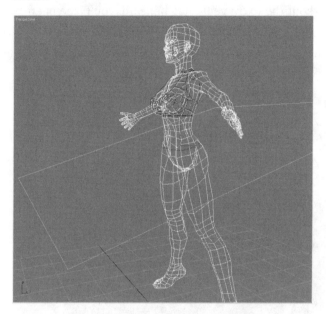

I deleted the vertices above the waistline, applied Push, and had instant pants. For the main geometry I didn't need to keep the underlying legs so I deleted the faces I didn't need but kept the immediate line of triangles closest to and beneath the pants line.

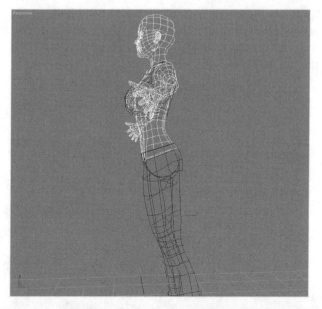

TEXTURING

I kept these triangles because with the Push modifier and the tweaks to the pants geometry to make it seem more like an article of clothing, there's a slight line around the pants you can see down into. Without the extra geometry beneath, you'd see open space instead of say...a thong...thong geometry, I mean. ;o

I applied the same material as I did to the top, and the pants are off to a good start!

There are many instances in which you can use Push. For example, if you've ever tried to render an image and make it look as if it's in wireframe you might get annoyed by the fact you can see through part of the mesh.

Hmmm. I *think* that's Callisto under all those lines.

In the past I've been anal enough to divide the wireframe up into pieces determined by what occludes what, render them in layers, and then recombine in Photoshop. Total pain in the ass. Now if you were to make a copy of the geometry you want to turn into a wireframe (clone but don't move it) (1), create and assign a material that is self-illuminated 100% and matches the background color (2), assign the Push modifier to those objects (3), and enter a value of −.002 (4), you suddenly get a *nested* set of geometry that serves as a matte object for your wireframe shell objects (5). (See the figure on the following page.)

TEXTURING

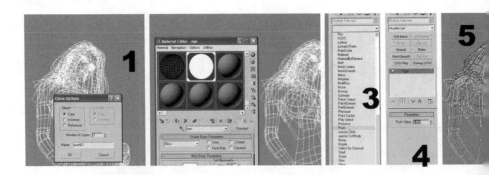

Render the "set" of geometry and you'll see a big difference:

Voilà. Looks much more like a wireframe *should* look. Her hair looks like some sort of funky dreadlocks or snakes! Speaking of hair, let's go over how I made that complex "do"...

Lofting Callisto's Hair

For cover Callisto's hair I used a lofting technique. Because I was going for a rendered image versus a real-time game character I had a lot more freedom to experiment and fewer limitations. Still, creating a real-time hairstyle using the technique I'm going to show you is practical and possible.

First, I settled on an angle that conveys what I'm after in attitude. I wanted this updated version of Cal to be more sexy and realistic. The cover of the first edition of this book never really felt right to me and I wish I had spent more time on it. So with the pose and angle right I'm ready to do the hair.

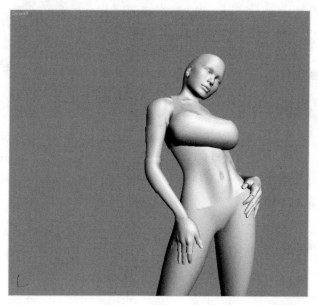

Don't ask me why I framed it this way instead of framing the book cover properly with text and her to the left. I have no clue. The mechanics of long hair is defined by gravity. It originates from hair follicles in the head and falls down. Product and styling and curly genetics help break the monotony of straight, stringy strands, but in simplest terms this is how hair works.

I wanted to make the hairstyle seem messy and fun and realistic so I went into it with layers in mind. So we'll begin the hairstyle by creating the loft paths for the hair strips at just above Cal's ears.

Create the Loft Paths

In the Front view I make a six-segment line out away from her head (a), then select all the vertices, right-click (b), and click on Smooth (c). This will give me a more natural, flowing line to work with.

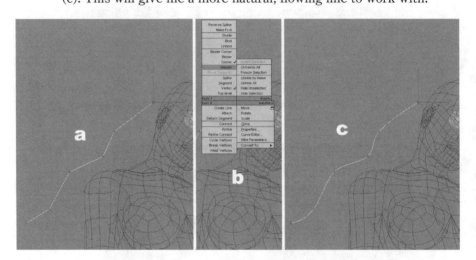

Now it's a simple matter of positioning the line and vertices of the line to resemble a group of hair strands in the hairstyle I'm after. To do this I change the Reference Coordinate system to Screen...

...and make sure Arc Rotate is set to Arc Rotate Sub-Object.

As usual, I work in one window, zipping around hitting Ctrl+R and dragging the view around with my middle mouse button. Eventually I place the first line where I want it, then clone it around the head until I have a decent number to work with when I loft the hair shapes.

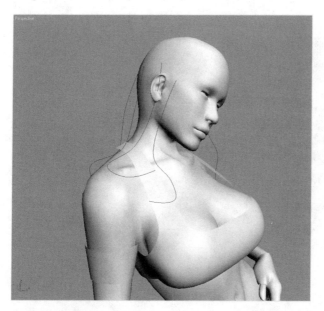

I know she looks like a sexy sister of Smeagol, but bear with me. The key to making convincing hair is layers — this is the first layer of three. Keep in mind the setup is different in a real-time vs. a rendered environment because the hair has to animate or simulate collision detection, but the approach should be the same.

TEXTURING

Create the Loft Shape

With the first set of loft lines done it's time to make the loft shape. I use a simple triangle because I'm going to apply MeshSmooth to create the high-res version and can keep the shape relatively simple.

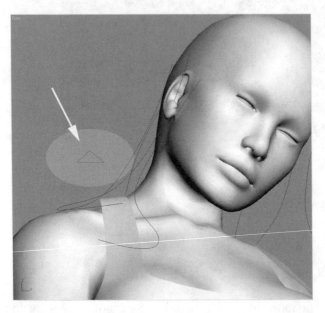

Try to keep the shape about the size you want the largest part of the hair strands to be. You can actually make it any size you want because of the ability to change the shape after the loft is created (we'll discuss this more later).

Loft the Shape

Loft path and loft shape created, it's time to make the loft object. Go to the Create tab, click on the hair spline (1), then on the small arrow to bring up a list of types of objects to be created. Choose Compound Objects (2).

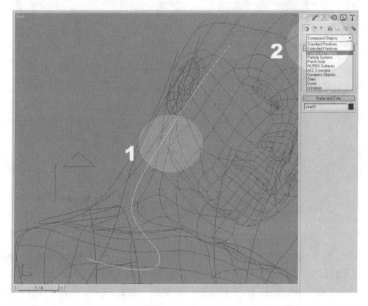

TEXTURING

With Compound Objects selected, click on Loft to make it active (1), click on Get Shape (2) and finally, click on the triangle (3).

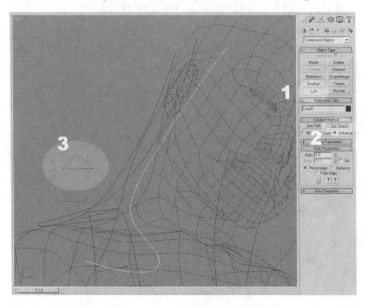

Notice how when you're in Get Shape or Get Path mode an ellipse with a line through it at an angle appears if you pass the cursor over a shape. This just lets you know you have a possible candidate for shape or path for the loft.

Note: The lofted objects are also new objects entirely. Splines and shapes used to create the loft don't go away, so they have to be deleted eventually.

Now we have the first loft object of the hair shape.

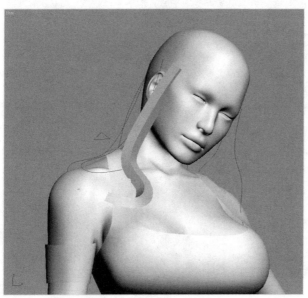

Adjust the Loft Parameters

However, there's plenty more work to do. First, keep in mind this object will have MeshSmooth applied to it so it doesn't have to be too high res. It also needs to conform to a hair-like shape so it needs to twist occasionally. These sorts of tweaks can be made in the Loft parameters. Select the loft object and click on the Modify tab. Expand all the subdirectories and it looks something like the figure on the following page.

TEXTURING

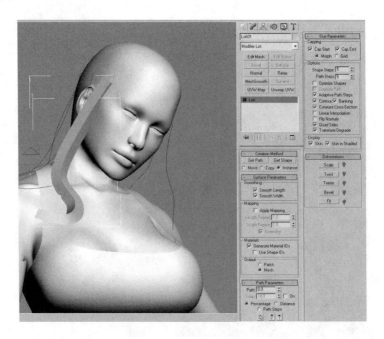

The first thing to do is to knock the resolution down by entering a value of 0 for Shape Steps and a value of 3 for Path Steps under Skin Parameters. Then *uncheck* Adaptive Path Steps (this evens out the distribution of segments as the shape is lofted down the spline path). Also make sure Optimize Shapes is unchecked.

Next, go to Surface Parameters and
under Mapping check the box beside
Apply Mapping. This applies mapping
coordinates to the shape that appear
uniform no matter what deformations
you apply to the loft object.

Deform the Loft Object

Speaking of which, now go to the Deformations panel and click on
Twist (1) to bring up the Twist Deformation window (2).

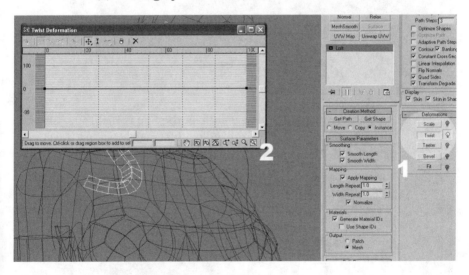

This gives you the ability to twist the lofted shape as it travels
down the path based on the shape of the line in the graph. As far as
max goes, the deformer windows have always been some of the
more intuitive tools to work with.

I want this strand to fall and twist slightly, then more so when it hits
Cal's clavicle. But first I need to adjust the loft shape so it starts
correctly. I raise the overall point (1) so that the shape turns and the
bottom of the triangle is flush with her head (2). Then I need to
keep the same direction with no twist before making it twist when
it hits her clavicle. To do this I have to add a control point about

TEXTURING

halfway down the line (3) and then drop the endpoint down to create the twist effect (4). This results in a slight twist, then a more severe twist as it lies on her shoulder (5).

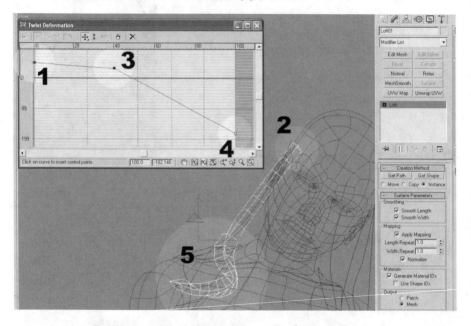

The cool thing about the edit points on the line is that they can be corner or smooth with Bezier handles. Just right-click on the point (1), choose Bezier-Smooth, and voilà — smooth line (2).

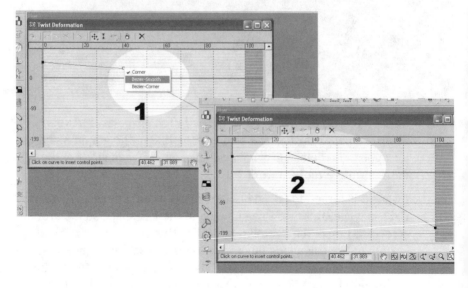

There isn't always a need to make the line a smooth curve versus a corner one, but I tend to use the smooth lines more when dealing with the Scale deformer than the other deformers.

Add Edit Mesh and Delete Backfaces

Because this hair strand will have MeshSmooth applied to it, the back and end faces of the triangle-lofted object need to be removed. This is because the hair strand will be two-sided and opacity-mapped. This makes getting rid of the backfaces even more necessary. It also makes adding a Scale deformer *unnecessary* since the strips of lofted geometry are really canvases for a hair texture and the ends will become points via the texture, *not* the geometry.

So add an Edit Mesh modifier (1), select all the back and end polygons (2), and delete them (3).

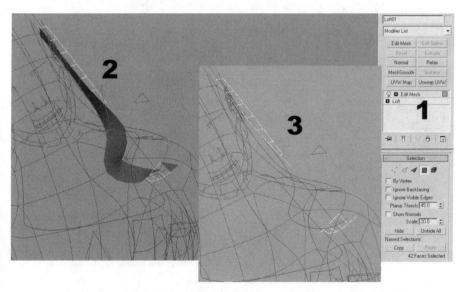

Remember, even though you've added an Edit Mesh modifier you can still go down the stack and adjust the parameters of the loft object and its sub-objects.

TEXTURING

Adjust the Loft Sub-Objects

The final thing to do with the loft object is to adjust the spline path to fit the geometry of her body. To do this you need to access the original path of the lofted object.

Note Lofted objects are composed of sub-objects just like a normal object is composed of sub-objects. Each sub-object of a lofted object in turn has its own sub-objects.

To access the lofted object *sub-objects*, go to the Modify panel and click on Loft (1), then the plus sign beside Loft (2), then the sub-object (in this case Path) (3), or click on the path itself inside the actual object (4). Then click on Line (5) and you have access to the vertices, segments, and splines of the sub-objects that were used to create the loft object.

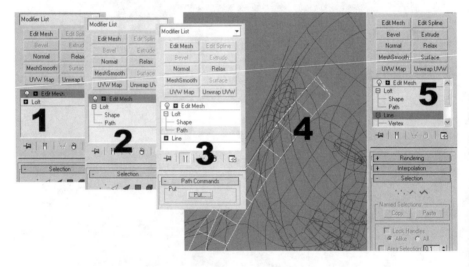

Next it's just a matter of adjusting the path using the same techniques used for creating the spline in the first place to adjust the loft object so it's not intersecting Cal's torso geometry. Apply a two-sided material if necessary to see the back side of the loft object.

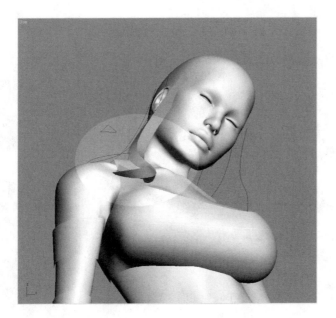

And that's how the basic hair strand object is created. I didn't use the Scale deformer because again the loft object is just a strip upon which to apply an alpha-masked texture of hair. The hair strand will be textured at this level so there's no need to apply MeshSmooth yet.

Now it's on to the rest of the first level strands.

Note: When working on the rest of the strands bear in mind that it's better to limit the basic tweaks to both path and shape to using deformers. Even though you can go into the shape sub-object, only do so to change the configuration of vertices in that shape. Use Scale and Twist to resize or turn the shape along the loft path instead.

TEXTURING

Once they're done they look something like this:

 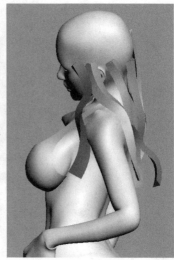

Creating the Other Hair Strand Layers

Another aspect of hair is the intertwining of the strands. With the first layer done, the second and third need to be created with this sort of interaction kept in mind. Now that I have a few stands done I could take any one of them, clone it, and move it into the right position. However, through experience, I've found that it's really just as efficient to make new splines and create new loft objects.

I make the splines for the second layer and position them just above the gaps made by the first layer.

I've color-coded the layers so they're easier to see. I've also scaled the lofted objects up by grabbing both endpoints in the Scale deformer and moving them upward. The final layer will be scaled even further to cover the "bald" spots at the top of her head. This building up of the layers is more time consuming than one overall "hood" of hair you often see in real-time characters, but it's well worth it.

The last layer is a bit more concentrated and overlaps more, looking like so:

Even though the last layer looks like the strands are almost too thick, they will have textures on them that are wispier than the other inner layers. This brings up some tips to consider when making hair this way:

- Make your hair strands in layers starting from low and inside.
- Clone splines so weight lines and strand length can be preserved.
- Align the start of the strand using Twist by moving both ends simultaneously.
- Adjust scale by moving both ends simultaneously.
- Always add some additional twist.
- Weave strands of hair in and out of other strands if possible.
- Give the impression of weight with the strands.
- Visualize the hair texture mapped onto the strands as you adjust them

Texturing the Hair Strands — Tweak the UVWs First

As in almost all aspects of creating digital content or game art, the process is very iterative. Oftentimes you find yourself going back and forth, tweaking *this* to fit with *that* so those *other* objects look right.

The first step to texturing the hair strands is to apply some random noise texture to it to get a relative average mapping coverage for all the strands. In Photoshop make a 512 x 512 "new" image file and add noise to it (filter/noise) with a value of 200%. Add a colored stripe across the top (I'll explain why in a minute) and save the file as "noise."

Then go back in max, make a material using noise.tif, and assign it to one of the strands (hiding the rest). Be sure to click the Show Map in Viewport button so the texture can be seen in view.

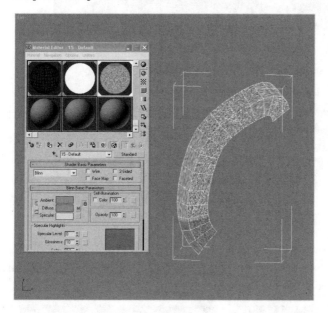

The texture seems to be squished together, which means the mapping is too *wide* for the object. Also, the colored stripe I put into the noise texture seems to be at the *bottom* of the shape instead of the top. To fix both problems we need to apply UVW Unwrap and adjust the UVs. Once the modifier is assigned, click on Edit to bring up the Edit UVWs window. Maneuver your view so you get a good look at the texture as it's applied to the object. As you tweak the UVs you want to be able to see the changes on the object.

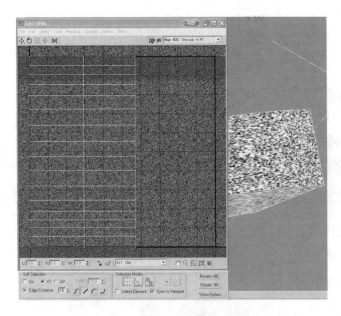

Now scale the UVs along the X or horizontal axis until the texture looks right (1), then rotate the UVs 180 degrees so the texture is oriented properly (2).

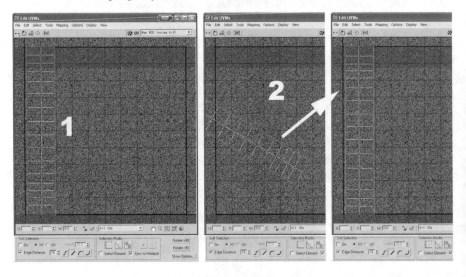

Another way to tell if the scale or orientation is right is to compare the way the UVs look in relationship to the polygons displayed in view. The should be at the same relative width and height when compared side by side (approximately).

Note: The only way to get precise rotations when working in the UVW Unwrap window is to turn on Angle Snap before working in the Edit UVWs window.

I actually did this for all the strands before moving on to the next step of the texturing process.

Get Good Hair Textures

Once the mapping is sorted for each strand you need to have a decent hair texture to map onto it. I like the decal approach, creating a dozen or so hair textures on one texture page that all the strands can use or reuse. Of course you can hand paint each group in Photoshop or whatever paint program you prefer. You can surf the net and find suitable pictures to cut and paste hair, too. Or you can coerce some hapless friend or relative into lying on the floor in front of your scanner while you arrange select locks, lay them on the scanner bed, place your foot firmly on the scanner lid, and digitize their precious locks into your computer group by group.

Guess which method I used? This is what I came up with after about 20 minutes of struggling with my victim, er…daughter:

The first thing I did with the hair texture is to invert it, desaturate it, and adjust the levels for it to be higher contrast to serve as an opacity map. This gives me the foundation to make the hair any color but still see how it's going to look on the hair strand objects.

TEXTURING

So armed with an opacity map I applied that texture to each strand, choosing a strand from the texture that fit where the strand was in the hairstyle. As I did this (applying parts of the hair texture to the strand objects) I also went back and adjusted the hair strand geometry. I mostly moved the path spline around until the meshes looked right together with a quick hair texture map applied.

I had to move strand starting and ending points and add extra strands to make the hair feel more real. Here's a comparison of what I started with and what I ended up with:

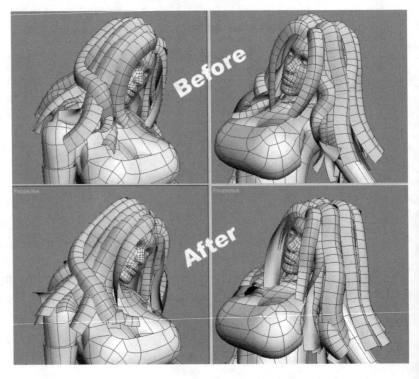

Notice I brought the strand level closer together and reduced the amount of "air" between strands. With the opacity map applied, the gaps were too great and the hair didn't look realistic enough. I also brought the starting point for the strands near the front of the face up so they obscured the naked scalp. You'll always have to make adjustments like these after getting your UVWs arranged and opacity map applied.

With the hair geometry sorted, it was time to make the brown locks blonde. After much cursing, tweaking, colorizing, levelizing, and (ahem) *hair pulling*, I ended up with a color version that better suited Callisto:

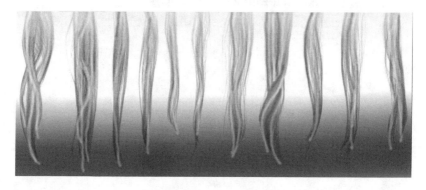

With all the textures applied and last remaining tweaks complete, she turned out like you see her on the cover:

TEXTURING

The forehead area is always a tricky place to work on. You usually need to combine a texture with physical hair geometry to make it look natural. For cover Callisto I just kept pushing geometry around until it looked right. Since this was only a rendered situation versus a real-time situation I had a lot more latitude to experiment and cheat.

That's it for me. I hope you found the extra stuff in this appendix useful and not confusing. Always feel free to email me if you get stuck on something in particular or just need a fresh pair of eyes for your art (paulst@microsoft.com).

Good luck and never stop learning. ;]

Index

About the CD

The companion CD contains models and texture maps necessary for chapter tutorials.

The models and texture maps are in the Callisto folder in the appropriate directory. For example, all the meshes are under Callisto\meshes. Please make corresponding directories on your hard drive.

The author can be reached via e-mail at paulst@microsoft.com.

!

Warning: By opening the CD package, you accept the terms and conditions of the CD/Source Code Usage License Agreement. Additionally, opening the CD package makes this book nonreturnable.

CD/Source Code Usage License Agreement

Please read the following CD/Source Code usage license agreement before opening the CD and using the contents therein:

1. By opening the accompanying software package, you are indicating that you have read and agree to be bound by all terms and conditions of this CD/Source Code usage license agreement.

2. The compilation of code and utilities contained on the CD and in the book are copyrighted and protected by both U.S. copyright law and international copyright treaties, and is owned by Wordware Publishing, Inc. Individual source code, example programs, help files, freeware, shareware, utilities, and evaluation packages, including their copyrights, are owned by the respective authors.

3. No part of the enclosed CD or this book, including all source code, help files, shareware, freeware, utilities, example programs, or evaluation programs, may be made available on a public forum (such as a World Wide Web page, FTP site, bulletin board, or Internet news group) without the express written permission of Wordware Publishing, Inc. or the author of the respective source code, help files, shareware, freeware, utilities, example programs, or evaluation programs.

4. You may not decompile, reverse engineer, disassemble, create a derivative work, or otherwise use the enclosed programs, help files, freeware, shareware, utilities, or evaluation programs except as stated in this agreement.

5. The software, contained on the CD and/or as source code in this book, is sold without warranty of any kind. Wordware Publishing, Inc. and the authors specifically disclaim all other warranties, express or implied, including but not limited to implied warranties of merchantability and fitness for a particular purpose with respect to defects in the disk, the program, source code, sample files, help files, freeware, shareware, utilities, and evaluation programs contained therein, and/or the techniques described in the book and implemented in the example programs. In no event shall Wordware Publishing, Inc., its dealers, its distributors, or the authors be liable or held responsible for any loss of profit or any other alleged or actual private or commercial damage, including but not limited to special, incidental, consequential, or other damages.

6. One (1) copy of the CD or any source code therein may be created for backup purposes. The CD and all accompanying source code, sample files, help files, freeware, shareware, utilities, and evaluation programs may be copied to your hard drive. With the exception of freeware and shareware programs, at no time can any part of the contents of this CD reside on more than one computer at one time. The contents of the CD can be copied to another computer, as long as the contents of the CD contained on the original computer are deleted.

7. You may not include any part of the CD contents, including all source code, example programs, shareware, freeware, help files, utilities, or evaluation programs in any compilation of source code, utilities, help files, example programs, freeware, shareware, or evaluation programs on any media, including but not limited to CD, disk, or Internet distribution, without the express written permission of Wordware Publishing, Inc. or the owner of the individual source code, utilities, help files, example programs, freeware, shareware, or evaluation programs.

8. You may use the source code, techniques, and example programs in your own commercial or private applications unless otherwise noted by additional usage agreements as found on the CD.

Warning: By opening the CD package, you accept the terms and conditions of the CD/Source Code Usage License Agreement. Additionally, opening the CD package makes this book nonreturnable